# CARDINAL RICHELIEU
## AND THE DEVELOPMENT OF ABSOLUTISM

France in 1630: additions after 1630 are marked with the date of accession; towns underlined were the seats of parlements.

# G. R. R. TREASURE

# CARDINAL RICHELIEU
## AND THE DEVELOPMENT OF ABSOLUTISM

ADAM & CHARLES BLACK
LONDON

FIRST PUBLISHED 1972

BY A. AND C. BLACK LTD

4, 5 AND 6 SOHO SQUARE, LONDON W1V 6AD

© 1972 GEOFFREY R. R. TREASURE

ISBN: 0 7136 1286 x hardback
0 7136 1287 8 paperback

To Melisa

PRINTED IN GREAT BRITAIN BY
T. & A. CONSTABLE, LTD., EDINBURGH

# Contents

# *Preface*

If nineteenth-century France was in some respects the France of Napoleon, *ancien régime* France was no less the France of Cardinal Richelieu. In the seventeenth century social and political institutions evolved in forms which the student of modern France may still recognise. At a time when many British people are thinking seriously about Europe, the life of Richelieu offers valuable insights. One should be chary however of attributing to statesmen the ability to act beyond the intellectual and material frontiers of their age. Nobleman, devout Catholic, writer and philosopher, diplomat and soldier, Richelieu was in all a man of his time. His stature is not reduced by placing him amid the toils of international diplomacy, the plots of nobles, discontents of office-holders or the revolts of the common people.

I hope that the reader will find that Richelieu emerges a more interesting person than he may have expected—and no less formidable. So far from being the inhuman architect of absolute monarchy, he is seen to be the harassed minister, fighting for survival, physically frail and sustained only by his strong will, fine intelligence and constant vision of the destiny of his country. He is one of many who contributed to the establishment of royal authority. Yet with the king's support and a growing concentration of powers he achieved an ascendancy greater than any French subject before him. It was a lonely eminence. His personality was strained by the demands of office; indeed, it may repel those who have not studied him closely or measured the problems he faced. Those who do so study him may come to appreciate his courage, respect his policies and see in him some of those civilised traits which have come to be thought of as especially French.

In writing this book I am indebted to many people: to the historians who have worked in this field and whose names are listed in the bibliography, and to friends who have read parts of the manuscript. Especially I thank Charlotte Park for deciphering and typing my script (and for her sense of humour), and my wife Melisa for her work upon copy and proofs.

HARROW
JANUARY 1972

# 1. The Young Bishop

Armand-Jean du Plessis de Richelieu was born on 9th September 1585. The event may have occurred at Richelieu in the family château or in their house in Paris: there is no reliable evidence either way. His father François was Grand Provost at the court of Henry III and Armand, the third son, was certainly christened in the Paris church of St Eustache on the 1st May 1586. François de Richelieu was a leading figure at court and close to the king, whose plight was no doubt a matter of anxious discussion in the Richelieu family. A month before Armand's birth the Spanish Army in the Netherlands had captured Antwerp and advertised once again their power. The effort of a French force under the king's younger brother to aid the Dutch had earlier collapsed in humiliating failure. At home King Henry III was so far from being master of his own house that he had to surrender to the demands of the House of Guise and issue an edict against the Huguenots, thus provoking a fresh outbreak of the civil wars which had been weakening the country for twenty-five years: this new and deadly phase was 'the war of the three Henries'. Henry III fought to rescue some vestiges of authority from Henry of Guise. The House of Guise, openly allied to Spain, ardently Catholic, dominated Paris through their organisation, the Holy League; they were bent on the destruction of the Huguenot party, led by the king's cousin, and heir to the throne since 1584, Henry of Navarre.

Armand's baptism was the occasion of an entertainment for the king and court: over the child's cradle was inscribed the legend 'Armand for the king'. But who was the king: Henry III, who could apparently find no solution to the political, economic and religious problems which beset him, or Henry of Guise, 'king of Paris' as he was known and as he effectively became after the Day of Barricades in May 1588 when the royal forces were divided and forced to surrender by the well-organised and militant citizens? In July Guise was made Lieutenant-General of France.

7

Abdication or assassination?—this is how the alternatives must have appeared to the king.

In December the Duc de Guise and his brother the Cardinal de Guise were murdered by the king's guards at Blois. It was not so much a solution as a gesture of despair, an act of moral nihilism, summing up in its cynical brutality the decadence of political life in the civil wars. While fanatics, priests and children marched round Paris with torches which they would symbolically dash to the ground as they chanted 'So may God quench the House of Valois', more sober Frenchmen questioned the sense of tearing France apart in the name of religion and dreamed of a strong king who could restore France's authority and frontiers. Henry III lacked the nerve, resources or reputation to do this. In August 1589 he in his turn was stabbed by Jacques Clément, a young friar acting probably on the instructions of Mme de Montpensier, sister of the Duc de Guise. François de Richelieu had been at Blois in 1588 and seems to have reacted violently after the murder of Guise. One account describes how the next day he rushed into the meeting of the States-General at the head of a troop of soldiers shouting 'Kill, kill, fire, fire'. When Henry was stabbed, he was at the king's side and he conducted the long inquest into the event. Whatever his personal feelings, he behaved with caution and soon joined the new king. In 1590 however, he died of fever while serving in Henry IV's camp outside Paris.

Henry of Navarre had to defend his claim against Catholics who would not accept him as Henry IV, the true heir to the Valois kings, in order to recover his capital and restore his country to peace and security. Military skill, patient and conciliatory diplomacy and the impact of an unusually shrewd and appealing personality contributed to his success in these tasks. His well-timed conversion to Roman Catholicism in 1593 was the turning-point. There was also a strong movement of opinion against fanaticism and faction, a patriotic, *politique* spirit which he was able to exploit to serve his policies of reconstruction. The economy was still buoyant, sustained by the steadily increasing volume of gold and silver in circulation, and Henry's minister Sully was able to balance the budget and promote schemes of reform quicker than might have been expected. Competent rule under favourable conditions brought about a degree of national recovery but could not efface at once the wounds and memories of the time of troubles. The France of Richelieu's childhood was

a deeply divided country which could easily relapse into anarchy
if the king was inadequate or too young to rule. The Edict of
Nantes in 1598 was a necessary but weakening surrender to an
armed minority whose separate and privileged existence was a
constant threat to peace. Lawlessness imperilled social order.
Henry IV was to die like his predecessor at the hands of an assassin, the schoolmaster Ravaillac. Reckless violence coloured the
country's political life. The history of Richelieu's own family,
not untypical of his class, illustrates this theme.

The family of Richelieu was well established and noble. 'Plessis'
means a pallisaded bailey and was a not uncommon name in the
Middle Ages among the numerous class of petty vassals. Richelieu's
ancestors had been vassals of the Bishop of Poitiers in the
thirteenth century. A cadet branch rose steadily in the fifteenth
and sixteenth centuries by marriage, war and service at court.
The name 'Richelieu' came to them with the acquisition through
marriage of the fortified manor house of Richelieu, built in about
1430 by the Clérembault family on a small island in the river
Mable, in the flat, green lands of Poitou. In this crude keep,
surrounded by a moat formed by the stream, and by acres of
woodlands, Richelieu spent his early years with his two elder
brothers; he was a frail but alert and impressionable boy. There
was food for thought in the contrast between the resounding
titles and claims of his family, and their frugal household. If not
ruined, they were left relatively poor after their father's death.
A sensitive boy must also have been intrigued, if not appalled,
by recent events in his family. One great-uncle, Antoine 'the
Monk', having refused to accept an abbey and been relieved of
his orders, became a captain in the Catholic forces of the Duc de
Guise and was the author of some unpleasant massacres of
Huguenots; he died in a street brawl in Paris in 1576. Armand's
grandfather, the elder brother, had married Françoise de Roche-
ouart, a great lady, extremely proud and bad-tempered; she was
early left a widow with five children. The eldest of these was
murdered after a squabble over precedence in the parish church
with the head of the rival family of Mausson. François, the second
son, was recalled from court where he was a page and incited
by his mother to avenge the family. He bowled a cartwheel at
Mausson's horse as he crossed a ford and killed the man as he
struggled in the water. He went into exile in circumstances which
actually furthered the fortune of the family, for the Duc d'Anjou,

whom he joined in Poland, became Henry III in 1574 on the death
of Charles IX, and François was made Grand Provost. He stood
apart from the more frivolous courtiers, the *mignons* who exploited
the king's fecklessness and instability. Loyal, devout in a somewhat melancholy way, conscience-stricken perhaps, but still prey
to sudden moods of violence, he was called 'Tristan the Hermit',
but he kept none the less a firm and ambitious hand on worldly
affairs.

Armand's mother had a greater influence upon the growing
boy, since he was only five when she was widowed. Born Suzanne
de la Porte, she came from a bourgeois family, but her father
had become a councillor of the Parlement of Paris. To the
arrogant, feudal tradition of the Richelieus she brought a valuable strain of discipline and civility. Hard work, intelligence,
self-control were the means through which the de la Portes
had risen in the competitive ranks of the urban patriciate;
these were virtues worth cultivating by a third son, without
estates or prospects, who had to make his own way in the
world.

When Richelieu's father died, the family sold his collar of the
Order of the Holy Ghost to pay for his funeral. The *seigneuries* in
Poitou produced little revenue: the combination of rents declining
in real value (for rents were paid mostly in livres and the livre in
1600 was worth less than half what it had been fifty years before),
the drain of François' expenses at court, the neglect of the farms
and the disruption of local life in the anarchic conditions of the
'religious wars' had affected the Richelieu family like thousands
of others. If one wanted to raise money, one must expect to pay
exorbitant interest. To secure an office or place at court one must
jostle in the queue with others in similar case. At the College of
Navarre, the aristocratic school to which Armand was sent at the
age of nine, and at the Academy, a cadet school in Paris run by
Antoine Pluvinel, a friend of his father, Richelieu displayed not
only a superior intellect but also a distinctive style of flamboy-
ance and courtliness which suggests concern about his image
in the world. Here he showed himself adept in the gentle-
manly and useful arts alike, horsemanship and mathematics,
fencing and fortification, courtly manners and military drill.
He was clever, vain, ordinarily self-conscious, extraordinarily
imposing.

His second brother, Alphonse, who was intended for the

bishopric of Luçon in the family gift, declined the responsibility and departed for the silent peace of a cell at La Grande Chartreuse. Armand was therefore summoned to Luçon and the Church for which he had hitherto expressed no vocation. He may not have been wholly reluctant to exchange the sword for the surplice. His health was wretched: already he was having a foretaste of future sufferings in the shape of migraines and paroxysms, perhaps epileptic, which affected him after bouts of work or at times when he was nervously overwrought. He was physically brave and he enjoyed the action and swagger of a soldier's life, but he may have doubted his strength. To become a bishop, even of the unregarded diocese of Luçon in the western fens, was to provide an opening to public life. Richelieu was attracted to power with all the craving of a masterful nature and a rapid, impatient mind; he was also inclined to use his mind in debate and study: an unusual combination.

The Church, in a period of exciting and fundamental reforms, and Luçon in a neglected area with a large number of Huguenots, offered a more promising arena than the army, where he was but one of many cadets, an uncertain career which a wound or plague could end at any time. So in 1602 he left the Academy, abandoned his courtesy title of Marquis de Chillou and embarked on theology at the College of Calvi. He was snubbed when he asked leave from the professors of the Sorbonne to deliver a philosophical lecture. He conducted a debate instead at the College of Navarre. His learning, his mastery of Church history, his espousal of the liberal theological ideas that he learned, among others, from the English Jesuit Richard Smith, impressed his fellow-seminarists as much as they did Pope Paul V, when he went to Rome for a dispensation to enable him to enter his diocese below canonical age. On 17th April 1607, he was ordained priest and consecrated bishop. He returned to Paris, passed his final theological examinations with acclaim, but then became seriously ill. By the summer of 1608 he was sufficiently recovered to be drawing crowds to his sermons. At court he attached himself to Cardinal du Perron and caught the ear of the king, whose morals he had defended in Rome before Paul V and who now referred to him as 'my bishop'. With a coolness that was to prove typical, he cut himself off from the smooth and promising way of the court. In December 1608 he borrowed an old coach from a friend and money to buy his episcopal purple, set out with no entourage beyond the few clerics and officials who met him at Luçon, and entered his diocese to celebrate Christmas.

Richelieu's life coincided with the flowering of the counter-reformation in France. The revival of Catholic faith and practice came relatively late to France because Gallican churchmen were suspicious of Rome and the Mediterranean emphasis of the Council of Trent. During the civil wars of the second half of the sixteenth century, crown and aristocracy maintained their grip upon the benefices of the Church. With the conversion of Henry IV to Catholicism in 1593 and the religious truce of the Edict of Nantes, the Catholics of France seemed to have triumphed. Weariness and cynicism were the prevailing moods, though there were stirrings of religious life and some outstanding individual examples of piety and fervour. With an upper clergy who were often indifferent and a lower clergy who were usually untrained, the Church was more a reflection of the society it was supposed to guide than a source of inspiration: the bishop was encouraged to be a courtier, the curé lived at the level of his peasants.

It was indeed a period of striking contrasts. To posterity this seems to have been the start of a golden age of the Church in France. To contemporaries it often seemed to be an age of disorder and impiety. They judged principally by the criterion of unity. Grave abuses persisted however despite the best efforts of the reformers. On the one hand there were some surprising constraints, at least in law, marks of the Christian state. Successive edicts dealt with such matters as the closing of butcheries during Advent and Lent, forbidding blasphemies, and making compulsory the celebration of the great religious festivals. On the other hand the Paris streets were as dangerous at night as those of modern New York. Brothels and gaming houses proliferated. Underground pornographic literature circulated extensively. In many country districts there was primitive licence, superstition, violence and squalor: sorcery was enjoying a dreadful vogue.[1] The letters

[1] The epidemic of Satanism towards the end of the sixteenth century was not only a French phenomenon. There was of course nothing new about the practice and persecution of witches: both were outlets for the fears and doubts of peasant communities beset by inexplicable catastrophes. What was new in this period was the tremendous public debate about possession, exorcism, and Satan himself: the Grandier case (pages 227-228) provides but one spectacular example of it. At the level of the intellectual élite there was an increasing rejection of sorcery, as might

of Monsieur Vincent reveal his depression about the condition
of France, and of Christian Europe. He favoured Christian
missions abroad in the hope that new lands might provide an
example to the old.

Seen against this background, the record of the seventeenth
century Church is astounding: it was indeed 'the great age of
souls'. In 1603 the Jesuits were admitted again to France. They
flouted the restraints placed on their activity, founded schools
and sent out missionaries. From these schools issued a flow of
devout laymen; some joined lay organisations committed to the
furtherance of the faith. The most influential of these was the
Company of the Holy Sacrament, founded in about 1630 by the
Duc de Ventadour, the king's lieutenant-general in Languedoc.
Strongly influenced by the Spanish school of mystics and notably
by St Teresa, he lived apart from his beautiful wife, who went into
a convent of the Carmelites, and he drew influential associates
into his movement for Catholic action. Another notable figure,
right on the line which divides religious commitment and ecstasy
from mania, was Duvergier de Hauranne, abbé de St Cyran, an
extremist indeed, but an influential director of souls.[1]Among those
who looked up to him as an inspired prophet were Pierre Bérulle
and St Vincent de Paul.

Bérulle was a leader of the *dévôts* and one of the group who came
to look to the intellect and the practical capacity of Richelieu to
promote their causes. In his rational and methodical mind, the
mystical devotion of the Spanish masters took a new Gallic
shape. 'Teacher of so many teachers, master of so many saints',
Bérulle founded the Oratory in 1611 to establish a new ideal of
spiritual life and a model for the priesthood. He also aimed to
take from the Jesuits their near-monopoly of Catholic education.
In his theocentric spirit, in what he called 'adherence to Christ',
lay his greatest significance. It is that spirit which we can identify
as the common inspiration of men and women as diverse as St

---

be expected of the age of mathematics. In 1640 the Parlement of Paris
made its historic decision not to pursue sorcerers, nor to let them be
condemned by judges of inferior courts 'without irrefutable proofs'.
Colbert's Edict abolished trials for sorcery altogether in 1682. This
subject is dealt with at length by R. Mandrou in *Magistrats et Sorciers en
France au XVII siècle. Une analyse de psychologie historique* (Paris, 1968).

[1] For his part in the growth of the Jansenist movement see pages
221-226.

Vincent, St François de Sales, St Jean Eudes,[1] the organiser of country missions, St Louise de Marillac, pioneer of St Vincent's nursing sisters, St Jeanne de Chantal, a founder of the *Visitandines*, an order of nuns, in St Francois's words, for 'strong souls with weak bodies', and Mme Acarie, Bérulle's friend, who was primarily responsible for the introduction, in 1602, of the Carmelite order into France and whose house became a centre of the *dévôts*, a religious *salon*, as it were.

Monsieur Vincent, as St Vincent was best known, is famous for his Ladies of Charity, founded in 1617 to help 'our lords the poor', better known in their later form as the Daughters of Charity. In their grey dresses and white cornettes they took the idea of charity into the streets, to the poor. Their founder's approach to life is revealed in his instructions: 'For your monastery use the houses of the sick, for your chapel the parish church, for your cloister the streets of towns or the rooms of hospitals'. The son of a poor peasant from the Landes, Monsieur Vincent was at different times a chaplain to the galleys, a curé in a neglected village where he encountered the squalor and hopelessness of the rural poor, and spiritual adviser to the powerful and pious Gondi. With the latter's money he started a college of priests, the Lazarists, who were trained to go out into the countryside in squads, preaching and catechising.

If St Vincent was the most radical figure among the Christian leaders, St François de Sales, Bishop of Geneva from 1602, a remoter figure, was no less influential through his writings and individual direction. For Mme de Chantal's *Visitandines* he wrote

---

[1] In his book *Les Missions de Saint Jean Eudes* (Paris, 1967) C. Berthelot du Chesnay throws light upon the motives and methods of the organisers of missions to the French countryside. Jean Eudes would spend about a month in each centre. With assistants he would teach and preach intensively in the evangelical, Carlo Borromeo manner. It was a work of education, and an important consideration in the minds of his backers was the need to establish order in the dangerous marginal districts, Brittany and Normandy for example. Many of those who gave money to the missions were members of the Company of the Holy Sacrament. Writing in 1648 to the queen mother, Eudes pinpoints one difficulty that confronted the missionaries: 'We have found that the Churches were often deserted on Sundays and Feast Days, even at the great festivals, because the inhabitants of those places do not dare to come to them for fear of falling into the hands of the collectors of the *taille*, who seize them at the very steps of the altar to drag them off to prison, an iniquity which would not happen even under the Turks.'

the spiritual masterpiece, *Traité de l'Amour de Dieu*. His manual of devotion, *Introduction à la vie dévôte*, published in 1609, ran to forty editions by 1656. His conception of the mystical experience of God as being available to all good Catholics was a Catholic version of Luther's priesthood of all believers. Its effect can be compared to that of John Law's *Serious Call* upon eighteenth-century England. St Vincent wanted his followers to read a chapter of the *Introduction* every day. François was a saint in the popular reckoning before his death, and the process of canonisation was begun at Rome only four years afterwards.

Such a brief selection of names and achievements can do little to convey the extent and flavour of the religious revival. Alongside the spiritual quality and genius of individuals there persisted moreover a worldliness and acceptance of double standards that mocked the efforts of the reformers. The force of reform can best be measured perhaps by the advance of the religious orders. Brémond compared France in the time of Henry IV to 'a part of the mission field in the first years of advance'. The urge to create new houses and new orders was too strong for the jurists of Parlement to resist or the cautious curia of Rome to delay. In 1631 the Parlement of Rouen declared that 'in the last twenty or thirty years more religious orders have been founded than in the last thousand years'. In the single diocese of Coutances there were six foundations in twelve years. Almost every order flourished—Franciscans, Dominicans, Capuchins, Calvarists, Feuillants, Premonstratensians, Carmelites and, most conspicuously, the Jesuits: the most severe of the orders, the Trappists and the Carthusians, both found recruits. That this was no passing phase can be seen from the history of the second half of the century. Whatever view is taken of the conflict of Jesuits and Jansenists, there can be no doubt of the sincerity of the combatants or of the passionate interest aroused by their theological arguments. The long crusade against the Huguenots, bitter though its outcome was to prove, was a natural fruit of Catholic devotion. Men like Fenélon and le Camus, at the end of the century, were as 'jealous of souls' as any of Richelieu's contemporaries, while at court the *dévôt* tradition persisted to the end of Louis XIV's reign.

Richelieu worked at the centre of this religious revival. Its effect on him, on his career and policies, was immense. Though he moved away from the inner circle of the *dévôts* and incurred the resentment of the faction of Bérulle and Marillac by his anti-Habsburg policies, he remained in close contact with some of the spiritual leaders of the time. Vincent de Paul had his ear, and it was Richelieu who asked the founder of the Lazarists to harness himself to the work of training priests. Accumulating benefices, gaining control where possible of the religious orders, he was able to defend himself by saying that he acquired key posts, such as abbot of Citeaux in 1636, in order to influence the direction of reform. The visitor of the Carmelites reported favourably to Rome on the use which he made of his commanding position. It was of course all part of his drive to concentrate power in his own hands. He was primarily concerned no doubt with the disciplinary aspects of reform. He did not however suspect enthusiasm for itself. He supported the work of the Company of the Holy Sacrament, on condition that a crown representative should belong and report to the king on its actions. He was only alarmed about movements of an other-worldly character which he felt to be outside such control. The central problems of his life arose from political decisions which he knew to be necessary, but which ran counter to the principles of *dévôts* of one sort or another, which either complicated or contradicted the promptings of faith and morality. He was not, as is sometimes suggested, insensitive to this problem, even though hardened by experience. He was, and remained in this own way, a *dévôt*.

Luçon lies in western Poitou, in flat and swampy country; a few miles away is the seaport of La Rochelle. From the start Richelieu was thus confronted in his diocese by the Huguenot problem in its most intractable form. This city, one of the chief fortified towns which the Huguenots had been allowed to keep under the terms of the Edict of Nantes, with its austere burghers and its hardy and reckless seamen, focused Richelieu's ideas on the subject of heresy. It gave point to his immediate mission and pricked him into thinking of the future. Thirty years later he was to write of how he 'often thought, in the deep peace there [at Luçon] of the various means for bringing La Rochelle into obedience to the king'. In other ways the young bishop found conditions which provided him with exercise on the small local scale in the greater problems of national government. Since the diocese had been treated for fifty years as a source of revenue to the Richelieu family and was, besides, in a poor district, the Cathedral was decayed, the canons were hostile, the parish clergy were woefully ignorant. With his usual concern for outward dignity, for 'the good of the Church and the glory of our House', to quote the words he had used to his mother when he had accepted the see, he at once ordered silver plates and tapestries, repaired and embellished his mediaeval palace, drove through a bargain which ended the long quarrel about the diocesan revenues, and secured money from the Parlement for the repair of the thirteenth-century naves and 'flamboyant' choir of his Cathedral of Notre Dame. Clergy and people thus felt the impact of his authority, the restless, probing activity of an impatient man. He impressed them with his sermons, mannered but systematic, and by his concern for secular matters: he secured a reduction in the tax assessment of the people and badgered the local authorities to take a stand against duelling. Though intellectual in his approach and happiest when he could argue and formulate on paper, he did not shirk the physical side of his work but travelled to outlying parts of the diocese. Whether because he was fired by concern of souls or simply driven on by his love of order and propriety—or even, as cynics may suggest, using Luçon as a showpiece of his administrative skills, there is no doubt that he was a model bishop.

After 1611 he was mostly at the priory of Coussay, near Poitiers, where he had a garden and found the climate better for his health than the Atlantic air of Luçon, but he continued to rule the diocese firmly enough through two *grands vicaires*. After 1614 he was more or less immersed in affairs of state. In this short time, however, the pattern of his religious life had been formed. It may be that, as Brémond said, 'he feared hell and loved theology; he was not indifferent towards the things of God but his kingdom was of this world'. He was also as close as a man of his essentially unmystical temperament could be to the piety of the time. He gave the English Jesuit Smith, of whom Robert Parsons said 'I never saw a man more heady and resolute in his opinions', a home in his palace when he got into trouble in England. A regular correspondent was Antoinette d'Orléans, a nun in the great abbey of Fontrevault nearby: she was later to found her own order, the Daughters of Calvary. It was through her agency that Richelieu met François le Clerc de Tremblay, Père Joseph as he is better known, the greatest Capuchin of his day. The contact was to have an importance very different from what they may have envisaged when the friar was first unfolding his plans for war against heresy. It was in Richelieu's episcopate that Bérulle founded his second oratory, in Luçon; Bérulle was to be an important ally for Richelieu, but at this stage he saw in him, like Father Joseph, a pastoral adviser rather than a political ally. Richelieu's religious convictions cannot be separated from his political designs; in his early career there was no inconsistency, for it was as champion of the *dévôts* that he was to make his mark.

## 2. Nadir of Government

After the death of Henry IV in 1610, his widow, Marie de Médicis, was left to rule France as regent. This self-indulgent Florentine, who was to have such an important part to play in Richelieu's political odyssey, was incapable of imposing her will upon the great nobles who had an interest in weak government. Her ample figure and rosy face have been preserved for us by the generous brush of Rubens and she monopolises a whole room in the Louvre, but in her time she was an ineffectual person. She had never been close to Henry nor learned much about the art of governing; she knew little about his foreign schemes and she had no interest in finance. Money to her was something to be spent on the arts and good living. If peace could be bought by money, she was ready to buy. In Richelieu's phrase, 'she ran after malcontents to satisfy them'. As a niece of the Duke of Tuscany she looked on Spain as a friend, but she could not have pursued Henry's policy even if she had sympathised with his aims.

Sully, Henry's admirable finance minister, retired in 1611 leaving a manageable debt of 196 million livres, reduced from 300 million under his surveillance, a reserve of about 20 million livres and an armoury equipped for war against the Habsburgs. The troops were recalled and the general European war that might have followed from Henry's decision to dispute the Clèves-Jülich succession was averted. Savoy was left to make the best peace she could while Marie signed the Treaty of Fontainebleau with Spain. It provided for a ten-year defensive alliance between France and Spain, against internal revolt as well as against external attack, and for a personal union in the shape of a double marriage, between Louis XIII and Anne, the Spanish Infanta, and his sister Elizabeth and Philip, heir to the Spanish throne. Marie's domestic problems could not be solved so easily. In the leaders of the League of 1614 against the regent we see the problem of 'the overmighty subject': Condé, the king's cousin and heir-presumptive to the throne, loathing the queen mother

and ready to further his ends by clutching at any ally, any cause
that promised to be useful—the Huguenots, Spain, a States-
General; Bouillon, lord of the principality of Sedan and virtually
an independent ruler, who had formerly played the part of the
persecuted Protestant but now made no bones about joining
the Catholics; Mayenne, the son of Henry IV's enemy; and
Epernon. Marie bought them off at the 'pacification of Saint
Ménéhould' in May 1614. In the following year, in a last-minute
attempt to prevent the Spanish marriage, Condé and Bouillon
bid for the support of the Huguenots: they were unwilling to
fight for them, though Rohan raised some troops in the south,
and Condé roused fury by allowing his own army to live off the
countryside. Louis XIII and the Infanta, Anne of Austria, were
married at Bordeaux despite him and in the following year, 1616,
by the 'treaty' of Loudun, Condé was given 1½ million livres and
a place on the council. He was soon talking openly of taking
the throne and Marie was able to have him arrested by smuggling
soldiers into the Louvre concealed in bales of silk. Dumas and
his imitators, who have written of this century in terms of court
intrigue, loves, feuds and light-hearted wars, may have done
French history an ill service, but they did not need to draw much
on their imagination for material.

In 1614 Marie summoned the States-General as part of her
agreement with the princes. It was to prove the last meeting of
this body until the Revolution, and a study of its debates goes far
to explaining why. The issues are, however, interesting: the
outcome may have been futile but the debates were vital. They
provided Richelieu with a chance to assert himself. He was
doubly fortunate at this juncture, in the unsettled pattern of
political life and in the leading part that churchmen were allowed,
even expected, to play at such a time.

Richelieu had already tried to sow the idea that he had larger
claims to influence than his diocese alone could satisfy. In 1610
he had startled the other bishops of the province of Bordeaux
by putting himself forward as their representative at a conference
of clergy in Paris: he was rejected. When Henry IV was assassinated, he tried a more direct approach, first writing to the queen
by way of his brother, who wisely refused to pass it on, then
coming to Paris, after selling some tapestries to pay for his
lodging, so as to be in a position to exploit any opportunity.
That he should thus press himself is not surprising. His father

had been a leading courtier, his brother had also been intimate with the late king; he was young and impatient; recurring illness, even perhaps a feeling that he had not long to live, gave point to his ambition. There is evidence at this time of his over-wrought state. In a correspondence to his deputies in Luçon he wrote with a rudeness and self-revelation that were equally unusual: 'Thanks be to God I know how to rule myself, but I also know how those under me should be ruled'. In 1614, however, he was to show that this was a reasonable claim.

Henry IV had never summoned a States-General. Before 1560, when it was called after the sudden death of Henry II, it had not met for sixty-six years; in the reigns of his sons, Francis II, Charles IX and Henry III, it became the instrument in turn of Catholic and Huguenot pressure groups. A fashionable view then was that the States-General was the embodiment of national sovereignty, the king merely a delegate. In Henry III's reign the Catholics, who by then dominated the States-General, played with the idea that the king got his powers from God, not directly but through the mediation of the people. The distressing results of weak monarchy, the partisan appearance of the last meetings and the débâcle at Blois in 1588, all helped to discredit the States-General and the shallow constitutionalism of those who had used it for party ends. The nobility expected to gain their ends through influence at court or the accumulation of estates and offices in the provinces. The clergy had their own assembly, while at least some of the privileged members of the Third Estate preferred the limited power and professional status they had in Parlements to the slights and insults they could expect from king and courtiers in the States-General. Whereas in England the crown had found it expedient to summon parliaments to hear grievances, raise money, confirm dynastic changes and rally support for controversial measures, in France there was little to gain by encouraging a representative principle which was in form and spirit a survival from feudal conditions. Judgements were given in Parlements, administration was the work of local officials and the French were used to paying their taxes, except in the *pays d'états*, without giving consent through a representative body. Roman law put more stress upon the duties than on the rights of the individual subject and did not foster the idea of communal responsibility. The fact that the privileged classes were largely exempt from direct taxation made it easier for the state to tax without reference to the wishes of communities. So the States-General was only likely to be of service at exceptional moments of national crisis. It was an ad hoc body, for all the elaborate ceremonial with which it met, irrelevant when the crown was strong, anachronistic even when it was weak.

The States-General of 1614 met with a clamour of rival interests and claims that ensured that it would be a failure. With the aid of his friend Rochepousay, Bishop of Poitiers, Richelieu was elected as a representative of the clergy of Poitou. On 26th October he walked with his fellow-prelates at the rear of a large procession, appropriately led by a rabble of beggars, which walked from the convent of the Augustinians to the Cathedral of Notre Dame for the mass which initiated the assembly. In the debates that ensued in the Hotel Bourbon in front of the Louvre, after the formal and solemn speeches of the leading representatives of the three Estates, several distinct issues were revealed. The animosity of the nobles towards the bourgeoisie found expression in an attack on the *paulette* which had regularised the hereditary principle in office-holding. The Third Estate were prepared to accept its abolition but demanded that the money lost to the government should be recouped by a reduction in pensions. Savaron, spokesman for the Third Estate, touched on a sensitive spot when he contrasted the money spent on pensions to *les grands* with the poverty of the ordinary people. The effect of the general attack on the government's financial policy was thus spoiled by the mutual antagonism of the privileged classes. A court was indeed set up to deal with corruption but this required the attention of experts for a long stretch, and the States-General was only to last for four months. All agreed, of course, that the *taille* should be reduced, but Jeannin, Sully's successor as *surintendant*, was in a strong position to refuse it, for no one could check his figures: there was no regular budget, no control over how the money was spent. The nobility stood to gain by this haphazard system and were not prepared either to administer the taxes or to contribute to them, while the clergy, as a body, deprecated the idea of public accounting. In the metaphorical style beloved of orators of the time they argued that, the state being a body, the finances were its nerves and should remain hidden under the skin. They too were concerned with preserving their rights, and they had other interests to defend.

The States-General witnessed an outburst of Gallican

sentiment.[1] The Catholicism of the subjects of *le roi très chrétien* represented a compromise between the claims of Pope and king, and a tradition which reached back to the fourteenth century when, during the Avignon captivity, the French crown enjoyed special privileges. The effect of this tradition was to keep France apart from the international Catholic initiatives and reforms. During the period of the 'religious wars', while Huguenotism was acquiring tradition and status, the Catholic efforts were weakened by failures of leadership and discipline at all levels. The claims of the reformed Papacy were represented by the Holy League, the faction of the Guises and especially by the ruthless Cardinal de Lorraine, who combined an ascetic life with restless ambition, and nominal adherence to Tridentine principles with shameless pluralism. Gallican feeling came therefore to merge in a wider patriotism. Many leading Catholics at the end of the century, and at the start of a new reign whose first great achievements were peace with Spain and with the Huguenots, took their tone from the *politique* stance of the convert Henry IV and the moderate humanism of Montaigne and his followers. To the traditional political claims of king against Church was added the fresh appeal of a broad-based national Church. The Gallican liberties, constantly re-examined, were made to give precise emphasis to the authority of the king. The Church, of course, was given to understand that it was dependent on the royal courts. The emphasis of the Sorbonne was naturally different, for the theologians were most interested in the right of bishops to regulate Church affairs. Bishops and lawyers agreed, however, that the king should be protector of the clergy, even though this was not stated so explicitly as in the reign of Louis XIV, 'patron and founder of the churches in France'. Cardinal du Perron indeed ascribed to kings a temporal sovereignty in which they 'depend upon God and recognise no power above them'. He was ultramontane, however, in his politics and held to be a supporter of the Jesuits. At this States-General he assumed the lead amongst churchmen who hoped that the enhancement of royal authority would not be at the expense of the independence of the Church.

Under the genial and oracular figure of Perron were ranged some of the younger bishops. Richelieu intervened effectively on

[1] This subject is treated more fully in pages 217-221.

a point of order and led a delegation to the Third Estate to persuade them to follow the procedure of the First. His chance to attract the attention of the court came, however, with a fierce attack by a group of bishops on the influence and power of the Concinis and their royal patron. Richelieu was put forward by his faction to defend the queen. His flattery so won her attention that she engineered the choice of the Bishop of Luçon to present the memorials of the First Estate at the closing session on 23rd February 1615. In front of the assembled notables and a crowd of courtiers who had invited themselves to the proceedings, Richelieu, bareheaded, spoke for an hour; his tone was obsequious but he made some telling points. He approved the policies of the Regent and especially the proposed marriages and alliance with Spain. He urged the crown to accept the decrees of the Council of Trent and demanded the establishing of Catholicism in Béarn, the southern province recently acquired upon the accession of Henry IV. With the boldness which he never failed to display at such times he advised the crown to bring an ecclesiastic into her councils on the ground that priests were, by their vocation and training, less tied than laymen to worldly interests!

In the event the crown would go no further than to promise the abolition of the sale of offices, reduce pensions and set up a special chamber to try financiers: empty promises, as it was to prove. Richelieu returned to his priory and to the intense study of theology. In 1616, roused by the purposeless revolt of Condé, which touched him personally when Condé's ruffianly troops plundered the family château, burned his papers and seized his possessions in Luçon, he went to court, where he had long talks with Father Joseph, who helped to make peace between Condé and the queen. He also secured, through an old acquaintance, Claude Barbin, an introduction to Leonora Concini. This could, as it turned out, have been fatal to his hopes.

In this transitional period in the development of government, between the limited, seigneurial, intimate and essentially personal kingship of feudal societies and the impersonal, bureaucratic structure of the modern state, the king's control over government was precarious; he was expected to act in a decisive, even arbitrary, manner but lacked the machinery to make his government effective outside his court. An important part could therefore be played by 'the favourite', *el privado*, the man behind the throne.

In some cases—Olivarez, Richelieu and Oxenstierna in the minority of Queen Christina are the most spectacular—he handled the levers of power so effectively that he became the director, if not the dictator, of his country. Others, notably Lerma in Spain and Buckingham in England, without ever reaching an unchallenged eminence, were able to exploit their position to the extent of creating a private empire: these may more properly be called 'favourites' and in this class were Concini and Luynes, who established themselves in turn as the influential figures behind Marie de Médicis and Louis XIII.

Concini, a good-looking Florentine, set himself up by marrying Leonora Galigai, Marie's foster-sister and intimate companion. At first he was restrained enough, as if concerned mainly with building and protecting his fortune. His appetite grew, however, with the feeding; he styled himself the Maréchal d'Ancre, started to collect provincial governorships and then bought the lieutenant-generalship of Picardy, on the northern frontier. This was alarming to those who were already concerned about the Spanish bias of royal policy. His style of living was as splendid as his rise had been rapid: he received petitions like a prince, disposed of patronage and was rumoured to want the high feudal office of Constable. In retrospect his authority seems to have been un-stable; even at the time he was held to be weak and he was certainly a man to buy off trouble rather than meet it head on. But Richelieu, as his subsequent patronage of Mazarin showed, did not think that being Italian disqualified a man for high office in France; he supported him at the time and later wrote of him with generous praise. Condé represented the view of the other grandees when he refused to take his seat on the council so long as Ancre continued to govern. Richelieu was anxious to avoid commitment to either party, since he realised that Condé might prove the winner; he corresponded with him and sent Condé's replies to the queen mother for perusal. He managed to persuade Condé to return to court, where the latter at once found himself the leader of all who wanted to dispose of Ancre, indeed talked openly of assassinating him. Ancre moved first and had him sent to the Bastille.

Condé's mother raised a crowd which sacked Ancre's house while Bouillon, Guise and Vendôme went to raise troops in the provinces. The Duc de Nevers, a Gonzaga from Mantua for all

his French title, son of the Princess of Clèves and grandson of a
Paleologus of the exiled house of Byzantium, was persuaded to
join their cause. Nevers was as vague as he was ambitious in his
plans. On the prompting of Father Joseph he had been on the
point of raising troops in Germany to go on a crusade to oust the
Turks from the Bosphorus and restore the Byzantine dynasty.
Now, in 1616, he led his *landsknechts* to the frontier and raised a
revolt in Champagne, the province of which he was governor.
Meanwhile Bouillon, another international figure and moreover
a Huguenot, had agents sounding out the intentions of England
and Venice, playing on current fears of Spain. Richelieu knew
Nevers through Father Joseph and he was sent to recall him to
his duty, without success. He was alive to the danger of domestic
revolt inviting foreign intervention and argued for decisive
measures: the royal army moved at once against Soissons, Nevers
and Rethel and the revolt was checked. On 25th November 1616,
Richelieu was rewarded by appointment to the Royal Council
as a Secretary of State. Already Nevers had recognised him
as the coming man by starting negotiations with him,
through his sister-in-law the Duchess de Longueville. With
Mangot and Barbin, the latter a resolute and experienced man,
Richelieu was apparently well placed to deal with the pressing
problems of state. All depended, however, on the survival of
Ancre.

On 24th April 1617, Ancre was murdered, in a courtyard of
the Louvre, by Vitry, captain of the guard, and three of his
men. By humiliating the king and by an arrogance and display
which surely revealed his sense of insecurity, Concini had invited
nemesis. His wife claims sympathy rather by her defiance under
torture and the ultimate penalty she paid for 'the black arts' which
she was alleged to have practised, than for her greedy, ambitious
life. As for the ministers, Mangot and Barbin were imprisoned.
Richelieu, however, went unscathed from successive ordeals. In
the Louvre he was snubbed by the young king but, owing possibly
to a good word from Luynes, who appreciated his talents, was
spared anything worse than dismissal. The next day when he
encountered a vicious crowd round the mutilated corpse of
Ancre, there was an awkward moment when it seemed he might
be recognised in his coach. In his own words he 'shouted them
down with the cry: "Long live the king!" Everyone joined in
enthusiastically and let my carriage through.'

It is not impossible that Richelieu might have stayed on to serve the king in some capacity. Instead he seems to have decided that he could be of more use as mediator between the king and the queen mother, who was sent to reside, in virtual exile, at the château of Blois. She was allowed some following and ceremony, as well as government in her province, but it was clearly the intention of the king to rule without her.

## 3. Louis and Luynes

'I am king now', Louis XIII shouted when he heard of Ancre's death. He was then sixteen, an awkward, moody boy, his personality marked for life by the circumstances of childhood when he had shown a wild temper for which his parents' usual remedy was whipping, administered by his governess. Alternately spoiled and bullied, flattered and slighted, expected to be the king on formal occasions such as the opening of the States-General, but left out of serious political decisions and given no regular training for responsibility, Louis looked vacant, slack-jawed, morose; he enjoyed playing chess and he composed music, but his greatest pleasures were physical ones, hunting, war, shoeing horses, making marzipan. Sometimes he found relief in unreasonable acts of violence. The coldness of his mother, not improved by occasional displays of sentiment, was reflected in his own shy and inhibited emotional life. He was capable of love affairs, as with Mme de Hautefort and Mme de la Fayette, but in these relationships, especially the crucial one with his wife, he seemed unable to show regular affection. Happier with men, like Luynes, St Simon or Cinq Mars when he could relax with easy talk about horses and hawks, he still lacked the self-mastery which could win their respect. He seemed to invite emotional scenes, as if he wanted to be humiliated. Mme de Motteville touched on this masochistic streak when she said that the only tender spot in him was the capacity for appreciating his own sufferings. He had his share of the Bourbon callousness which came out so strongly in his son. Unlike his son, however, he was also a martyr to ill-health.

The *mauvaises humeurs,* moods of hysterical depression when he was almost unapproachable, may have been the cause or the effect of his chronic disorders. In his twenties he contracted the tuberculosis which brought him to the grave at the age of forty-one. He was a hypochondriac on the grandest scale: in one year he was bled 47 times, took 212 medicines and 215 purges; even

28

so, he was something of an athlete, happy on horseback or sharing the life of his soldiers. In all he is a figure of some pathos, one of the more wretched of the human beings whom fate has called to the exposed and lonely task of kingship. And yet he was to prove in certain respects the right king for France at this juncture. His withdrawn, jealous spirit went with a great obstinacy and pride. He had the invaluable quality of resolve, in unpleasant crises. When Montmorency was sentenced to death for treason in 1632 it would have been easy, and comfortable, to have pardoned him. By his own lights Montmorency was a good man; he was also one of the greatest of his subjects. But a principle was at stake: the interest of the state demanded that subjects should not be allowed to rebel with impunity. The greater the subject, the greater the danger, and the more necessary to uphold the principle.

It was not a sensitive king that France required, or an imaginative man, but a just one; if he could assume a coldness and calm, and keep men at a distance, so much the better. Louis was convinced of the destiny of France, in a mystical, somewhat superstitious fashion an extension of his idea of kingship as divinely ordained; along with his own sense of personal inferiority this made it possible for him to accept the tutelage of an abler man. His partnership with Richelieu makes one of the more unlikely combinations of political history: it proved effective because of Richelieu's adroitness, his willingness to play the courtier, and Louis XIII's understanding of certain basic needs of the state for which he cared so much.

This lay in the future of which in 1617 there was no hint beyond the young king's excited determination to be master in his house. He leaned primarily upon Charles Albret, Duc de Luynes, whom he regarded as the instrument of his emancipation. Luynes had come up from Provence to be Henry IV's page; he then became Louis XIII's master of falcons. Skilled enough to rouse the king's interest in hunting, tough enough to provide him with an example of virility, sensible in a rough-and-ready way and not afraid to take chances, Luynes promptly filled the place of Ancre. He was energetic but lacking in knowledge of affairs. True or not, the story that at the height of the Bohemian crises which precipitated European war he asked in council if Bohemia were on the sea reflects what Louis' subjects thought of the new favourite! His father had been a Provençal squire; he was now chief minister, duke, and Constable of France. If he had not died in 1621 at the siege of Montauban, it is likely that he would have gone the way of the former favourite. The servants found playing picquet on his coffin provide a wry epitaph on the Duc de Luynes.

Richelieu had insured his position during his months of office by attentions to Luynes and the two men continued to be outwardly civil while Richelieu attended to the business of Marie, and to his bishopric. Each man was in different ways insecure, and realised that his future was bound up with the other's. Richelieu went to his diocese to keep clear of the trouble that was certain to emanate from Blois. He occupied himself with two works of theology, published in 1618 and 1619. *Les Principaux Points de la Foi de l'Eglise Catholique* (The Principal Points of the Faith of the Catholic Church) was a reasonable, objective and penetrating study of Protestantism, written in French rather than the usual Latin of theologians. The book was a well-timed foray into the great debate which had begun the year before with a work by the king's confessor, P. Arnoux, suggesting that the Protestants misused the Bible, and it was widely read. Richelieu's second book was less controversial but no less influential. In form a catechism, with special stress upon the Commandments, it is authoritarian in tone and makes notable use of the idea of Divine Right: with its rejection of Bellarmine's idea that subjects may depose a king who is deliberately evil it put a significant gloss upon accepted ideas of kingship. The *Instruction* was translated into several languages and for a century parts of it were read from the pulpits of parish churches at mass on Sundays. The book was written from Avignon whither in April 1618 Richelieu, with his brother, was ordered into exile on the pretext that he was intriguing with Marie against the king. Luynes was mistaken in this and when, in February 1619, Marie escaped from Blois and joined Épernon, who was leading a cabal with familiar ramifications, he was persuaded by Bérulle and Father Joseph to use the bishop as peace-maker. So in March Richelieu left the Papal city, without regret, to practise his diplomacy on the queen mother. On 4th May she accepted terms which seemed to be favourable to her in that she was granted the governorship of Anjou and the town of Angers. The government was ready to be generous in order to detach her from a confederacy which could use her name to secure Spanish support.

Richelieu's position was enhanced by his diplomatic skill, while he was also able to establish his family in key positions in Anjou: his uncle Amador la Porte was made governor of Angers and his brother-in-law, the Marquis de Brézé, captain of the guards, for the latter, the decisive move in a career which was to lead to his being marshal. As for himself, he knew that the king had asked for a Cardinal's hat. Luynes, who wanted to keep Richelieu in suspense on this score, had also seen to it that Rome was informed that he was unfit for it. More harmful than Luynes' double-dealing, however, was Marie de Médicis' indiscretion. Lacking as she was in patriotism and sense of proportion, she allowed herself to become the centre of renewed plotting. This had been encouraged by the release of Condé from the Bastille, which Luynes hoped would be construed favourably as an act of confidence. The spring and summer of 1620 saw a mustering of magnates in east and west: Longueville in Normandy, his hereditary governorship; Vendôme in Brittany; Épernon's son in Metz. Since the great nobles kept up small permanent forces of their own it is hard to fix a point at which legitimate pressure became open revolt. To this, however, things were drifting, with Luynes undecided and courtiers quietly leaving for the provinces when, at a council on 4th July, Louis suddenly determined to lead an army against the rebels: 'In the face of so many dangers we must march against the greatest and nearest, and that is Normandy! Let us go!'

Confronted with such resolve, the numerous advisers of Marie lacked either nerve or plan. Richelieu, at least according to a pamphlet published soon afterwards, urged her not to fight against Louis: 'There will not be one of your faithful subjects who will advise you to revolt against your son'. The advice was certainly in line with his ideas about rebellion and his likely estimate of the outcome. Louis' small army was big enough to deal with the rebels at a battle fought in a heat haze, such an anti-climax that it became known as the 'drôlerie de Ponts de Cé'. Neither Longueville nor Mayenne was present. Richelieu, who was rewarded for his part in the subsequent negotiations with the pledge of marriage between his niece and Luynes' nephew, had seen how handicapped were the nobility in a direct confrontation with the crown. As he was later to say: 'Those who fight against the power of the state will always be defeated by their own imagination, since behind the enemy they cannot help seeing the executioner'.

Encouraged by their victory, Louis and Luynes decided to mount a long-delayed operation: the restoration of Béarn to Catholicism. The province was the fragment on the French side of the Alps, of the kingdom of Navarre that was left in 1512 when Ferdinand of Aragon joined the rest to Spain. As it was an independent state there had been no obstacle to the furious onslaught upon the Church launched by Jeanne d'Albret and her husband Antoine de Bourbon, father of Henry of Navarre. Henry endowed France with Béarn but needless to say the province did not follow him into the Roman Church. The restoration of the province was one of the conditions on which the Pope had given Henry absolution; he did no more, however, than to appoint two bishops to the sees of Oleron and Lescar. Meanwhile a constitutional debate developed over the status of Béarn. Was it a personal union of crowns or was Béarn, as the States-General claimed in 1614, an integral part of France? In 1617 the Estates of Béarn claimed that their constitution could not be touched by a king of Navarre without their consent, and their cause was adopted by the Huguenot assembly of La Rochelle. The monarchy then decreed that Church property be restored; the commissioners who went to execute the edict were chased out. After the battle of Ponts de Cé Louis made a triumphal tour of the south to overawe the Huguenots; a Jesuit college was founded and the decree executed. Like Bohemia after the Habsburg victory of the White Mountain in November 1620, Béarn was to be restored to the faith. The result was a general Huguenot rising in the winter of 1619-20.

Richelieu at this stage believed that the Huguenots were moved more by fear than a policy of separatism. In the context of European events he saw the danger of a prolonged civil war which would immobilise France at a time when the Habsburgs were exploiting the revolt of Bohemia to good effect, occupying the Palatinate, subjugating Bohemia and resuming the war with the United Provinces on what seemed to be favourable terms. But he was in no position to influence the council, which decided to send an army to crush the Huguenots. Luynes, as Constable, commanded. He captured Saumur, St Jean d'Angely and laid siege to Montauban, under the veteran Duc de la Force. The royal army was checked, the artillery was ineffective and assaults failed; the troops died of typhoid. Luynes was beset by bitter recriminations. When he too died in December the siege had been abandoned. Lesdiguières, lately converted to Rome, took the Constable's sword, captured a number of southern towns, St Antonin, Carcassonne, Narbonne, then led the negotiations with the Huguenots. In October 1622 the Peace of Montpellier provided a compromise which few thought could last. The crown promised to respect the independence of eighty-odd fortified places which remained to them. La Force and Châtillon were consoled for defeat by marshals' batons. Rohan was given a substantial pension but this did not deflect him from his design of turning the area round La Rochelle into an independent republic. Montpellier was not the final solution.

The removal of Luynes was convenient to Richelieu; it was followed by the death of Cardinal de Retz. Since it was traditional for France to have four Cardinals there could be no further valid objection to him. In September 1622 he became a Cardinal; in an ensuing ceremony when he received the broad red hat, he placed it at the feet of the queen mother with the courtly gesture that rarely failed him, as 'a reminder of the solemn vow I have taken to shed my blood in your service'. He gave up his bishopric of Luçon, while retaining a pension of 5,000 livres, and took up a stance at the edge of the council, using Marie as his mouthpiece. La Vieuville, who had emerged as head of the council in 1623, did his best to keep him at bay, offering him ambassadorships in Madrid and Rome. Richelieu had too much in his favour now to be fobbed off with anything less than a place on the council. There was the loud insistence of Marie de Médicis, the possibly more cogent argument of Father Joseph. The ministers seemed to be fumbling and their policy of appeasement looked weak as the Habsburgs moved from strength to strength. Father Joseph realised that before his cherished dream of the crusade could take shape there must be some degree of European unity; Spain would not think in these terms so France must take her place. Richelieu pressed his views through the pens of pamphleteers, notably Fancan, who wrote in 1622: 'The passage of the Rhine is now in the power and disposition of the Marquis Spinola. . . . In a night he can be at the gates of Strasbourg. . . . On the other side Spain has seized the passes of the Val Telline . . . the realm of France will be entirely blockaded.'

While the impact of his message came from this *politique*, nationalist assessment of the European crisis and his awareness of the danger that France might be encircled by the Habsburg

C

alliance, for tactical purposes Richelieu was able to use the argument that the ministry neglected the interests of the Church. The Treaty of Compiègne settled the terms of French support for the Dutch, but la Vieuville failed to obtain from them a guarantee of freedom of worship for Roman Catholics. Even the negotiations for marriage between Prince Charles of England and Louis' sister Henrietta Maria, Richelieu contrived to use against the minister, though the marriage was something of a coup in view of the fact that England had been proposing a Spanish match the year before. He urged that the English should be made to concede the same rights to their Roman Catholics that they had been made to concede in Madrid. Since those concessions had caused a storm in England at the time, there was little chance that they would be repeated. Not without reason, therefore, did la Vieuville complain that 'these infernal priests would spoil everything'. The combination of the *dévôts* and the *politiques* proved too much for him. On 12th April 1624 Richelieu took his seat in council. The very next day he arrived with a prepared document setting out his claim to precedence as a Cardinal. The conflict for power went on through the summer, la Vieuville being undermined steadily by pamphlets, courtiers and not least the popular voice as it expressed itself in successive revolts in the provinces, notably in Lyons, Figeac and Cahors. Before long Louis was convinced that Richelieu was the better man by his reasonable and authoritative statements of France's problems, his confident projections of policy. On 13th August la Vieuville was dismissed and Richelieu summoned to be chief of the council, his official post being only Secretary of State for Commerce and the Marine.

He was thirty-nine years old. Since his early twenties he had lived through crises, both personal and public: he had administrative experience, an intellect of great natural power, sharpened by study, argument and writing, intense concentration and a nervous energy which had so far triumphed over all physical weaknesses. All these attributes he and France now needed. For the acute dangers of the external situation were but an extension of domestic problems of the greatest complexity. Richelieu inherited a crisis of authority which was in itself not new: its origins lay in the 'religious wars'. Nor was it peculiar to France. England, Spain, even to some extent Sweden and the United Provinces were affected. In France there was a specially urgent need for effective and sustained government; the Calvinist minority could exploit the weakness of the state, the class interest of the nobility seemed to demand the continued dispersal of authority rather than its concentration at the centre, and the slowing down of the economy, as was shown by frequent popular revolts, was a weight to be reckoned with on the delicate scales of order and disorder; and there was not least the risk of outside intervention. The civil wars of the later sixteenth century could have reduced France to the condition of a larger Switzerland, or another Germany in which the king's authority was no more effective than the emperor's. Less disastrous, but no less disturbing to Frenchmen to contemplate, was the prospect that provinces in the south and east might be lost—Béarn, Picardy, even Champagne. We should remember too that Richelieu and his contemporaries had neither the advantage of hindsight nor sophisticated techniques of economic measurement to reassure them about the real strength of Spain. In 1624 she looked unprecedentedly strong and menacing.[1]

[1] The struggle for power and Villeroi's career and policy are analysed more fully on pages 183-186.

## 4. *Anarchy or Absolutism?*

The country whose affairs Richelieu was to direct for eighteen years had only recently reached anything like its present shape and was still essentially mediaeval in character. Archaic, Celtic Brittany was finally secured in 1532. Many Bretons could still speak no French. The treaty of Câteau-Cambrésis in 1559 began the process of consolidating the north-eastern frontier by the acquisition of rights of garrison in Metz, Toul and Verdun, while Calais was wrested from the English. The rivers Somme, Meuse and Saône made a frontier on the north-east and east. Despite some pioneer work upon linear definition and fortification, the frontier in Henry IV's time was still conceived of in terms of regions and estates. Provinces such as Franchecomté, Artois, Flanders, Roussillon on the western shore of the Mediterranean, were all links in the Spanish chain. Alsace was Imperial, Lorraine half a French vassal, half-independent under its dukes. To the north-east, east and south, France was very exposed. In the north-east the crucial fact was the proximity of Paris to the Spanish frontier, about 100 miles, under a week's march. The eastern provinces of Champagne and Burgundy lay open to the determined invader, as Richelieu learned in the year of Corbie. Though Henry IV's acquisition of Bresse and Bugey padded out the southern frontier, the Lyonnais and the Dauphiné in the south invited the attention of the Duke of Savoy. The population was about sixteen million, rising slowly if at all; by the end of the century it had reached eighteen to nineteen million but this was mainly to be accounted for by new territory. Spain, by contrast, had but eight million (with Portugal, ten) and her population was actually declining; England had five million, Holland under three, Sweden about one and a half.

Relatively densely populated, having after Italy and the Netherlands the highest proportion of inhabitants (thirty-four) to the square kilometre, with both climate and soil combining to produce a high level of natural fertility, France's potential was immense. But as the history of Poland was to show, size alone was no guarantee of success in the struggle for survival. The very size of France posed problems of order more acute than, for instance, those of England. The outlying provinces of France— Languedoc, Brittany, for example—should be seen as analogous to Scotland and Ireland rather than as counties like Yorkshire or Cornwall or, for the Spaniard, as Catalonia is to Castile. One should recall, too, the way in which France had grown up, as an accretion of provinces, by marriage and conquest round the heartlands of the Île de France and the Loire Valley. The provincialism of France went beyond peasant customs and differences of *patois*. They differed usually in their weights and measures, law, taxation; they might be divided by internal tolls and customs. The country was divided broadly into two systems of law: the *custumel* which prevailed in the north, Roman south of the Loire. There were still independent territories between Lyons and the mouth of the Rhône, like Avignon and Orange, ruled respectively by the Pope and the Prince of Nassau. There were private jurisdictions, private armies, private tolls. The Clermontais, with 40,000 inhabitants, belonged to the Prince de Condé who collected and kept its taxes. Towns such as Marseilles and Bordeaux were virtually self-governing; Marseilles was a 'free port' exempt from dues.

Above all the Huguenots were, in Richelieu's own phrase, 'a state within a state', armed, privileged and separate. They were but the largest of the special situations where the crown was forced to compromise with local interests. At the level of their leaders, men like Rohan, la Force, Soubise, the Huguenots were one tough shoot of the plant of feudal independence, old, rotten in parts, but deep-rooted. The task of monarchies everywhere in the sixteenth and seventeenth centuries was to increase the authority of the central government at the expense of the aristocracy with whom the crown had long been forced to share, bargain and compromise in order to survive. In England, the great dynastic conflict, the Wars of the Roses, was fought out before the Reformation, which might have added fanaticism to party feeling and exacerbated a sufficiently bloody war by the emotional and dogmatic rivalry of creeds and churches. This accident, together with the high proportion of casualties in a relatively small and compact noble class, made the task of the Tudors easier. They were also an exceptionally capable house, and they managed to use the Reformation proceedings to strengthen the resources

of the monarchy. Even so, during Elizabeth's reign, the crown
steered with difficulty, and some luck, between the extremes of
religion and party: the factors of civil war were present. In France,
during the same period, from the death of Henry II in 1559 to
the accession of Henry IV in 1589, the crown was weak; Francis II
and Charles IX were minors. Henry III was inconstant and
neurotic, a disastrous ruler for all his ability and fitful periods of
resolution. Catherine, the queen mother, was tenacious and clever
only in devising short-term solutions. The prolonged struggle
between the crown and the factions temporarily checked the
advance of absolutist theories of government which had been
favoured under Francis I and Henry II.

The Huguenots justified their stand in two treatises on the
right of resistance to a tyrant. The *Franco-Gallia* of 1573 rested
upon the quasi-historical argument that the Valois kings were
imposing a foreign, Roman system on a Frankish people. The
Gauls, according to this thesis, had released the Franks from the
tyranny of the Latins and put in its place the sovereign authority
of the Estates. The more profound *Vindiciae contra tyrannos* of
1579 gave a philosophical basis to the need to resist unjust rulers,
by use of classical and scriptural examples. One wing of Catholic
thinking, represented by Mariana and acted on by the Guises
and the Holy League, used the same arguments to justify tyranni-
cide. Such arguments carried in them the seed of reaction.[1]
At the time, however, they corresponded to political realities
for, as is usual, political theory tended to rationalise an existing
situation.

Resistance to the weak crown was a valid attitude, a profitable
activity at all levels. The Huguenots moved after the massacre
of St Bartholomew's Eve into an overtly revolutionary position.
The League set itself up as an independent body with the aim of
furthering Catholicism in France and excluding Henry of Navarre
from the throne. It was organised on an urban basis, with groups
in most of the larger towns. The success of Leaguers in capturing
key public offices and the zealous partisanship of its clerical
sympathisers made the League a more effective body than its
numbers would suggest. Like the Huguenots they drew on aid
from outside the country: in return for their support of Philip II

[1] See pages 41-50 and 240-241 for a more detailed account of the
trend of political ideas.

they received a subsidy and later an army. There was talk in these years of re-establishing the middle kingdom of Lotharingia: the Guises were in a position to implement their own propaganda since they controlled eastern France from Rheims to the Dauphiné. At the end of his reign Henry III even lost control of his capital.

The alliance in 1588 of Henry of Guise, the only faction leader ready to play demagogue, and the *Seize*, the secret organisation based upon the sixteen sections of the city, pledged to overthrow the leaders of Parlement and even to assassinate the king, was the nadir of monarchy in France—at least since the English wars. In the States-General which ensued, the Third Estate demanded, among other things, that the subsidy granted to the king was to be controlled by a special commission elected from the Estates. It was evidently the aim of Guise and his faction to control the state without radically changing the political or social structure of the country. But they were travelling along a dangerous road, for the elements of a revolutionary situation existed in France as in the Netherlands. Until its recapture by Henry IV in 1594 the *Seize* controlled Paris by methods which provided a foretaste of a greater revolution. The city which had already witnessed one cruel pogrom in 1572 experienced another reign of terror. The climax was the arbitrary execution of Brisson, Premier Président of the Parlement, with two other judges, for failing to convict one of the men they accused. By such methods, however, the *Seize* scared and alienated noble and bourgeois leaders and prepared the way for the reaction.

The claim of the Guise faction that the States-General was 'the brain of the state', although wildly unconstitutional upon any strict consideration of precedents and traditions, was valid comment on the breakdown of royal government. The fact that some prominent bourgeois were prepared to throw in their lot with the aristocratic leaders of the League, and that some, follow-ing the lead of Louis Turquet de Mayerne[1] in the reign of

[1] Louis Turquet de Mayerne was a Huguenot: his father was a merchant and banker, originally from Savoy; his son became Henry IV's doctor and later went to England to be doctor to James I and Charles I. Louis himself displayed the originality and radicalism, which seem to have been traits of the family, in his writing. He wrote in 1591, but did not publish till 1611 when the circumstances of the minority no doubt suggested that it would be well received, *De la Monarchie aristodemo-cratique*. The book was seized by order of the council and only the fear of upsetting the Huguenots seems to have deterred the Regent from

Henry IV, took into the new century their determination to resist royal authority, shows the extent to which the solid, propertied and professional classes of France were disillusioned by the events of the last Valois reigns. For the lapse into provincial autonomy, the fragmentation of France into semi-hereditary fiefs, menaced law and order and the well-being of the economy. The same disillusionment which made some want to resist royal power made others all the more anxious to support it.

---

taking action against the author himself. He was in advance of his time and representative of but a small minority. His ideas are interesting however as suggesting a direction that bourgeois thought might have taken if anarchy had been prolonged. They also contain elements which we usually associate with the 'Enlightenment' of the eighteenth century. Human society, he held, was under natural laws like the physical world. Society should be classified according to talents, not race or birth. 'A poor nobility is useless to the state' but (his solution is the opposite to Richelieu's) the remedy lay in opening the ranks of nobility to the people ('la pépinière de la noblesse'). By 'people' he meant of course the bourgeoisie and specifically the merchants, whose skill, diligence and integrity peculiarly fitted them to lead the state. Sovereignty lay with the people and kings held their fiefs from God—but through the intermediary of the people. Sovereignty rested on two contracts, that of the people with God, which produced society, and that of the king with the people which produced the polity. (This was only a variant of orthodox Calvinist thinking at this time, represented for instance by Hotman and Duplessis-Mornay; advanced League thinkers also reckoned that the king ruled conditionally and accorded him the status of magistrate, an executor of laws.) The States-General was to be the natural guardian of the laws of God and nature (one may add the bourgeois social order) and this body even had the duty of surveying the king's private conduct. So the upper bourgeoisie administer the country, exercise legislative power, and, although the king is left with the right to make decisions, control the executive.

Mayerne saw in mathematics the method par excellence by which the human spirit could attain to truth. He was a deist (he scarcely mentions Christ in his writing). He seems to have been considering France as an abstract or model rather than as a living society, and his notion of society rested on a utilitarian concept of merit and status. At a time when the main ambition of most bourgeois seems to have been to ape the nobles, and secure land and titles, Mayerne may appear to be an isolated figure in this as in so much else. We can see however why the government thought it necessary to suppress his work.

This subject is explored in an important article by R. Mousnier, 'L'Opposition politique bourgeoise à la fin du XVI siècle et au début de XVII siècle—L'Oeuvre de Louis Turquet de Mayerne', *Revue Historique*, 213, 1955.

During the religious wars a party grew up who called themselves *politiques* and undertook not to put religious considerations before those of the country. Chancellor l'Hôpital (who died in 1573) was their first important political representative, Montaigne and Bodin their philosophers, the author of the *Satire Ménippée* their leading and typical propagandist.[1] L'Hôpital was a moderate, whose saying that a man does not cease to be a citizen because he has been excommunicated might be taken as the motto of the *politiques*. He opposed force on grounds of conscience but he could not maintain a consistent position when confronted by the Huguenot threat: 'The division of language', he said, 'does not divide kingdoms, but that of religion and law does and makes two kingdoms out of one'. Montaigne was a sceptic and stoic who was convinced that the main cause of the suicidal wars of religion was an excessive trust in reason, which led men to try to translate religious mysteries into fixed creeds and exclusive parties. Bodin dwelt sombrely on the decay of political life in France in his *Republic* (1576)[2] and concluded that it was necessary to divert men from civil struggles by providing them with a goal or enemy outside themselves: his message was therefore one of aggressive nationalism in commerce as in politics; nor did he shrink from the conclusion that, since it was 'almost impossible to maintain subjects in peace and friendship if they are not at war', it could be accepted as a principle that 'the best way to preserve a state and guarantee it against rebellions and seditions . . . is to have an enemy against whom they can dress themselves'.

The weakness of the *politiques* was that the last Valois kings failed to provide a strong lead or a satisfactory image. Henry IV,

---

[1] The *Satire Ménippée* was originally circulated in manuscript form at the time of the States-General of 1593 and was printed afterwards. Several authors seem to have contributed to its violently partisan, anti-Spanish, anti-Papal pages: the principal, without doubt, was Pierre Pithou.

[2] Jean Bodin wrote the *Six livres de la République* in 1576. The essence of his teaching, which was very influential, in England as well as in France, was that the state was the only organisation with power sufficient to direct men to their ends. Laws of the state must conform to natural and divine law—by which he meant that the state must secure the conditions under which men may worship God undisturbed. Believing as he did in a universal moral order, he required the state to establish a regime in which citizens could find justice. But to the ruler was reserved the right to decide upon matters of religion.

aided by the divisions of his opponents and by the maladroit interference of Spain, was able to provide both. That he was, until 1593, a heretic in the eyes of most of his subjects came to matter less than the fact that he ruled by hereditary right. The author of the *Satire Ménippée* put this in words which must have evoked strong feelings at the time and which seem, like so much of the *Satire*, to be quintessentially French, tenderly romantic, arrogant—or as one might say today, Gaullist: 'We want a king so that we may have peace, but we do not want to imitate the frogs. We want a natural, not artificial king, already made and not still to be made. In this matter we do not wish to take the advice of the Spaniards, who are our inveterate enemies and who wish to tutor us by force. . . . The king we ask for has already been made by nature. He was born in the real garden of the flowers of France, a straight green shoot from the stem of St Louis. Those who speak of making another are mistaken. We can make dozens of marshals and peers but not a king. He must be born of himself.' When this 'natural' king established himself, not only the *politiques* but former Leaguers like Villeroi and Jeannin rallied to him and affirmed their faith in hereditary monarchy.

There were undoubtedly strong centrifugal forces at work in France, challenging the authority of the king and the unity of his realm. Yet the seventeenth century saw a great advance in the status of monarchy and the concentration of power in a centralised administration. In this process, we shall see, Richelieu played a vital part. He was heir to the *politiques*, profoundly influenced by their ideas and by the historical events out of which those ideas had grown. Like Henry and Sully before him, he was assisted by a pronounced movement of opinion in favour of discipline and order among the articulate and responsible citizens. 'Things fall apart, the centre cannot hold, mere anarchy is loosed upon the world . . . and everywhere the ceremony of innocence is drowned.' The words are those of a modern poet, W. B. Yeats. Do they not describe the experience of civil war from the point of view of those who were at the centre—and felt they had most to lose? Pascal later expressed what many of his contemporaries undoubtedly believed: 'The greatest of all evils is civil war. The evil to be feared from a fool who succeeds by right of birth is not as considerable nor as certain.' The opportunity to reinforce the powers of the crown existed in 1624, after another period of civil disturbance, as it had in 1598 at the end of the religious wars. Richelieu took the opportunity with ruthlessness and *éclât*. But the development of absolute monarchy cannot be seen merely in terms of the personality of the ruler or the opinion of the ruled. Monarchy had strong roots in France. By their laws and institutions as well as by their traditions Frenchmen were prepared to accept royal authority. When the king was weak, interested parties took advantage of the fact and found apologists to justify their attitude. Even when a strong king tried to enlarge his sphere of authority there was sure to be resistance. But this resistance lacked constitutional machinery to make it effective, as is demonstrated by the fiasco of the States-General and the uninspiring record of the Parlements in this century.

A French king could draw on a fund of loyal sentiment as old as the dynasty of Capet, deriving from centuries when the kingdom was relatively small and beleaguered and when the king was seen as the protector, the embodiment of unity, and the source of justice. With the awareness of mutual dependence that is characteristic of feudal monarchy went an element of intimacy and family spirit. As a French ambassador at the Spanish court at this time observed: 'The Spaniards love their state more than their rulers while the French love their sovereign personally'. Bignon[1] wrote of this informality and accessibility of French kings: 'It is this which attracts and wins Frenchmen's hearts and makes them affectionate and devoted to their prince . . . without force or constraint'. There was an outcry when, in the sixteenth century, the prefix of Majesté was introduced: 'What are these mimicries, these idolatries, these barbarous fashions?' demanded one critic. There was nothing new about ceremony; indeed, the court of Francis I was far more magnificent, and in relation to the total expenditure of the crown more costly, than that of Louis XIII. But the regal style which Louis XIII learned how to assume and which was second nature to Louis XIV, and the elaborate rituals which were perfected in the court of the latter were alien to the French tradition: Byzantine in origin, Spanish in manner, an

---

[1] Jerome Bignon was one of the cleverest men of his time. An ardent royalist, a humanist who was friend of such men as Pithou, Grotius and Scaliger, and a successful royal official who became *avocat-général* in the Parlement of Paris, in 1625, he wrote about monarchy in terms which betray the sentimental Parisian as well as the dedicated careerist, in his *De l'excellence des Roys et du Royaume de France*. Paris, 1610.

exotic growth indeed, but suited to an idea of kingship which reached its highest point of acceptance and exaltation in the second half of the seventeenth century.

The king stood for continuity. Legitimacy was crucial. Since the right of the Valois had been uncertain from the start and contested by the English kings as co-descendants from Philip V, it was all the more stressed by their protagonists. The ultimate victory of the Valois kings was hailed as God's blessing on the dynasty. The misfortunes of the fifteenth century helped to reinforce the image of the royal saviour—when France was saved. Literary arguments embellished the Scriptures when patriotic scribes presented the case for the legitimacy of the Valois and their claim on the obedience of their subjects. If miracles occurred, as in the case of Jeanne d'Arc, that was only to be expected. In the fourteenth century the *oriflamme*, the scarlet silk banner of St Denis, and the *fleur de lis*, the lily on the banner of France, originally the arms of Philippe Auguste, both acquired miraculous origins. The king himself was more than merely human, miraculously endowed from the moment in the coronation at Rheims when he was anointed with the holy oil of Clovis (which had descended in a phial from heaven for that king's baptism and had ever thereafter been miraculously renewed). When the king was crowned he wore his tunic 'like that of a sub-deacon at the Mass': his mantle was 'raised on the left, as one raises the chasuble of a priest'. *Le roi thaumaturge*, thus set apart, was constantly assured that he was like a prelate, 'the first in your kingdom after the Pope, the right arm of the Church'. He was *très-chrétien*, a description which became almost a formal title. He touched for the 'king's evil', scrofula. Francis I, in whose reign the latent powers of the crown were exploited to the full, made a regular practice of it; he was even asked to carry out a healing ceremony when he was a captive in Italy. Louis XIII was also assiduous in carrying out this picturesque rite at the great Church festivals. In the year 1620, he touched 3,125 people. It made good publicity for the crown, but it also seems to have been taken seriously by all concerned.[1]

[1] Marc Bloch, in his masterly study, *Les Rois Thaumaturges,* Paris, 1924, quotes a bishop of Evreux, Robert Ceneau, as saying: 'The majority of the kings of France cannot be called mere laymen. Of this there are diverse proofs: first the holy unction which takes its origin from the sky itself; then the celestial privilege of the healing of the

In the succession of a line that was, according to a speaker at
the States-General of 1468, 'singularly decorated with grace and
celestial prerogative', Louis IX, St Louis, the Christian knight
par excellence, had pride of place. He believed in kingship as a
trust for which its holder was responsible to God alone. Removed
from the context of thirteenth-century feudalism with all its
limitations on arbitrary power, the ideal of the Christian prince
was made to serve the cause of absolutism. Du Boys[1] declared
that kings were the image of God, 'masters in the obedience that
a subject owes them; seigneurs, as owners of the goods and lives
of men; sovereigns, as having no one over them; protectors, as it
were a shield and buckler'. Indeed men could do nothing without
kings, for 'human life would be no more than confusion and
disorder. They have been placed above men in the same way that
God is above the angels. . . . They are like a second soul in the
universe, a rainbow which sustains the world.' Duchesne[2], his
contemporary, wrote in the same vein: 'Kings of France are
specially chosen by God . . . kings who by the divine character
which His hand has implanted have the honour of being at the
head of all the kings of Christendom'. In 1625 the Bishop of
Chartres went so far as to say in the name of the Assembly of
Clergy: 'Prophets announce, Apostles confirm and Martyrs confess that kings are ordained by God, and not only that, but that
they are themselves Gods'. The words anticipate Bossuet and the
full flowering of the theory of Divine Right. Louis XIII may have
taken this fulsome stuff with a pinch of salt. But he applied himself
devoutly, with sometimes agonising self-appraisal, to his *métier
du roi*, and his confessor seldom appealed to his conscience in
vain. In his exalted view of kingship he had much to support
him besides the arguments of theologians.

In Louis XIII's reign, a party came into being who called
themselves '*bons Français*', signifying that they pursued a policy

---

scrofula . . . and last, the right of the *régale*, above all the spiritual *régale*.
Louis XIII's doctor, Hérouard, recorded numerous occasions when
the king 'touched' gatherings of invalids (*Journal de Jean Hérouard*, ed.
Soulié and de Bathelemy 1868). The ceremony usually took place in
Paris in the grand gallery of the Louvre. It was announced by sound of
trumpets several days before.

[1] H. du Boys, *De l'origine et autorité des Roys*. Paris, 1604.

[2] A. Duchesne, *Les Antiquités et Recherches de la Grandeur et Majesté des
Rois de France*. Paris, 1609.

inspired by nothing other than the good of the crown, as against the *dévôts*, who put first the international interests of Catholicism. They held that the king should be obeyed as the supreme incarnation of the state, and some even went so far as to say that between state and king no distinction could be made. They were the heirs of the *politiques* of the religious wars, when Gallicanism had become a sort of patriotism. At the start of the seventeenth century the Catholicism of a majority of the court and magistracy, and a large part of the Church hierarchy, was staunchly Gallican. Henry IV, so recently converted for what seemed to be reasons of state, was an argument in himself. There was a widespread suspicion of Spain. In Parlement the lawyers cherished a long tradition of opposition to Rome. It was an axiom with them that there could be no ecclesiastical exception to the royal authority. The 'Gallican liberties' which expressed the special position of French Catholics with regard to Rome were constantly being examined and restated, as for instance during the controversy over the entry of the Jesuits into France. In what might have been a nursery of constitutional opposition *parlementaires* devoted themselves to establishing the dependence of the Church upon the protection of the king's court, and therefore enhancing the spiritual and secular authority of the king. Though not accepted by all, the axioms of Roman law lent themselves to absolute government. The same is true of the canon law of the churchmen.

There were several interpretations of the nature and extent of royal power. Absolutists, who seem to have been the prevailing influence, claimed that the king, as God's viceregent on earth and as embodying the state, was the sole law giver and bound by no human ordinance or control. In the words of Loyseau[1] 'Sovereignty consists in absolute power, that is to say perfect and entire in all particulars. . . . As there can be no crown without its being a complete circle, so there can be no sovereignty if there is anything lacking in it.' The sovereign therefore has the power to make laws, give privileges and remove them, make and unmake officers, render justice, coin money and levy taxes without the consent of the Estates. Loyseau concludes: 'the power of a prince extends as well over goods as over persons: it follows then that he can command the goods as well as he can the person of his subjects . . . for the proper necessity of his people'. The

[1] C. Loyseau, *Traité des Ordres*. Paris, 1613.

Parlement of Paris would not go so far. While admitting that authority resided in the king's person, it did not accept that he was free to dispose of the kingdom as he wished. He was not owner but administrator and was subject to fundamental laws which guaranteed the rights of his subjects.

What were these fundamental laws? Another way of putting the question is: how did Frenchmen envisage the rights of the king and of subjects within the state? The state was customarily described as a body of which the king was head and the people of the three orders the limbs, all together comprising the *corps politique et mystique*[1] which is so made that if one part suffers, the whole suffers as well. An organism, unlike a mechanism, operates according to the natural laws of its being. Ideally there was no conflict of interest between ruler and people. But it was recognised that the ideal was not always realised. Then political theorists produced doctrines of resistance drawing upon contract, natural law and historical precedents. How empty these were when there was no constitutional machinery to give effect to them! While in England, in the reigns of the early Stuarts, the crucial battles about sovereignty and the control of finance—the tactical weapon which the French monarchy held so strongly in its grasp—were being fought between king and parliament, in France monarchy was compelling acceptance of its authority. The best that le Bret[2] can say, in answer to the question about resistance to an unjust authority, is that the sovereign courts should make 'serious remonstrances to the prince and try by all sorts of means to turn

---

[1] The description is that of Guy Coquille in his *Discours des Etats de France*, 1588. The phrase *corps mystique* also appears in Seyssel's treatise, *La Grande Monarchie de France*, 1519 (ed. Jacques Poujol, Paris, 1961). It has an interesting history. *Corpus Mysticum*, meaning the Eucharist, was replaced in Church usage in the twelfth century by *Corpus Christi*, to stress the doctrine of real presence. *Corpus Mysticum* was thereafter used more to describe the Church. The secular state then acquired this description as befitting its transcendental status. It soon came into the political arena. In 1615, Chancellor du Prat told the deputies of Parlement that the well-being of the realm was the well-being of the king because it was a 'corps mistique dont le Roy est le chef'.

[2] Cardin le Bret, *De la souveraineté du Roy*, Paris, 1632. In le Bret's work we can see how hard it was in practice to maintain the validity of the 'fundamental laws'. His idea of sovereignty, although anchored to 'the common good', was 'a supreme power bestowed on an individual, which gives him the right to command absolutely'. He believed that all institutions and customs could be changed by the royal authority.

him from such policies'. Set this alongside the edict of 1641 forbidding the courts to consider affairs of state without special command of the king and it will be seen how feeble in practice mere 'remonstrance' might be. The preamble to the edict begins: 'A monarchical state cannot suffer any hand to be laid on the sceptre of the sovereign or to share his authority'.

Yet Frenchmen did not think that their government was despotic. Loyseau rejected the notion of seigneurial monarchy, in which the king enjoyed complete control of the goods and persons of his subjects, as being barbarous and unnatural. What then, we may ask, of violations of individual liberty, imprisonments by *lettre de cachet,* confiscations and trials before special tribunals? (The latter was a feature of Richelieu's administration.) These acts were usually treated as exceptional and rare extensions of the king's authority as supreme justiciar and custodian of public safety, and therefore justifiable when that safety was endangered by plots, rebellions and war. If we apply this criterion to Richelieu's invasions of private liberty we find that it holds good. Indeed, nothing is more impressive about Richelieu's statecraft than the discrimination with which he used his arbitrary powers. True that 'the public interest' is a dangerous excuse when it is one man or party that decides what is the public interest. But this arbitrary element is an integral part of the French system. As le Bret said, 'It is the glory of a great prince to be secret in his counsels'.

Effective sanctions did not then lie in single institutions so much as in the character of the whole. The basic sanction was the Salic law, 'engraved in the hearts of Frenchmen' (Bignon) according to which the succession passed from male to male by the rule of primogeniture: the king could not choose amongst his offspring, nor could there be an election. He was restricted, and so were his subjects, by that unwritten law which Frenchmen had 'taken from nature itself'. Once he had come to the throne in this legitimate way, the king, consecrated and anointed, submitted to no one but to God. In the seventeenth century this was accepted as natural and fitting, almost, one is tempted to say, taken for granted by ruler and subject. In a society that was deeply penetrated by religious ideas and sentiments, submission to God was more than a polite phrase. Louis XIII and Louis XIV both consistently spoke and acted as men aware of their responsibility to a supernatural being with awful powers of favour and punishment. Victories, contentment and material prosperity were marks of God's approval of a good ruler. Defeats, famines and plagues signified that he was displeased with the king's behaviour or decisions.

However seriously king and subject took the sanctions of religion, the fact remains that all the powers of government, legislative, executive, judicial, were concentrated in the hands of one man. Was this not a dictatorship? Were the restraints of nature and tradition anything but pious fictions when in practice the ruler could be as arbitrary as he pleased? The answer lies in the fact that the majority of intelligent Frenchmen wanted a strong monarchy as the only alternative to disorder. Absolutism was generated by conflicts within a society of separate and privileged orders and interests. Only the king could command the allegiance of so many different bodies and individuals. The feudal rights of the seigneur, the independent status of towns, the privileged rules of the religious orders, universities and guilds, the particularism of provinces, made the king necessary if the country were to remain whole. In an age that witnessed the slow passing of feudal society, with its essentially personal notions of allegiance, and only knew faint stirrings of a conception of national sovereignty, awareness of the *patrie* was a vague sentiment rather than a dynamic force in men's lives. In the absence of any true organic unity, only the person of the king unified France. Resounding claims were made on his behalf but they indicate the weakness of his authority in practical terms of what government could achieve.

This was a fragile and insecure society, in which more than half the population lived at a bare level of subsistence; a jealously divided society in which civil disturbance was endemic and in which every advance of the central government was met by bitter resistance. The France of the *ancien régime* was also an unequal society in which the privileged were able to protect their rights, and the others had to rely upon goodwill and fortune. In such a situation the emphasis should not be on the rights that individuals lost by accepting the sovereignty of the absolute king but rather on the security they gained. Absolute monarchy grew out of particularism and violence. Privileged bodies, aristocracy, Parlements, were too concerned with sectional interests to offer a national solution. A strong monarchy, centralising and egalitarian, could do so. It was limited all the same by the conditions out of which it grew. The government of Louis XIII and Richelieu

D

was absolute in theory and increasingly effective. Yet it may well seem to be less arbitrary—and effective—than even the 'democratic' governments of today! One recalls de Gaulle's aphorism: 'Every Frenchman desires to enjoy one or more privileges. It is his way of asserting his passion for equality.'

The tradition of feudal independence and the separatism of the provinces went together in the position of the provincial governors. What this could amount to in their heyday can be seen in the splendid figure of Anne de Montmorency (1493-1567), the greatest landowner in France and the Constable, grandfather of Richelieu's antagonist, the last duke, who was executed in 1632. When he attended a meeting of the royal council at Fontainebleau in 1560, 800 followers attended him, a private army and a *clientèle* that would include many young sprigs of the *noblesse* who saw as much chance of advancement in the service of a magnate as in that of the king. The Constable's eldest son, François, was governor of the Île de France and was protector as well as representative of the king. For his nephew Coligny, who was governor of Normandy, the Constable secured the parallel feudal office of Admiral. Coligny became the Huguenot leader in the civil wars and his daughter married William the Silent. These family groupings were international and even transcended religious differences. In France Montmorency's power and direct patronage stretched from Languedoc to the Channel coast. There was a comparable position in the east, where the Guise family ruled from the Dauphiné to Champagne: here a key figure was the Cardinal of Lorraine, Archbishop of Rheims.[1]

Religious differences gave faith and cohesion to the rival parties and it is right to call these civil wars 'religious wars'.

---

[1] Marc Bloch, in his book *Feudal Society* (Paris 1939-40; translated by L. Maynon, 1961), gives impressive evidence of the survival of feudalism in seventeenth-century France, which will come as no surprise to students of English history in the same period. 'Even in France of the early Bourbons the nobleman who, in order to make his way in the world, became the servant of a great man, assumed a status remarkably akin to primitive vassalage.' 'One *belonged* [my italics] to Monsieur le Prince.' In June 1658 a Captain Deslandes addressed himself to Fouquet: 'I promise and give my fealty to my lord the procurator-general . . . never to belong to any but him, to whom I give myself and attach myself with the greatest attachment of which I am capable'. This echoes, says Bloch, the most absolute of the formulae of commendation.

But we must recall how contemporaries saw them. Evoking the feudal quarrels of the families of Guise and Châtillon-Montmorency, the author of the *Satire Ménippée* declares: 'For all the bloody tragedies which have been played out on this pitiful French stage arose from these first quarrels, and not from differences of religion'.

The nobility had lost the profits of war by the Peace of Câteau-Cambrésis in 1559, but not the appetite that had grown with the feeding, the habits of violence, the sense of emancipation from civil restraints. In a period of rapidly rising prices and conspicuous consumption they fought now for the offices and pensions to be wrested from the crown. In this age of ruffs and rapiers, slashed doublets and jewelled cloaks, when entertaining, above all building, was fiercely competitive, men threw away fortunes in a few months at court, mortgaged and sold their estates, duelled and brawled with a recklessness and violence that reflected fundamental uncertainties of place and purpose. In the States-General, in its occasional meetings, in provincial Estates, in Parlements, in Huguenot synods and colloquies, even in peasant gatherings in country lanes and market places, at all levels they strove to maintain a privileged place in an increasingly fluid society. By defeating the Guise party, reducing the power of individual nobles, treating with the Huguenots, destroying unauthorised strongholds and in general by asserting the precedence of the crown, Henry IV and Sully had gone some way towards solving the problem. That this achievement was impermanent was shown, however, by the events of the minority when, as we have seen, the nobility levied blackmail on the crown. 'What is now happening', wrote Sully, who saw his patient efforts undone after the 'peace' of St Ménéhould in 1614, 'is simply a pact guaranteeing that the rebels will get millions and lordships and fortresses whenever they want'. The situation was made worse by the existence of the royal bastards, Henry IV's unfortunate legacy, with pretensions to royalty but no secure place, inevitably an uneasy element: two of these, César, Duc de Vendôme, and Alexandre, Grand Prior of Malta, were both to be thorns in Richelieu's flesh.

Overmighty subjects, too great in estates, connections and offices, these 'satraps', as a contemporary called them, provide the spectacular element in the struggle of the crown against privileged classes. As Richelieu recognised, they got prestige

and followers from the depressed condition of the ordinary
*noblesse d'épée*. From his relatively detached viewpoint he was a
keen-eyed analyst of the values and faults of his class and sympathetic to their claims for privileged treatment in the stringent
aftermath of the price revolution. The inflation of prices had
affected the landowners' position throughout the sixteenth
century in every country in Europe. In Poitou, on the reckoning
of Raveau,[1] the purchasing power of the livre fell between the
reigns of Louis XI and Henry IV by more than three-quarters.
Producers suffered little. It was the smaller landowners, who
lived on rents, and day labourers, whose wages lagged behind
prices, who suffered most.

[1] P. Raveau, *L'Agriculture . . . dans le Haut Poitou*, Paris, 1926.

## 5. *The Condition of the People*

In 1569 the Venetian ambassador described the *noblesse* as 'crippled by debts'. François de la Noue, voicing the nostalgia of his class for the days of 'our good kings Louis XII and Francis I', said that 'out of ten noble families one will find eight inconvenienced by the alienation of some property, by mortgage or other forms of debt'. As Richelieu found when he took over the management of the family estate from his elder brother, this was exactly the case with his family. Often rents were fixed, as when the land was let in perpetuity in the mediaeval years of land shortage to prevent its going out of cultivation altogether. Usually the seigneur would not farm all the land himself but would let out more than half *en métayerie*, the *métayer* or share cropper working the land and paying a percentage of the proceeds, usually in kind, in return for the money for stock and seed. The seigneur's revenue was precarious, depending upon all the imponderables of country life, but he was more successful than his counterpart in England in retaining his privileged status. He enjoyed an imposing array of rights: the *lods et ventes*, a tax upon tenants' land changing hands; the *redevances en nature*, percentage tax in kind upon all crops raised on the seigneurial land; the *péages* or tolls on goods passing through their estates; the *corvée*, entitling him to claim the labour of peasants on his domain land for a week or so in the year; the *banalités* by which he could compel each tenant to bring grain and grapes to his own mill and wine press, not to mention the host of minor perquisites from which a keen bailiff could squeeze some extra revenue. Hundreds of pigeons would fly from his dovecote, returning to roost at night after gorging upon the peasants' corn. The *droit de chasse* enabled him to pursue his game in the open fields and woodlands, regardless of standing crops. That an edict as late as 1669 forbade hunting over land when the corn was in stalk, while at the same time renewing the ban on hunting by all *roturiers* (commoners), even on their own land, gives an idea of the menace of the *droit de chasse* on some estates.

Often, however, the privileges were poor things to set against the material problems of the seigneur's existence. Everything expected of his rank had to be paid for: a commission for his son or a place at college; for a girl a dowry for marriage or for a convent; fine clothes for himself and his servants if he wished to visit court. Accepted custom, which hardened into the law of *dérogeance*, by which he stood to forfeit noble status, prevented his adopting a career in law or in trade. If he took to soldiering he had to provide for his family. The majority of seigneurs lived close to the peasants, in a more mutually dependent position than might be expected from a mere recital of their privileges. Evidence from the records of the raising of the *arrière-ban* show that a great many noblemen had an annual income of less than 300 livres. Some exploited their rank to rob and abuse their peasants but others settled to the simple life. Educated at the same school as his peasants, attending their church, leading them out in hunts, joining in feasts and dances, only perhaps the sword he wore, the leisure he enjoyed, his simple manor house with its dovecote and stables, distinguished the seigneur from the richer peasants. If he lived in one of the provinces of *taille réelle*, he had to pay tax on an estate that was *roturière*. Otherwise he was exempt from direct tax. He was, however, affected by the *aides* and other indirect taxes, and by the *arrière-ban*, originally a feudal summons to military service, which became a levy of money rather than of troops. Such a man was an *hobereau*, to use the contemptuous expression of the courtiers.

Only a minority of the nobles went to court. There the prizes were alluring but failure to secure them meant ruin. In 1627 the court nobility were described as being 'in the most pitiable condition they have ever been in. Poverty overwhelms them, enforced idleness makes them vicious, oppression has reduced them practically to despair.' Exaggeration no doubt, but an echo of the resentments which gave these men a vested interest in war or, if there was no foreign war, then in the ventures of his feudal superior or patron. Life for them was reduced to the level of a gamble. With impotent resentment they watched the bourgeois growing prosperous in office or trade, and important in government. They sold their estates to rich merchants and tried to recoup their fortunes by arranging marriages, *mésalliances*, with bourgeois families. It was the growing discrepancy between the apparent privileges of the *noblesse* and their real powerlessness that made them so anti-social. Their condition explains some aspects of Richelieu's policy towards duelling, towards the provinces, and the Huguenots; and his concern with colonies and commerce. He appreciated that it was impossible to have an effective foreign policy so long as revolts against his authority could assume the character of large-scale popular risings against the state. The ambitions of the magnates, the discontents of the *noblesse* made two parts of this threat: a third was the plight of the peasantry who would be the raw material of any popular insurrection.

As elsewhere in Europe the economy of France was essentially agricultural: nine out of ten Frenchmen lived on the land. The village was the cell of collective life for the vast majority, close-knit, with understood traditions and obligations, a common rhythm of seasonal labours and festivals, with customs about grazing rights and crop rotation as ingrained as the dirt on a peasant's hands. Within the village there was a hierarchy, complex in some areas, simple in others, but always more subtle in gradation than the categories of the social historian lead one to expect. The difficulty of defining the 'peasant problem' is that the status and income of peasants varied so widely within the village, between one district and another, and from year to year. There was a great difference between farming in one of the relatively fertile districts of the north, the Beauce or Picardy, for example, and the poorer districts of southern, western and central France, Quercy, the Limousin, or Brittany. That there was poverty and suffering on a vast scale is beyond doubt. The widespread indebtedness of villages, repeated defaulting in tax payments, furious peasant risings and periodic famines in which large numbers actually died of starvation, bear witness to the gravity of the problem. The weight of misfortune fell unevenly, but all were affected to some extent by the forces that checked the development of agriculture.

The population was always rising past the point at which subsistence was possible, and being brought back by famines and plagues. Economic circumstances no doubt induced some parents to accept voluntary restraint, but artificial birth control was unknown and families of ten or more were not uncommon. The population could therefore have doubled within half a century had it not been for a rate of mortality almost past belief to the fortunate citizens of the twentieth century. There would be a small increase in numbers during a period of years when there was no natural disaster. Then a sequence of wet summers, ruined harvests, and the epidemics which usually followed, produced famine conditions and the mortality rate would rise. First the old, the weak, and little children would appear in the parish burial registers; but then as disease and hunger took their toll, even the able-bodied would succumb. By spring, always the worst season after a bad harvest, the population might have been reduced by a tenth or even a quarter; there would then be fewer marriages and births, and it would be some years before numbers began to rise again. So nature maintained the balance between population and food supply. It was only the periods of prolonged famine (1647-51 and 1691-4 were the worst of this century) which retained a special place in the collective memory of village people, for they lived with death as a natural and regular occurrence: a private calamity which everyone had to expect, and even a public necessity if the community as a whole was to have a tolerable life.

Since the fourteenth century there had been no radical change in methods of farming. Because wheat yielded less in bulk per acre than the secondary crops it was these, rye, maslin (a mixture of wheat and rye), oats, maize and *blé noir*, or buckwheat, that were mainly grown, though wheat bread remained the staple food of the northerner. Subsidiary crops included beans and a large pea called *bizaille;* vines were, of course, of paramount importance in the wine-making districts. Apart from cabbages, green vegetables were little known; the same is true of root crops and potatoes. From about the middle of the sixteenth century, common land was coming under pressure: enclosures were bitterly but unavailingly resisted; sometimes the peasants themselves sold commons to pay their debts. A high proportion of the land was left uncultivated because of shallow soil, poor drainage, hunting rights, the need for common pasturage or, in some frontier districts, the ravages of soldiers. Because of the impoverishment of the soil by the unvaried sequence of cereal crops and shortage of manure, land was left fallow by the rotation system which Arthur Young found still practised in places in 1789: 'the barbarous course of 1. fallow, 2. wheat, 3. spring corn, the product of this spring corn being beneath contempt'. Small holdings meant shortage of capital and in this respect the process by which peasants had acquired land in tiny parcels was unfortunate.

In the Beauvaisis,[1] in about 1670, 80 per cent of the peasantry owned plots of less than five acres; only about 3 per cent held more than twenty-five acres. In many villages larger blocks of land, the estates of absentee landowners or the Church, were leased to tenants, *laboureurs-fermiers* or *reçeveurs de seigneurie*; at most there would be only one or two such men. They were unduly influential, able to evade their proper share of the *taille*, lend money, buy more land, and generally exercise a degree of economic power that caused bitter resentment. In the long term, however, it was only by the concentration of land in the hands of a few peasant capitalists or by the equally unpopular penetration of bourgeois landowners that the necessary concentration of small strips, enclosure or other improvements in agricultural practice would come about, for there was little sign of a growth of interest in farming amongst the noblesse. Where small strips of land were let out to peasants, the system usually adopted was that of *métayage*, whereby a proportion of the rent was paid in kind; this suited the landowner, for it protected him against price-changes and strengthened his hold on the peasant. It is in contracts of *métayage*, especially favoured by the *petit bourgeois* landowner, drawn up with minute detail about payments and services, that we see the characteristic—and for the peasant, humiliating—relationship between master and man in French society.

Ploughs and other implements remained crude, usually of wood banded with iron. Because of the absence of turnips and beet for winter feeding, most stock was killed off in the winter; this meant that there was a shortage of dung. Open fields made selective stock breeding impossible. There were insufficient sheep, so that France was actually an importer of wool. In Poitou there was a surprising reluctance to keep sheep, although the country is suited to them and it would have been easy to acclimatise the Spanish merino type. In the same province Raveau notes that the peasants were more backward than their

[1] Pierre Goubert's classic study of this area, predominantly corn-growing but supported by a local textile industry, not only presents a detailed picture of the peasant economy in one place, but sheds light on certain aspects of rural life throughout the country: P. Goubert, *Le Beauvais et le Beauvaisis de 1600 à 1730*, Paris 1960. Also there is a good picture in miniature in his article, 'The French Peasantry of the 17th century', in *Crises in Europe, 1560-1660* (ed. T. Aston). London, 1965.

remote ancestors of Roman times: he instances their failure to use marl and lime, with which the Picts had once improved the fields. In the south the horse was a scarce animal and only the richer peasants owned one anywhere. A good plough horse was worth 60 livres, equivalent to the price of twenty sheep; the rare *laboureur* who possessed one was in a strong position, as creditor or master; the ordinary *manœuvrier* had to hire a horse for his own ploughing and carting. When large numbers of horses were required for the army they had to be imported from Germany. The cattle and pigs would seem poor creatures to the modern eye. Relatively few *manœuvriers* were able even to keep a pig, though most would have a few hens. It is a feature of arable farming that the demand for labour is seasonal rather than constant. Even in good seasons there was therefore a fair number of casual labourers and vaga- bonds and in bad seasons this might swell into a beggar horde, which charitable abbeys or frightened town authorities could do little to help. Then *la mendicité*, beggary, became a problem of government.

Where there was an alternative job, for example lace-working in Brittany or textile-weaving in Picardy, there was a certain built-in resistance to the cruel, arbitrary accidents of nature. But demand fluctuated with the level of prosperity and soon after a bad harvest, spinners, carders and combers might find themselves out of work. Since they usually owned neither tools nor raw materials but were dependent for these, and for their orders, upon the merchants of the nearby towns, they were powerless to remedy their situation. It was best to live in a district where there was a variety of occupations, as for instance in the land bordering the Île de France to the north-west, the country round the Oise and Thérain, where there were vines and woods, good grazing and patches of fertile soil, independent peasants, market gardeners supplying the needs of the towns, wine-growers, cattle-drovers and peasant craftsmen. In such a district Arcadia might be found. It was exceptional.

At the heart of the matter is the fact that very few peasants had any substantial margin above what was needed for mere survival in good years, reserves to fall back on in bad ones. At the top of the pyramid were the *fermiers* and *reçeveurs*, if any, and the *laboureurs*. Taking six villages in the Beauvaisis, Goubert finds only 29 *laboureurs* out of 428 households. Only about one in fifteen! This man was a proprietor, marked off from the rest by possessing enough stock, land and tools to be independent, to be an employer and a creditor. He would be able to dress his family well, his children would wear shoes and his wife would have some finery to show off on market days. They would eat off pewter and tablecloths. With luck he might even save enough to buy an office, to secure some education for his son, perhaps, so that he might become a priest or enter the ranks of the bourgeoisie. How different was his lot from that of the *manœuvrier*, who owned a cottage, a small garden and a plot of two to five acres. The *manœuvrier* might also be a craftsman, a smith, wheelwright, cooper or mason, but this would give only part-time employment. He would be unlikely to own a plough and would therefore owe money or service to his creditor which put him in a chronically dependent position. There were men poorer than he, who were assessed in the tax rolls at the nominal sum of a sou, who had no possessions and worked at best as casual labourers: these were the *journaliers*. But it is the *manœuvrier* whom we must study if we are to gauge the state of the peasant and village. How did he live? On one calculation it required the produce of five acres to feed a family adequately; allowing for the rotation system this figure must be doubled at least. Then there were deductions: seed for the following year, a sixth; the *taille*, which might amount to more than a tenth; the *gabelle* in some provinces, as much again. The Church took six to nine sheaves of every hundred in tithe and the seigneur the same, as *droits de champart*, apart from other dues. Since few peasants, as we have seen, had more than fifteen acres, it will be evident that most were under-nourished even in good years. To feed their families and pay their taxes they competed fiercely for extra work, another acre to rent, usually *en métayage*, another job, cutting wood, spinning hemp, making baskets. Some scavenged for nuts and berries, gleaned forage and poached game. In bad years the weakest fell out of the race.

Living in a hovel of wood, dried mud and straw, subsisting largely on bread supplemented by soup, porridge, beans, occasional eggs, seldom any meat, the peasant was likely to be small and scrawny; his resistance was low and he was susceptible to deficiency diseases such as scurvy. Some of these people would seem to us to be very different from the plain but pleasing subjects of Louis le Nain's wonderful peasant studies, more, perhaps, like the awful faces that leer out of the canvases of

Breughel and Bosch. Half the children died before they were a year old and among those who survived it was common to die before forty. After forty a man was a veteran. The fact that many districts, notably the Landes, were swampy had an important effect on health and to this we may ascribe the tertian and quartan agues of contemporary records. The diseases that they suffered from, dysentery, plague, typhus and cholera, are usually associated with armies or urban slums rather than with country people working in the open air. Because town authorities were able to stock reserves of food and make special purchases, mortality was usually higher in country than in town, but the poorer town workers endured conditions similar to those of their country cousins.

Agricultural prices fluctuated but with a downward trend after 1620; after 1650 there was an unrelieved depression of demand until after the turn of the century and prices only rose in years of scarcity. From this situation the richer peasants actually gained, as they were in a position to profit from occasional high prices, to strengthen their position as creditors, buy land from debtors and take on new leases. Bourgeois, too, were steadily buying land, sometimes whole estates from impoverished nobles. As Colbert observed: 'Families can only keep up their position if they are backed by substantial properties in land'. This was generally beneficial to the economy as a whole for, with capital, came a degree of rationalisation and high productivity. But the new landowner tended to make more of his feudal dues: if these were questioned in local parlements the peasant had little satisfaction, for the lawyers were also landowners!

The position of the peasants was grim enough in Richelieu's time, though the evidence is incomplete and there are some puzzles. Why were the revolts against the crown confined, except for Normandy, to the centre, south and south-west? Why, if conditions were truly desperate, was it so difficult to find recruits for the army? The peasants' lot undoubtedly worsened as the century proceeded: as the depression went on, landowners, particularly the new ones, squeezed all they could from their dues and the government became more efficient in collection of the *taille*. But it would have been little consolation to the peasants of 1630 to be told that conditions would actually get worse. Since some men were evidently immune and others even benefited from their plight, while the king, Church and seigneur, their traditional

protectors, were unable to help them, they may be forgiven for
thinking they were the victims of an organised conspiracy. The
truth is less dramatic. In an almost static economy the peasant did
not possess the bargaining power to defend, let alone to improve,
his position. He did not at once abandon the conservative position
of centuries: reverence for the curé, a peasant probably like himself
but representative of the Church whose physical presence and
moral authority still dominated his life, and respect for the
seigneur, especially if he were resident. He accepted the precarious-
ness of life as part of the natural order of things. One feature of
the peasant revolts is that they were directed less against the
seigneurs than the taxmen. Indeed, seigneurs often incited and
joined the revolts themselves and there was a degree of local
solidarity in the face of the central government. Trouble arose
when the peasant felt that he was alienated from his natural
protection: when the seigneur was a local townsman or represented
by a *fermier*, a vulgar *coq le paroisse*; or when the peasant was
caught in the toils of *métayage* or crushed between the millstones
of feudal dues and royal taxes; or when to survive he had to buy
from the seigneur's mill corn that he had delivered as his due only
a few months before.

The system of taxation was haphazard and unfair in a way
that reflected the uneven growth of the country, the long struggle
of central government against local interests and the enormous
gap between the claims of monarchy and its actual powers.
Indeed when one considers the size of the state, the scope for
resistance and abuse (often encouraged by vested interests), the
chronic shortage of coin and the persisting tradition that the king
should 'live of his own', it is remarkable that the crown fared as
well as it did in its efforts to make Frenchmen pay the price for
political and military supremacy in Europe. The price was a heavy
one, not only in the amount levied but also in injustice. From
1610 to 1714, except for one decade when Colbert was able to
embark upon reforms, ending with the outbreak of the Dutch
War in 1672, the financial authorities lived with the spectre of
insolvency. In an atmosphere of emergency, purposeful planning
took second place to improvisation; the state regularly took the
easier course of deferring to powerful interests and penalising
the weak. Richelieu was aware that this was so and regretted it.
As the instigator of policies which entailed an ever-mounting
expenditure, he incurs a share of responsibility for the cumulative

fiscal failures which threatened social order and retarded economic progress. If, as he would reasonably claim, his policies were necessary to France's survival, it must also be said that he took on commitments, such as subsidies, without a very clear idea how they were to be paid for—to the exasperation of his *surintendants*. He was in fact the prisoner of a system which he did little to improve. But he went so far in asserting the authority of the central government that he opened up possibilities for his successors. Mazarin and Fouquet were content to work within the existing system. Colbert made it work better but even he did not reduce privilege significantly, and this failure was shown to be crucial when Louis XIV's wars placed unprecedented burdens upon the taxpayer, and the state suffered a fiscal calamity from which absolute monarchy never recovered. The failures of Mazarin, Colbert and his successors put Richelieu's performance into perspective.

The *taille* was established as a permanent tax in 1439. Charles VII's assertion of the right to levy a tax which had previously been granted annually was a victory for monarchy with immense implications for the future. The amount was small, less than two million livres, but the principle was one on which later kings could enlarge. At the beginning of the sixteenth century the *taille* amounted to about three million. By 1640 it was more than forty and Mazarin raised it to fifty-five million. The total amount to be collected each year was decided by the *surintendants* and council and then apportioned in *généralités, élections* and finally parishes. The previous autumn the *trésoriers* and *élus* had made a tour of their district and estimated the taxable capacity of each village. At all levels the system was riddled with exemptions and bent to satisfy local interest and traditions. There was a vital distinction between the *taille personnelle* and the *taille réelle*. The former was a personal tax and was paid only by the unprivileged. Not only nobles and churchmen were exempt but also royal officials, members of the sovereign courts and universities, and a host of fiscal and municipal office-holders. There were certain privileged towns, nine in Normandy alone, that were wholly exempt, and a large field was open to private influence: a powerful seigneur or royal official might secure exemption or reduction for his own estate, but not for any benevolent purpose, for the *taille* was resented by nobles, who saw it as infringing upon their rights of taxation, as well as by the peasants who paid it. The *taille réelle*

was confined to the *pays d'états* of the south and south-west and
was levied on land; it was less arbitrary in that it applied to all
*roturier* land whether held by nobleman, commoner or churchman.
Within the *pays d'états* usage varied again: in Languedoc the tax
was collected in two forms, the *aide* and the *octroi*, and in Brittany
and Provence, where the estates voted an annual sum, this was
known as the *fouage*. Later in the century John Locke provided a
valuable view of the operation of the *taille*: he was objective,
statistically-minded and interested in how things worked. Writing
of a province in which the *taille* was personal and fell principally
on those least able to pay it, he noted that when 'a bourgeois or
tradesman that lives in the town, if he have land in the country,
if he keep it in his hand or set it out to rent which is the common
way, that pays noething; but the paisant who rents it, if he be
worth anything, pays for what he has'. In the *pays d'état* he
noticed a further inequity since 'the *terre noble*, which is about
one-twentieth, pays nothing' and there was pressure to have
*roturier* land given noble status. 'And so the burthen still increases
on the rest'. He concludes: 'This is that which so grinds the
paisant in France. The collectors make their rates usually with
great inequality. There lies an appeal for the overtaxed, but I
find not that the remedy is made much use of.'[1]

Indirect taxes, customs duties and *aides* should have been
fairer since they fall in theory on all. The principle is impaired
straight away by the fact that the nobility and Church enjoyed
exemption for the products of their demesne lands. The *pays
d'états* raised their own indirect taxes and paid a contribution to
the crown. Customs duties were levied not only at the frontiers
of the country but also between certain provinces. The diversity
of customs barriers was a major obstacle to trade. The *aides*
were levied principally on drink; also on the sale of certain
selected commodities such as fish and wood. To complicate the
picture, extra *aides* were imposed, notably the *annuel* of 1632, the
*subvention* of 1640. The most important *aide*, an elaborate wine
tax, embracing the whole process of production from grape and
cooper to the village innkeeper, suffered from the normal dis-
advantages of taxation: it took an army of functionaries to collect
it, it was widely evaded, and it was subject to the law of diminishing

[1] Ed. J. Lough, *Locke's Travels in France* (pp. 137, 147-8). Cambridge,
1953.

returns. It is sad to discover that the French peasant, unless he lived in a wine-producing district, could not afford to drink wine!

If one had to select one institution as typifying seventeenth century administration at its most strenuous and complicated, the *gabelle* would be a strong candidate. The word applied originally to all indirect taxes but came to be applied to the salt tax as sixteenth-century kings developed this basic source of revenue to the point at which it occupied, along with the *taille*, a central place in the royal finances. The basic advantage of the tax was that salt was needed by everybody, especially for preserving fish and meat. The tax, like the *taille*, reflected the way in which the kingdom had grown. So the *pays des grandes gabelles* in the north and centre of France corresponded to the areas that were unoccupied by the English when the tax was started in the fourteenth century. In these provinces the salt was collected in royal *greniers* and sold at a price which was designed to give the producer, merchant and, of course, the crown a fair profit. Smuggling flourished despite efforts to stop it by stringent penalties, making purchase compulsory and poisoning salt that was designed for such purposes as tanning. In the *pays des petites gabelles* collection was so difficult that the government had to be content with a smaller duty, while certain areas, notably Brittany, were exempt altogether. Of course there were further exemptions and reductions within the provinces which paid the tax; some towns paid less and many individuals had acquired the *franc-salé*. An army of officials was employed to collect the tax and prevent smuggling but by the end of Richelieu's time the yield from this tax alone was 13 million livres, after all expenses of collection.

The administration of finance had grown layer upon layer so that by the seventeenth century the system appears to be more complicated than it really was because offices survived after their functions had been replaced. Francis I had established a central treasury, the *Trésor de l'Épargne*, in 1523, to receive all revenues, whatever their source. In 1543 the same king replaced the former divisions by sixteen *recettes générales*. In each of these *généralités* a *reçeveur-général* was put in charge of the collection of all revenues, with authority over the *trésoriers*, *élus* and *collecteurs*. Later in the century *trésoriers-généraux* were established; first one, then two more. After 1577 *Bureaux des Finances* were established in the *généralités*. By the middle of the seventeenth century there were 457 *trésoriers* and the office was becoming a redundant ornament since the *intendants* were taking over their work. It was still much in demand, for it usually led to the acquisition of a title, but it yielded only a moderate return on the capital laid out in purchase. The rise of the *intendant* also affected the *élu*, his work, fees and therefore the value of his office. Though ultimately their interest lay in loyal service rather than revolt, the discontent of *trésoriers* and *élus* played some part in the outbreak of the Fronde.

The extent to which private enterprise co-existed with state control can be seen in the way the government actually raised the taxes. This work was done by tax-farmers, *traitants* or *partisans*, as they were called, at first in the sixteenth century, usually local business men but by Richelieu's time a small group of rich capitalists, specialists in the technique of money-raising; they sometimes acted in a consortium, as in the farm of the *Cinq Grosses Fermes*, an organisation responsible for the collection of five royal taxes in a large part of central France. The *gabelle* was also farmed out to a group. As the tax-farmers came to be more prominent they became more unpopular, focusing upon themselves the resentments of the taxpayer and the social prejudices of the traditional upper class. They were the 'dirty souls' of la Bruyère's bitter characterisation. The public instinct was at least right in divining that this class of plutocrats held, though on a precarious basis, real power in the state. In a sense they throve on the state's needs. But they provided also an essential service as the entrepreneurs of the fiscal system, taking great risks to earn great fortunes.[1]

[1] In his article 'Un Traitant sous Louis XIII; Antoine Feydeau', *Revue d'Histoire Moderne*, 13, 1938, P. Heumann amplifies our picture of the gains and risks of the *traitant's* career. Feydeau came from a leading family of lawyers and financiers: starting as a *receveur des tailles* at Noyon he rose to be the director of the *ferme générale des aides* (1611) and *des gabelles* (1622). He was receiving interest at one stage of the order of 1,200,000 livres a year, representing a capital sum of at least 20 million. After the fall of La Vieuville his situation deteriorated. He was an extravagant man, and his wife was a celebrated and lavish hostess; he bought *seigneuries* and built a great château at Bois-le-Vicomte. But the basic cause of his embarrassment was the difficulty of making sufficient profits out of his elaborate organisation to sustain his position and his private army of functionaries in the face of dwindling returns from a depressed economy and the pressure on margins applied by the government for economic and propaganda reasons after 1624. In a desperate move to cover himself he bought the office of *trésorier* in 1625

Like the *traitants*, the *trésoriers de France* seem to have been unjustly criticised for the failure of the fiscal machinery to produce the sums required in wartime conditions. In fact its faults, notably the exemptions, were those of society, fundamentally unequal and hierarchical, with degrees of privilege which may have been as natural to people of the time as was the landscape around them—a society of orders rather than of classes. In this setting the achievements of the *trésoriers* were not negligible. At the top Sully stands out amongst *surintendants* for his probity and skill. This has obscured the fact that some of his predecessors, notably Bellièvre, were also honest and capable men. The complicated process of assessment and accountancy went smoothly. Some *trésoriers* made an excessive profit out of their operations, but they were operating in a very different milieu from that of a modern bureaucracy. Governments publicly defaulted on their debts and juggled with interest rates. Office holders paid large sums for their *charges*—even an *élu* might have to pay 10,000 livres—and of course looked for a good return on what could be a risky investment. When the *surintendant* was as efficient as Sully, abuses were kept in check, but when he was casual like Bullion, or Fouquet (*surintendant* 1653-61), they proliferated and the state lost millions. So it was a venal and irregular organisation which Richelieu had at his disposal, but capable all the same, if well-regulated, of providing a steady growth in revenue.

The instability of the economy was worsened by international price movements which had a direct bearing upon foreign trade. The flow of precious metals, upon which prices largely depended, was not suddenly cut off. From 1601 to 1620 the world produced 422,000 kilograms of silver and 8,250 of gold; thereafter the decline was slow. These amounts did not, however, increase relatively to the growing total: the percentage increase, which in the middle of the sixteenth century had been 3·8 was by 1600 only 1, by 1700 only 0·5. The forward impulse of western Europe had been nourished by the bullion of the New World; it was slowly pinched by its relative decline. Though the problem was not

---

for 800,000 livres! It was too late. He became bankrupt and died, aged fifty, in 1627, leaving nothing but debts. His was not an isolated case. It was possible for men like Feydeau, Moisset and Payen (two other *traitants* who suffered a similar fate) to become prisoners of an empire of their own making. Essentially they were gamblers, and the stakes were enormous.

crucial until the second half of the seventeenth century when it was the main factor in the ruthless statism of Colbert, the first half was also a period of contraction, felt the more keenly by contrast with the buoyant economic conditions of the previous century. Some writers go so far as to relate this economic process to the puritan mood of the time of Olivarez and Richelieu. Court manners, dress, literature, architecture, show a common tendency towards austerity and restraint, markedly different from the careless splendour of the late Renaissance culture. There is plainly some connection between the restriction of credit, the caution of business men, the retrenchment of court and government, and the ideas and sensibilities of educated men. We should perhaps beware of pushing the connection too far. In its way, the art of the baroque is as extravagant as anything of the Renaissance, though more disciplined; nor was there anything pinchbeck about the court of Louis XIV. There can be no doubt, on the other hand, about the effect of the contraction upon economic activity. Price movements were erratic, moving within a wide bracket which was even more discouraging to investment than the steady downward trend of the second half of the century. This is one reason for the remarkable growth in office-building.

More than the government's need for ready cash, more than the bourgeois' concern for status, certainly more than administrative needs, it was the opportunity for a relatively secure investment that made available vast funds for this method of state finance funds which, in a more dynamic economy, would have found their way—as in England and Holland—into commerce and industry. The Frenchman who wanted to make money looked to finance, the lucrative tax farms and loan-mongering (the *rentes*), for these were the growth sectors of the seventeenth-century economy. At the top were the *noblesse de la robe*, the exclusive caste of magistrates and councillors, the leading tax officials; below them stretched a swelling host of functionaries. This was no civil service in the modern sense, for the office-holder regarded his office as a property providing social position and an inheritance to pass on to his descendants. Multiplicity of offices was specially a feature of the Roman law countries modelled upon the elaborate hierarchy of Byzantium. There was, however, a roughly parallel development in common law England, where the sale of office was openly practised, but where there was of course much less scope. Its extension in France to the point reached by Richelieu's time, when the government could hardly exist without it and it could provide a vast field of investment, was the product of special factors.

Sale of office had first been systematised in 1522, when the *bureau des parties casuelles* was set up to act as a clearing house. Selling became widespread and reversion was allowed although attempts were made to limit it by stipulating that it should take place within forty days of the seller's death. By an edict of 1604, the rule was waived in return for a small annual payment to the crown, which gained thereby a regular revenue. This system of sale on easy terms was soon called the *paulette* after Charles Paulet, the official who first farmed it for the crown. Henry IV had envisaged the *paulette* as providing a small but steady addition to the revenues; inevitably it became a pillar of royal finance and a regular expedient in times of emergency. In 1610 he anticipated later form by putting a block of new offices on the market. The more ambitious operators began to build up large holdings in office. In 1622 seventeen commissioners of the *taille* in Normandy shared 969 offices between them. Prices rose steadily in response to demand, as much as 600 per cent in some offices in the first twenty years.

Twenty years after the inception of the *paulette*, when Richelieu came to power, he considered abolishing it: it was, as he said in a memorandum to the king, 'prejudicial to your authority and to the purity of justice'. It was not only the exigencies of war finance that made him reconsider this view and make indiscriminate use of the system. The state bought political security in this market. In place of the private clientele it created its own gigantic interest, parasitic but amenable. He believed indeed that Henry IV had been influenced more by his experience of the power of the Guises in this sphere than by necessities of revenue, and it is true that his bargain with the office-holders was generous. The bourgeois acquired a stake in the state which paid, but could also withhold their dues. Condé discovered this when he failed to secure the sympathy of Parlement for his campaign against venality. In his *Testament* the Cardinal justified his policy of inertia in revealing words: 'Prudence does not admit action of this sort in an old monarchy whose imperfections have passed into custom and whose disorder forms part of the order of the state'. As in other fields he was ready to pay a high price for the security and order which, in his view, was the first priority of the statesman.

## 6. Europe: Elements of Conflict

The historian has often to write about a country's external affairs as if they were conducted in a separate compartment, unaffected by domestic concerns. This is because he has to make sense of complicated events. To relate Richelieu's European policy, at every stage, to the pressures to which he was subjected at home would be to obscure the foreign issues. It is evident, however, that the problem of security was indivisible in the statesman's mind: the measures he adopted to assert his authority at home and to make France great in Europe were of a piece. During the years 1624-8 his whole foreign policy was jeopardised by the revolt of the Huguenots and the conspiracy of his enemies at home, and important designs were postponed until he could take effective action against them. The Huguenot rising and the Chalais conspiracy were both international events; conversely Richelieu's designs upon the Val Telline had far-reaching domestic repercussions.

If we compare the situation of France in Europe when Richelieu came to power with her situation in 1661, when Louis XIV began his personal rule, or even 1715, when Louis' reign ended after a sequence of defeats, it will be seen that the term 'crisis' can be applied to the international field as well as to the domestic. Richelieu's policy has to be weighed against the outlook of the early twenties, when the House of Habsburg appeared to dominate Europe as never before. It appeared that France was invested by the Habsburg powers and that in Germany at least they were irresistible. The last German Protestant forces were being chased off the field, the Val Telline was open to the passage of Spanish troops. Few can have guessed that there would be twenty-four more years of war in one theatre or another before the Thirty Years War finished, though long before 1648 this had ceased to be primarily a German war. It is important to be clear as to the nature of the complex struggles which historians have labelled the Thirty Years War—sensibly enough, seeing that thirty years elapsed between the Bohemian revolt against Habsburg rule and the Treaty of Westphalia which ended military operations in Germany. If this title imputes any sort of unity to a number of conflicts, then it is indeed misleading. So is the equally naïve view that the problems of 1618 were novel ones or that they were all settled by 1648. In some respects this was a German war, in others a religious war. At all levels it was concerned with political power; at the level of the giants it was a phase, and a crucial one, in the contest of Habsburg and Bourbon which went back to the Italian Wars of the sixteenth century, which was renewed again in 1609, and which was not resolved until the Peace of the Pyrenees in 1659. From the end of the Italian Wars in 1559 to the accession of Henry IV, France's influence in foreign affairs had diminished to a point at which she had almost ceased to exist as a European power. Henry IV's reign brought the assertion of old claims and some striking diplomatic successes. He died when France was about to become involved, it seemed, in a European war over the Clèves-Jülich succession. To understand this affair and the reason for France's involvement in what could have been a disastrous adventure, it is necessary to look at the European picture as a whole.

From Francis I to Louis XIV the effectiveness of French diplomacy depended largely upon the availability of an ally outside Germany to adjust the balance against the Habsburgs. Francis I used the Turks, Richelieu was to use Sweden, Louis XIV returned to eastern Europe and flirted with the Magyars of Hungary. It was a feature of the first decades of the seventeenth century that there was relatively little interference from non-European powers. In the east, the Russia of Ivan the Terrible, after great successes against the Mongol tribes to the east and south, had been checked in her attempts to establish herself around the Baltic. Despite the contacts achieved by Chancellor by way of the White Sea, the formation in England of the Muscovy Company to exploit them, and the establishment of a degree of centralised control by the autocratic czar, it was generally felt in the west, as Sully wrote in his *Grand Dessein*, that Russia's interests lay in Asia rather than in the west. After the death of Ivan in 1584 there ensued 'the confused time'—*smutnoe vremia*—a prolonged nightmare of succession conflicts which Ivan began when he slew his son with an iron staff, two years before his own death. Muscovy was exposed during this time to the invasion of bands of Poles,

Swedes, Cossacks and Tartars. The accession of Michael Romanov in 1613 and the restoration of a semblance of national unity meant the end of Poland's attempt to bring Russia into western Christendom as a Roman Catholic power under a Polish sovereign. Until the arrival of Peter the Great at the end of the century it remained true, however, that the western powers did not have to take Russia into their calculations. No less significant was the decline of Turkey in this period. Suleiman the Magnificent (1520-66) had followed his victory at Mohacz in 1526 by over-running Hungary and turning Transylvania into a puppet state; with a series of conquests he turned the eastern Mediterranean into a Turkish lake. After the death of the Grand Vizier Mohammed Sokoli in 1579, only the preoccupation of the western powers with their internal problems prevented them from recovering lost ground, for the Turks lost the will to conquer and their administration was incompetent. Venice was absorbed in pursuing her commercial interests and the rulers of the Empire had their hands full with Germany. Father Joseph's dream of a united crusade against the Turks may not have been practical politics, but it was based on a realistic assessment of Turkish weakness.

In the past France had made use of Poland, whose elective crown offered regular chances of intervention and influence. Henry III had been king of Poland for thirteen months before he acceded to the French crown in 1574. His successor, Stephen Bathory, *voivode* of Transylvania, reigned for eleven years. Sigismund III, son of John of Sweden, not only ruled himself from 1587 to 1632 but was followed by two sons in succession. His reign saw the peak of Polish power as well as its incipient decline. Since the Union of Lublin, in 1569, had merged the kingdom with the Grand Duchy of Lithuania, it surpassed all neighbours in population, commerce and agriculture. Besides present-day Poland and Lithuania, it included Latvia, Byelorussia, the Ukraine, East Prussia and Danzig. The towns benefited from the activity of small colonies of Jews and German immigrants, while the *szlachta* or country gentry were usually competent farmers of their large estates. In the border wars against Turks and Muscovites the light cavalry earned the reputation of being the best in Europe. In Sigismund's reign the country afforded the counter-reformation with its most spectacular triumph after fifty years of Lutheranism. The duchies of Prussia, Courland and Livonia, fiefs of the Polish crown under their own rulers, remained

Lutheran; their loose attachment underlines the real weakness of Poland at a time when her material resources should have enabled her to dominate northern Europe, and accounts for the surprising success of Sweden in the wars of 1621-29.

Like France, Sweden was threatened by the constriction of rival powers. The eastern frontier of Finland provided her with an open frontier to the north, but to the south and west she was hemmed in by the joint monarchy of Denmark and Norway. Denmark then possessed lands which are now part of Sweden, such as Jamtland, Malmöhus and Kristianstad, while her possession of both shores of the Sound excluded Sweden from access to the North Sea. Danish Gotland and Bornholm menaced Swedish communications in the Baltic, and from Oesel the Danes could launch an invasion of Estonia. Since Gustavus I had led Sweden into independence in 1523, Swedish policy had been dominated, therefore, by the need to obtain access to the German and Polish shores of the Baltic and safe passage out of the Baltic. The decline of the Hanse and the corresponding increase in the activity of Dutch and English merchants only intensified the competition for the rich prizes of Baltic trade. Western Europe needed the products of the northern countries: the copper and iron of Sweden, the hemp, tar and timber of Russia, the grain of Poland— all passed through the Sound whose dues were a large part of Denmark's revenues. The fight for *dominium maris Baltici* owed nothing to religious differences. The aims were strategic and economic: control of the ports and estuaries of the long coastline and, to secure this control, conquest of the Polish fiefs of Livonia, Courland and Prussia, the German duchies of Pomerania and Mecklenburg, and the free cities of the Hanse such as Riga, Danzig and Stralsund.

In the careers of Christian IV of Denmark (1588-1648), of Charles IX of Sweden, who ruled as lieutenant-general from 1595 but did not assume the title of king until 1604 and died seven years later, and of his more famous successor Gustavus Adolphus (1611-32), we see variations on this theme played by gifted and resolute rulers. There is a contrast, however, between the splendid image of Christian, the Henry VIII of the North, and his actual achievement. He impressed his merchants by his enterprises, his East India Company (1614) and the foundation of Glückstadt (1616) as a trading rival to Hamburg; his reign saw some successes in the Kalmar War against Sweden (1611-13) but these were overshadowed by his disastrous foray into Germany (1625-29). He died in the year of the peace treaties which put their seal upon Swedish supremacy in the Baltic. By contrast, Charles IX had to struggle to maintain himself in a fierce civil war with the magnates who attempted to take advantage of the connection with Poland, in the person of Sigismund who was already king of Poland when he inherited the crown of Sweden. He broke the power of Sigismund's followers, made a treaty with Muscovy which gave him useful support against the Polish invasion of 1610 and founded Göteborg to take advantage of trade with Russia. At his death, however, he was faced by a war with the combined forces of Denmark and Russia.

His successor Gustavus Adolphus, aged sixteen, began his reign with widespread concessions to the aristocracy; these could have rendered the Swedish monarchy ineffectual but for his military talent and the consummate skill of his Chancellor, Axel Oxenstierna, who, in the next thirty years, was first lieutenant and then virtual ruler of Sweden. The peace of Knäred (1613) brought Sweden with modest gains out of war in which her troops had been worsted by the Danes, and the peace of Stolbova (1617) ended the Russian war and brought Karelia and Ingermanland, the one securing the eastern approaches to Finland, the other making a bridge between Finland and Estonia. Gustavus was then left free to attack Poland in a war which was to have an important bearing on the German conflict. His country's war potential was greater than its size would suggest. The importance of naval power had been grasped; now it was to be the turn of the army, to be forged by Gustavus into a formidable instrument of war. Industrial developments were afoot: iron and copper were already being exported; cheap labour, plentiful water-power and helpful government concessions tempted foreign entrepreneurs.

The military presence maintained by Sweden from 1630 to 1648 provides a remarkable example of what could be achieved by good government. One of the lessons of this century was that the small, integrated state, with resources intelligently exploited and an army well led could be disproportionately effective. As Poland's history shows, size itself was of little account.

When in March 1618 the Protestant nobles of Bohemia committed themselves to open revolt against Imperial authority in the traditional Bohemian manner by throwing out of the window of Hradcin Castle in Prague two of the Catholic royal governors and their secretary, they created a situation which invited intervention from both camps. The judgement of James I of England, who was sceptical about the prospects of the rebels, proved to be sounder than that of his son-in-law Frederick, Elector Palatine who accepted the throne of Bohemia in August 1619 in a spirit of optimism wholly unjustified by the lukewarm spirit of his supposed allies. The States-General of the United Provinces was concerned primarily with the imminent end of their truce with Spain and sent a niggardly subsidy and about 5,000 men. The Duke of Savoy sent a regiment of mercenaries whom Mansfeld had collected to invade Spanish Milan. Gustavus Adolphus began negotiations which came to nothing with Russia, with the idea of providing a diversionary attack upon Poland. James I would not be drawn in at all but stood ready to act as referee.

Very different was the prompt activity of the Catholic party. Cardinal Khlesl, who was working for compromise with the Estates, was arrested and imprisoned, and his fortune used to pay the expenses of the first campaign. When the death of the Emperor Matthias was followed by the election of Ferdinand II, two days after the election of Frederick to the Bohemian crown, only the Bohemian representatives, who were voteless anyway, protested against the elevation of the former king of Bohemia, who was known to be a ruthless and dedicated exponent of the twin ideals of the counter-reformation: absolutist rule and religious conformity. This strong-willed, Jesuit-trained prince, who believed implicitly in the Church and in the Habsburgs, had repressed the Protestants in the province of Upper Austria as thoroughly as he was later to repress the Protestants of Bohemia after the end of the revolt. This came in 1620 with the battle of the White Mountain, on 8th November, when the Imperial general Bucquoy beat Frederick's intimate adviser and commander, Christian of Anhalt. Meanwhile Catholic initiative had extended the theatre of war in such a provocative way, that Protestant retaliation was inevitable. How had this happened? Why did a local quarrel within the Habsburg family, important as it admittedly was, develop into a general war?

The heart of the problem lay in the condition of Germany, the patchwork of territories whose rulers owed nominal allegiance to the Holy Roman Emperor, a texture of many threads and colours, torn by the rivalries of the privileged groups, the electoral princes, and the dukes, counts and margraves below that coveted status, the princes and the representative estates, and overall by the religious divisions that were the legacy of the Reformation. The 'Final Compact' of Augsburg (1555), one in a line of settlements of the religious wars that ensued upon Luther's historic defiance, proved to be neither final nor binding. It satisfied the aims and aspirations of neither Catholic nor Lutheran and specifically excluded the Calvinists. Further, it provided no machinery by which doubtful clauses could be interpreted or decrees enforced. An attempt to halt a fluid situation upon arbitrary lines was preferable to a further sequence of wars that invited outside intervention. But it could only succeed if one side was passive and the other restrained. In fact the Catholics gained heart and clarity of purpose with the reform of the Papacy and the decrees of the Council of Trent. They yearned to recover their losses, and in the Jesuits they had an instrument expressly designed for missionary work; only the caution and weakness of the emperors supplied restraint. The Lutherans meanwhile expanded throughout central and northern Europe, while Calvinism was established in the Palatinate and Brandenburg, threatened the establishment in Bohemia, acquired alarming links with the Calvinist communities in France and Switzerland and with republican Holland, where Calvinism grew with successful resistance to Spain. By the turn of the century there were signs that a general conflict was inevitable.

The truce of 1609, so far from settling the issue between the United Provinces and Spain, gave both sides a rest to repair their arms and finances; it was not expected to last for the stipulated twelve years. The weakness of the Imperial Constitution, Diet, Chancery, Aulic Council, Imperial Tribunal, and the ten Imperial Circles, all belonging in spirit to the Middle Ages or the constitutionalism of the early 1500s and dependent upon a willing cooperation in common policies which it was now futile to expect, was paradoxically the weakness of the princes as much as that of the emperor, for he was compelled to exploit his own ancestral lands and to make his alliances in the open market, using the honorific counters at his disposal to build up his own following He was the better able to do this because potential rivals lacked strength or character. The history of Europe would indeed have been different if John George of Saxony had been a strong, ambitious personality or, one might add, if Maximilian of Bavaria had not been a Catholic. Maximilian was the ablest of the princes, careful, wary but ambitious for his Wittelsbach house, which had been rewarded for its loyalty to Rome by the cession of rich bishoprics and a large measure of control over the Church; he had family connections with prominent states outside Bavaria, notably Cologne after 1583 and Jülich-Berg after 1613, and he was the moving spirit of the Catholic League, founded in 1609 in response to the Protestant Union of the year before.

Lutheran Saxony was the largest and richest of the Electorates but John George, whose reign (1611-56) spanned the Thirty Years War, was timid and sluggish. His vaunted patriotism consisted largely in aversion to outsiders, Sweden, France, Spain, but it was his failure to coordinate a constitutional party, to restrain or resist the emperor, that enabled the outsiders to make Germany their battlefield. He was thoroughly conservative and recoiled with repugnance from the Calvinists of Holland and the Palatinate. One suspects that Calvinism, so clear-cut in its theological, moral and social principles, was viewed with something of the myopic, legend-ridden awe and mistrust that Communism arouses in many of its opponents today. Certainly the Lutheran feared the Calvinist as much as did the Catholic; in 1619 the Lutherans, led by John George, attached themselves to the Imperial cause. Brandenburg, in the person of George William (1619-40) followed tamely. The string of territories from Memel in Baltic Prussia to Clèves on the border of Holland, obtained in 1614, suggested nothing but weakness. The opportunistic state building of later Electors belongs to a future, to a decay of Imperial authority, and to a dominance of French diplomacy, as well as to a quality of statesmanship in successive Hohenzollern rulers, which could not yet be foreseen. Outside the close group of the seven Electors the most important houses, Brunswick and Hesse, were both reduced in influence by repeated partitions. A telling example of this process is provided by Hesse, whose landgraviate was divided into four in 1567 among the sons of Philip of Hesse, after which the two younger branches were reduced to the negligible status which was the lot of most of Germany's petty sovereignties, while the two elder were consumed in jealous rivalry. The richer part, Hesse-Cassel, became Calvinist in 1605 and entered upon close relations with Holland and France, while Hesse-Darmstadt remained Lutheran and

Imperialist. In Hesse we can see on a small scale the problem of Germany and the reason why, as in the Balkans before the First World War, or the Middle East today, minor issues of constitution or succession could provide the material for major wars. This is what happened in Clèves-Jülich when its ruler, John William, died in 1609.

In this case there was an accretion rather than subdivision of lands. Duke William of Jülich-Clèves-Mark-Berg-Ravensburg, who died in 1592, had been known as William the Rich, quite appropriately since his lands contained some of the most prosperous manufactories in Europe; textiles, paper, ceramics, powder, swords and knives, along with the busy Rhine ports of Wesel, Duisburg and Düsseldorf, made this an economic proposition of the first importance. No less significant to the outside powers was the strategic alignment of these lands which bordered upon the Guelph duchies—Hesse, the United Provinces and the Spanish Netherlands—and surrounded Cologne on all sides. At the same time the duchy was weak, for Duke William was followed by a half-wit, John William; the Estates, and in the Estates the nobles, took full advantage of his weakness; moreover the country was split upon religious lines, Jülich and Berg remained Catholic, Mark and Ravensburg became Lutheran, Clèves Calvinist.

Duke John William was childless but had four sisters: the sons of the elder two, the Elector of Brandenburg and the Count of Neuberg, claimed the estates. Inevitably there was confusion, sufficient to justify the emperor's intervention, for which there were sound precedents, although he was far from being a disinterested observer. To the Emperor Rudolph II the Protestant claims were a challenge to authority and faith which could not be evaded. He must divide the lands or impose a Catholic ruler. To the Evangelical Union, on the other hand, it was a test case. The Dutch watched the Spanish jealously for any move to exploit the question. To Henry IV it was a tantalising invitation to break a lance with the Habsburgs. For some years he had been restrained, against his naturally reckless gambler's inclination, by the clamant needs of the people and the treasury, impressed upon him by Sully. He was concerned with the delicate balance of the religious settlement: the path that lay between goading the Huguenots to revolt under the impression that they were being betrayed to Rome, and impressing the mass of his Catholic subjects with the sincerity of his conversion, was hard enough to follow without foreign complications. He had been angry, therefore, with the Protestants of Germany for their support of the rebellious Duc de Bouillon and disposed to side with Maximilian of Bavaria in the hope that dynastic rivalry, Wittelsbach against Habsburg, would prove stronger than the bonds of religion, as it was in the case of France and Spain. To the chagrin of his envoy Bongars and the Protestant princes, he had allowed the Catholic candidate, Charles of Lorraine, to secure the bishopric of Strasbourg, the Imperial Free City commanding the vital Rhine crossing. In 1606, however, Bouillon had given up and in 1607 Maximilian had shown where his loyalty and hopes of advancement lay by obeying the Imperial summons to occupy Donauwörth in retaliation for an anti-Catholic demonstration there; this incident had provoked the formation of the Evangelical Union, whose members raised an army and looked to Henry for patronage.

By 1609, therefore, Henry was both more confident of his strength and more sharply concerned about the German situation. At first his diplomacy was of the type that we know in our world of east-west block alliances. It was dangerous to embark on a war when he could not be sure of the reaction of the *dévôts*; at any rate such a war must seem to be a retaliatory operation in defence of French strategic interests. To avoid war he had to be able to show that he was not afraid of waging it. So he negotiated for alliances with Switzerland, the Dutch, Savoy, the Evangelical Union. Unfortunately his timing, even his intentions, were affected by an incident, absurd enough in itself, the folly of an ageing gallant, but crucial in its effect upon a crisis which called for calm nerves. Infatuated with a sixteen-year-old girl, Charlotte de Montmorency, he arranged for her marriage to the Prince of Condé, hoping apparently that she could then become his mistress. Condé resented being made a cuckold and went to Brussels to put his bride under the protection of the Spanish court there. Henry, 'a man with a bandage over his eyes', in Richelieu's phrase, was roused as lover, patriot and prince, jealous of Condé and of his rejected authority. After this there was no mention of the 'general European peace' which had appeared in state documents up to this time. Sully, like Colbert after him, an economist who believed that wealth was amassed to be used in war for the security of the state, and an ardent Protestant, was not averse to preparations for war, but cautioned Henry when he realised that he had something bigger in mind than a limited operation in the north-east. His view was that nothing should be done about the Condés since the archduke Albert would soon want to be rid of them. He was instructed, however, to raise an army of 30,000 men. Since Henry was assassinated in the rue de l'Arsenal by Ravaillac when he was paying a farewell visit to Sully before joining his army, we shall never know exactly what his intentions were. It is hard to believe that his old shrewdness had quite deserted him. It may be, however, that he was seriously under-estimating the military strength of the Habsburgs. The Dutch, who had good reason to fear it, and had just negotiated a truce in the previous year, were willing only to commit their troops to fighting in Clèves. Savoy was intent upon a hard bargain, promising only three towns which the Spanish were occupying anyway. It is almost certain that Henry's death avoided a European war, and possible that it saved France from a military disaster. The affair reveals the way in which France was likely to be drawn into German politics, and the tensions in Germany which were exacerbated by the hostile positions of Bourbon and Habsburg. It throws light upon the realistic policies of appeasement pursued by successive ministers up to the advent of Richelieu, and it was a warning to him of the dangers involved in too direct a con-frontation. For him the indirect approach was more attractive, attacks upon the Habsburg lines of communication rather than open war in Germany, at least so long as it could be avoided.

With both the Regent Marie de Médicis and the new Emperor Matthias (1612-19) advising caution, for a few years the 'general peace' seemed to be possible. The imperial cities of the Union secured the disarmament of the forces of both the Union and the League. Wolfgang William, son of the Count of Neuburg and one of the two 'possessing Princes', became a Roman Catholic, married Maximilian's sister and set about converting his subjects. By contrast John Sigismund did not try to impose his Calvinism upon his Lutheran subjects. At last, under the mediation of the great powers, including the French, the two princes agreed in the Treaty of Xanten upon the division of the country. To Neuburg went Jülich and Berg, while Brandenburg, with con-sequences beyond the ken of the diplomats of 1614, took Clèves, Mark and Ravensburg. The settlement was not so neat as it seemed, for both heirs continued to claim the whole parcel and the Estates wanted to preserve its unity. Administration of the provinces, such as it was, remained with the central authorities. After 1619 they were involved in the war between the Spaniards and the Dutch: the Spaniards took Jülich and kept it until 1660, the Dutch, Clèves and Wesel.

## 7. The Challenge of Spain

When Richelieu came to power his most pressing concern was the future of the Val Telline, the pass which carries the river Adda from its source to Lake Como, linking the Tyrol with northern Italy and providing a ten-day journey from Milan to Vienna. This was the only route which did not involve breaking the neutrality of Venice and Switzerland and it was the most convenient way of getting supplies to Belgium, all the more important if the Dutch or English were able to close the Channel to Spanish shipping passing to and from Antwerp. Control of the pass, sixty miles long, at most three miles wide, was therefore an axiom of Spanish policy. The Val Telline's population of eighty thousand were tough and for the most part poor; like the Scots, their young men were very willing to serve in foreign armies and Henry IV recruited thousands of them. They were Catholics but they were ruled by the Grisons, a federation of leagues of mountain dwellers who, though divided themselves, were mainly Protestants and, furthermore, of an aggressive and missionary type. While they ran their own affairs, they ruled the inhabitants of the Val Telline through officials who, being unpaid, were encouraged to exploit their position. This odious overlordship was naturally of concern to the Spanish. Even the constitutional procedure of the leagues encouraged foreign intervention since, on the plea of public danger, any group of three hundred could meet in a *Strafgericht* or tumultuous assembly. Here was a situation far removed from the fertile, prosperous estates and towns of Clèves-Jülich, but alike in that local trouble could spread into a general war.

An important part in French calculations was played by Savoy. Surrounded by France in the west, Milan and its Spanish garrisons in the east, Genoa in the south, free from pressure only in the north where it bordered on the Swiss, the dukes of this mountainous state, infinitely stronger in diplomatic currency than its size and resources would suggest, sought to exploit the enmity of

F

France and Spain. Change of sides was a dangerous but almost inevitable game: Charles-Emmanuel I (1580-1630), wiry, hot-spirited and restless, played it with relish and skill. Having married Philip II's second daughter, he travelled first with Spain, tried to enlarge his duchy by occupying Geneva and fished in the French pond during the latter stages of the civil wars. In 1590 he had entered Aix-en-Provence at the request of the Leaguers and stayed there for nearly a year, fighting Henry IV's general, Lésdiguières; he got no help from Spain and so, seeing the League faltering and his flank exposed, he occupied Saluzzo. The Treaty of Vervins perforce excluded Saluzzo, the Pope failed to arbitrate, the duke tried to draw Biron, the governor of Burgundy, into his plans, and Henry IV waged a forceful campaign against him. Biron remained loyal, though he was later to be executed for complicity in plots, and Charles-Emmanuel was soundly defeated. By the Treaty of Lyon (1601) he ceded Bresse, Bugey and Gex, a useful extension of France's south-eastern frontier, while keeping Saluzzo. Henry's decision to concentrate on strengthening his mountain frontier and to avoid commitment beyond the Alps was justified in that it pushed Savoy against Spain in the Milanese; expansion could only be at the expense of the Spanish or Swiss. Hoping once more for Spanish support, Charles-Emmanuel again attacked Geneva, but the Genevese, with help from Berne and France, carried the war into Savoy. In Italy, however, Henry's influence owed more to diplomacy than to arms. With Savoy hostile, Mantua and Modena feeling abandoned to Spain by the cession of Saluzzo, and the Grisons refusing to renew their French alliance, the attitude of Venice and the Pope was import-ant. Henry got money by his otherwise condescending marriage to Marie de Médicis, niece of the rich Duke of Tuscany, and moral aid from the approval of the Pope, Clement VIII, who was delighted by the return of Henry to the Church and no less by his mediation in a quarrel over Church matters with Venice; from Venice, which had been the first state to recognise Henry as King of France, he received aid for his dealings with the Grisons.

In 1603 the Grisons had come to an agreement with the Vene-tians and felt strong enough to prevent the Spanish from using the Val Telline as a supply route. Fuentes, the Spanish governor in Milan, had built a fortress near Lake Como to block the mouth of the valley. The Grisons could try to strangle Spanish trade, but the Spanish could starve them out. In 1616 the course of events persuaded them to use this weapon. Venice found itself at war with Spain after an attack by her ships on some pirates in Segna, which was territory of the Archduke Ferdinand. Faced with ruin, the Serene Republic turned to Savoy and to the Dutch; the latter sent 4,000 troops. France had a treaty of mutual defence with Venice. To complicate matters further, Bouillon and Nevers had been trying to raise Venetian support for their rebellion against the crown. Richelieu, in his few months as Secretary of State in 1616-17, was faced, therefore, with a dilemma. If France honoured her commitment the *dévôt*, pro-Spanish party might turn against the state; it was the spectre of the League again. To do nothing was to accept Spanish domination of northern Italy and to risk a lasting alienation of the independent Italian states. He tried to settle the war by diplomatic means but his hand was forced by the abrupt and unauthorised action of Lésdiguières, governor of the Dauphiné, 'le roi dauphin' as Henry called him, by virtue of the splendour of his château and private army and the arrogance with which he treated the royal government. The old Huguenot was persuaded by Charles-Emmanuel to make a demonstration. He raised 7,000 troops, marched them over the snowy Alps and appeared in Piedmont for Christmas. 'That will put the Spaniard's nose out of joint', said Louis XIII, pleased by an action which had made hay of the government's policy.

Richelieu may have been exasperated, but he decided to use the coup to introduce a change of policy. Now resolved on arbitrating himself, he presented it to the Venetians and Dutch in the guise of a gesture of aid and to the Spanish as a reminder that it was not sensible to rely too much on the Catholic sentiments of France where her strategic interests were concerned. Richelieu was dismissed and had to watch from the wings while first Luynes, then Vieuville, groped for a solution to a question which became urgent with the development of the European war after 1618. The envoys of the Grisons, as exasperating to their allies as to their enemies, accepted a treaty in 1617 which guaranteed Spain the right of passage over the mountains to the Tyrol and the Upper Rhine, and the right to recruit in the area, formerly the preserve of France; but their democratic assembly refused to ratify the treaty and resolved instead to launch a missionary drive in the Val Telline. When they opened a Protestant church in Sondrio, the new Spanish governor Feria armed the Italian

Catholic refugees and in July 1620 they ranged through the valley, killing 400 Protestants. The Swiss retaliated but at Tirano encountered the regular Spanish troops. Severely defeated, they retreated to the mountains while the Spanish proceeded to set up forts along the valley. Meanwhile Luynes, hard pressed with the breakdown of his agreement with the queen mother and the recalcitrance of the leading nobility, ill at ease in the widening circle of his responsibilities, had sent the Duc d'Angoulême to negotiate an armistice in Germany. The Peace of Ulm in June, on paper, confined the struggle to Ferdinand and Frederick, but the parties who there promised that they would not fight one another reserved the right to assist one or other of the combatants. So while the Spanish were taking over the Val Telline, Spinola attacked the Lower Palatinate with 25,000 troops and Maximilian of Bavaria moved his troops into Bohemia.

The Battle of the White Mountain in November only empha-sised the failure of French diplomacy. Luynes was unable both to mount an operation against the Huguenots in France and to send an army to relieve the Val Telline. He chose to take the less risky course and, as Richelieu's subsequent experience showed, with wisdom. While his envoy Bassompierre secured from the Spanish, generous in victory, the restoration of French rights and a guarantee of the Catholic position in the valley, he marched against Saumur. The Grisons again refused to ratify and the Catholics appealed against the prospect of further overlordship. With the support of the Pope the Habsburg powers responded with impressive force and speed. Feria from Chiavenna, and the Archduke Leopold from the Tyrol, crushed the Grisons in a pincer. Now they had to renounce their suzerainty, open the passes to Spain, admit the practice of Catholicism in their own lands and give up the Lower Engadine to Austria. The French could do nothing until the Peace of Montpellier had brought an end to the Huguenot war, in October 1622. Early the following year a treaty was signed with Venice and Savoy with the aim of driving the Spaniards out of the Val Telline. Spain, which had more to gain from placating the French than from any stand on titular sovereignty, suggested that the Val Telline be occupied by Papal troops. This took place in May 1623; in November the Pope put forward proposals which were rejected in turn by Spain and France, as they leaned towards one side or the other. This was Richelieu's inheritance when, in August 1624, he became once more Secretary of State. A month earlier, Vieuville had ordered the army of the Marquis du Coeuvres to mobilise on the frontier.

Richelieu's first important essay in international statecraft reveals clearly both the nature of the problems that he confronted and the resources of will and intelligence which he could deploy. From the start, whatever accidents befell him, it was plain that France had a minister who could take the initiative and keep it, plan for distant results and follow the plan consistently, but not so rigidly as to jeopardise the chance of immediate advantages. The combination of nervous energy, intellectual control and tactical sense, the will to sublimate personal ambition and feeling in service to the state, and a disconcerting loftiness towards the individuals who stood in his path, are among the first impressions we receive. Through all runs the courage of a man whose confidence was regularly tested by plots and threats, who knew that he stood on shifting ground at home and that he could be sure of little: not of the king, not of the army, not even of his own health. It is misleading to see the relationship of statesmen to events in images such as the spider and his web, or the puppet-master and his dolls. The historian must be mindful of the importance of the accidental, the small things that decide the course of battles and sway the reasoning of diplomats. The shot that killed Gustavus Adolphus in his prime, the failure of Anne of Austria to produce an heir for twenty years, the Francophil feelings of Pope Urban VIII—these factors and many more must be weighed. Similarly the temptation to make a pattern out of coincidences of dates and lives must be resisted, attractive though it is. No more in history than in art is the picture made by the frame. We are none the less drawn by the dramatic effect of such coincidences, as here by the way in which the career of Olivarez complements that of Richelieu.

When the Cardinal came to power Olivarez had recently assumed the direction of Spanish policy under Philip IV(1621-65). He was overthrown a few months after Richelieu's death, as a direct result of the Battle of Rocroy (May 1643), which set the seal upon Richelieu's efforts to end Spanish supremacy. Olivarez epitomised this supremacy, and sought to further it by domestic reforms and by aggressive use of military strength. Richelieu was convinced that the security of France could only be assured by the defeat of Spain. The two men undoubtedly saw their struggle in personal terms. To Olivarez Richelieu was the evil genius, the apostate who called in the heretical powers of the north to dispute the righteous cause of the Habsburgs; as the advantage leaned towards France his concern grew into an obsession. Richelieu was more objective in his appraisal of Spanish policy, but with good reason he believed that it was Olivarez' policy to support intrigues against his position, even his life. Statesman and charlatan, imperialist, dreamer and social reformer, ever bustling amidst a welter of papers, a vivid, noisy ebullient personality whose conception of civic virtue was yet intensely puritan, the Count of Olivarez, or *Condé Ducque* as he came to be known after winning a dukedom in 1625, combined in himself two traditions and sought to implement the policies dictated by both. He was the heir to the *arbitristas,* the reformers whose programme took on a new urgency after the first two decades of the century and Lerma's rule, characterised by waste and inertia. As such he sought to reduce offices, to control dress, to close brothels and to prohibit the import of foreign manufactures. Of this ambitious programme (based surely upon the assumption so characteristic of the seventeenth century that morals and economics were related, if not indistinguishable from each other and codified in the articles of 1623), came little beyond the disappearance of the ruff. When he tackled the finances Olivarez met the same opposition of private interests and public apathy. He wanted to set up a national banking system to reduce the dependence of Spain on foreign bankers and, by imposing a ceiling on interest rates, to force money from loan funds into more productive investment. He also tried to replace the *millones,* taxes on consumption which bore most hardly on the poor, by a direct tax, assessed upon the towns and villages of Castile. The *Cortes* of Castile, vigilant and negative, a strong check upon the executive, forced him to abandon these schemes. Indeed the *millones* were extended in range and doubled in yield.

Olivarez' financial difficulties reflected two fundamental conditions which fiscal measures alone could not cure. The economy was sick from the failure of exports owing to the price rise of the last sixty years, the steepest in Europe, the accompanying decline in manufacturing industries, and excessive dependence upon imports of bullion from the New World which were now starting to decline. The expulsion of the Moriscoes at the beginning of the century had probably only a marginal effect upon the economy, but the loss of a quarter of a million inhabitants aggravated a trend toward depopulation. The barren uplands of central Castile and the great sheep ranges controlled by the monopolist Mesta; the once flourishing places like Medina del Campo, Burgos, Toledo, falling back into the decayed state of provincial market towns; the beggars loafing in the squares of Seville and Madrid; the innumerable priests, monks and friars, the magnificence of baroque altarpieces, church plate and vestments mocking the poverty outside; the growing army of officials parading a little Latin to secure some niche in a swollen bureaucracy, anything better than farming the dusty, shallow soil; and the hidalgoes, a tenth of the population by some accounts, privileged in law, exempt from tax, jealous of their status even when it had been recently bought—all these aspects of declining Spain have one thing in common: they were unproductive.

With declining returns from Castile, Olivarez was bound to turn to the political condition and a political solution. Castile was one of ten provinces of Spain, a loose confederation because of the way in which the original union of Aragon and Castile had been effected by a personal union of sovereigns, and the subsequent acquisition of distant territories such as Naples, Sicily, Milan and Flanders. It provided, however, a disproportionate part of the royal revenues. In an integrated state, *una regna et una lex*, Olivarez saw the beginnings of a solution to his financial difficulties, as well as the strength that might come from a co-operative venture. In 1626 he produced his scheme for the 'Union of Arms', a common reserve of 140,000 men to be supplied and maintained by the states of the monarchy in fixed proportions. To Aragon, Valencia, and especially to Catalonia, the scheme appeared as a threat to their cherished liberties, and against the opposition of their respective *Cortes*, Olivarez was able to secure only small concessions from the first two, and nothing from the Catalans. With the inauguration of this decree, a reform of the coinage and the suspension of payments to the bankers by which Olivarez hoped to end the grip of a small group of Italian financiers and work with a more amenable consortium of Portuguese, together with the encouraging successes of Spanish arms and diplomacy abroad, Olivarez was optimistic in these years about the chances of his reform programme.

With Richelieu embroiled with the Huguenots, England and the other opposing powers virtually *hors de combat*, in the years 1627-28 the moment was as favourable to Spain as it was depressing to France. It may have seemed to Olivarez that he could be faithful to the imperial tradition of militant activity in Europe without jeopardising his domestic plans. As Richelieu was later to find out, however, an aggressive foreign policy cannot be budgeted in precise terms; commitment cannot be limited. To this extent his two aims were incompatible. And when Olivarez became involved in the war of the Mantuan Succession in Italy, after the almost casual decision to endorse the action of his governor in Milan, Cordoba, who had occupied Montferrat in March 1628, he set in motion a train of events which was to be disastrous. French troops came back into Italy to uphold the claim of the Duc de Nevers and Richelieu was taken a step nearer to the open war which he wanted to avoid. The Pope was confirmed in his mistrust of Spanish aims and induced to lend his moral authority to the enemies of the Habsburgs in a way that contributed to the hardening of Richelieu's attitude, the steeling of his conscience to the point at which he was able to consider open alliance with heretics. Spain, meanwhile, became committed to a partnership with the Emperor which became expensive after the entry of the Swedes into the war in 1631 and which so dissipated the Spanish resources that the war against the Dutch, which should have been the main objective, and which Spanish troops were near to winning after the capture of Breda by Spinola in 1625, developed into a costly stalemate. This extended commitment gave Richelieu a chance to use military and diplomatic action effectively, cutting the supply routes and subsidising the Swedes; it also forced Olivarez to squeeze more money out of an economy which became ever more debilitated, to turn increasingly to the use of special *juntas*, emergency measures, and ultimately to take the desperate actions which provoked rebellion in Catalonia and Portugal.

Telescoped in this way, the events and stages in the decline of Spain take on a look almost of inevitability but here the historian has an unfair advantage over the statesmen of the time. When Richelieu pondered the courses open to him in 1624 he could do no more than accept the facts of power as they were represented by the disciplined *tercios* of Spain, in control of strategic points around France, threatening encirclement, and the disarray of the Protestant states. In a threatening world he had to move warily, and act boldly only when he thought he could win.

His first action on replacing Vieuville was to send Père Joseph to Spada, the Papal nuncio, to air the French proposal that the Spaniards should only be denied the Val Telline passage for 'grave reasons'. The nuncio was baffled by the secretive and elusive manner of the friar, who probably knew that these negotiations were intended only to be a distraction. When the latter reported that the Pope would not yield, Richelieu ordered Coeuvres to invade the Val Telline. Between November and February, aided by Venetian siege guns, he secured all but two of the forts. Lésdiguières, meanwhile, crossed the Alps and joined Charles-Emmanuel, who provided a diversion by besieging Genoa. Rome reacted with predictable anger and unusual speed, and Spada demanded the restitution of the forts. While Père Joseph parried his claims, the ground was cut from under his feet by the news that the Huguenots were in revolt again. Soubise had seized a French fleet and Rohan, his brother, was raising troops in the south.

Not apparently understanding the finer points of Richelieu's policy, the Huguenots had given timely aid to Spain and reminded the Cardinal that he would not have a free hand abroad until he had dealt with his enemies at home. Richelieu now tried to spin out negotiations by proposing to the Pope that the Spanish should have access on condition that the forts were destroyed. Père Joseph was sent to Rome, where the general chapter of the Capuchins was holding a meeting, to announce that the French were suspending military operations for two months as a mark of goodwill, and further that they would be on the side of the Church in the larger struggle against heresy: in this at least the Huguenot intervention was helpful. Meanwhile the legate Barberini was sent to Paris by his uncle the Pope, ostensibly to bring dispensation for the marriage of Henriette Marie to Prince Charles of England, but really to impress upon Richelieu that the Pope was in earnest about the Val Telline. The arrival of the young legate, who entered Paris in May 1625 on a white mule in traditional imitation of Christ's entry into Jerusalem, touched upon some delicate spots. The *dévôts* were already uneasy at the sight of a Cardinal waging war against the Church and the political opponents of Richelieu were given a handle against him; on the other flank, Gallican prejudice was roused by this visible reminder of Papal authority. Indeed the legate had a boisterous reception when he rode past Notre Dame at the head of a sumptuous procession; in the Rue St Jacques women tried to kiss his slippers, but outside Notre Dame students from the Sorbonne broke through the guards and made off with his mule, leaving the legate to pick himself off the ground and hurry into the Cathedral. In this way the Parisians demonstrated the hot feelings that lay beneath the pedantic disputes of Ultramontane and Gallican parties. Fortunately for Richelieu the Pope was not a man to go to extremes. Imaginative, interested in poetry, profoundly spiritual, but cool enough in his judgement of political issues, he was anxious to preserve peace and also much taken with the personality of Father Joseph, who brought with him a poem on the crusade for the Pope's delectation. He was in fact more open to argument than his legate, who broke off the negotiations in August 1625 when Richelieu refused to abandon the Grisons.

Richelieu's dilemma was painful. 'Never in the midst of the great enterprises which it has been necessary to undertake for the state have I felt so near death as when the legate was here', he was later to write. If he consented to an arrangement which gave uncontrolled use of the Val Telline he would damage the war effort of the Dutch at a critical phase, and he relied on them for ships to deal with Soubise, which they were willing to lend in the belief that France was an essential member of the anti-Habsburg front. Furthermore he might spur the English to aid the La Rochellais as a gratifying gesture against the Pope. Yet he could not forget that he owed his position largely to Bérulle and the *dévôts*, with whose point of view he was still largely in sympathy. A clue to the direction of his thinking at this time is, however, provided by his summoning a Council of Notables composed of leading figures in court and administration, whose vehemently anti-Spanish feeling suggests some careful selection on Richelieu's part. It took little to rouse such feeling, however, among politically conscious Frenchmen, especially those who were old enough to remember the presence of Spanish troops in France during the civil wars. An incident roused feeling, especially among merchants, to fever pitch. The Duc de Guise, governor of Provence, intercepted a convoy of silver being sent from Barcelona to Genoa and then seized three Genoese ships off Marseilles carrying further money. The bankers offered the Spanish government a reward for recovering the money which the Spanish themselves could ill afford to lose. In April 1625 Olivarez decreed the sequestration of French property in Spanish ports to the value of the silver; Richelieu answered by closing the Spanish frontier to trade and Olivarez retaliated by sequestering all French property in Spanish lands. That Richelieu was seriously thinking of war at this point can be deduced from a memorandum of May in which he argued that, Spain being short of cash and its people restless, especially the Catalans from loss of French trade, the country must succumb before simultaneous attacks launched with 'French fury'. The publication at this time of *The Catholic of the State*, a work in which one of Richelieu's paid pamphleteers, perhaps Richelieu himself, argued that wars might be necessary for the peace of subjects and the security of states, and that the moral rules guiding private behaviour are not always applicable to the state, conveys the Cardinal's thinking at this time. It is likely however that Richelieu's mood was less bellicose than such arguments would suggest: it was plainly important not to give the Spaniards, or his enemies at home, the impression that France could not afford to fight.

In the event Richelieu's hand was forced once again by the action of a subordinate. The Comte de Fargis, ambassador in Madrid, was persuaded by his wife, who had been influenced by the *dévôts*, that he should make peace at once; in January 1626 he signed a treaty with Olivarez containing the condition that the Grisons should forfeit their claim to the Val Telline if they could not fulfil the other conditions. This was clearly impracticable but the remarkable thing, an indication of the problem of effective government at this time, was that Fargis should have signed the treaty without authority and without having informed the king of its contents in advance. Richelieu had to use the treaty as the basis for a hurried settlement, for he could not repudiate his ambassador; fortunately for him, the Spanish too were eager for a settlement and accepted his modifications. The resulting Treaty of Monçon, in March, confirmed the independence of the Grisons but in terms so ambiguous that both sides could interpret it as they pleased, or as they were in a position to implement. The Spanish were not debarred from using the passes, though the French hoped that the acknowledgement of the Grisons' authority would have this effect. The Spanish put their trust in clauses protecting Catholic rights in the Val Telline and giving its people virtual self-government under the merely nominal over-lordship of the Grisons; furthermore there was no mention of French rights of passage and recruitment in the valley. The demolition of the forts saved Richelieu's face, for it was the erection of these forts that had precipitated the crisis in the first place. Since the Spanish secured the right of passage, and the French could not object to this without laying themselves open to the accusation of breach of treaty, the treaty was a gain for Spain in the strategic terms that mattered. Not only had Richelieu deserted his allies, Savoy and Venice, he had also made it impossible for them to cooperate effectively with France so long as the pass remained under Spanish control. It was a lesson to Richelieu, that he remembered four years later when faced by a similar *fait accompli* at Regensburg, in the importance of clear and unmistakably binding terms. His own complacent comments in his subsequent memoirs, written after later success had healed the wounds of time, should not blind us to the fact that this treaty was a set-back for France and for the Protestant cause, whose effects were felt right up to the climax of the Spanish military success at Nordlingen. In that it encouraged Olivarez to believe that full-scale military aid to his Austrian cousins was feasible, it can be said also to have contributed to the ultimate misfortune of the Habsburgs.

## 8. *The Huguenots and the Fall of La Rochelle*

The Huguenot question eludes straightforward definition. The Huguenots did not occupy one corner of France but were dispersed throughout. They were a minority, about one in ten, but their strength was much greater than the figures would suggest because of the relatively high proportion of nobles and substantial bourgeois in their ranks. Where they were most numerous and militant, in the south and the south-west, the crown was also most ineffectual, because of the problem of communication and the virtually autonomous position of local governors. They cannot be isolated as a specifically French problem since they were part of the international body of Calvinism; no more could the French government deal with them without reckoning on repercussions abroad. Henry IV had found himself in an ambivalent position after his conversion since the Huguenots expected him to be their protector while Catholics looked for some rigour as a mark of the sincerity of his conversion. The experience of the Duc de Luynes, who had at least grappled boldly with the problem, showed what dangers attended a purely military solution. But Richelieu found that he could not be sure of a free hand in foreign affairs so long as they could revolt when they pleased.

These considerations reveal the extent of the challenge posed by the separate, armed existence of the Huguenots, a state within a state, indeed a republic inside a monarchy. There was nothing new about this challenge. There is a greater continuity, both in the attitude of the Huguenots and in the measures taken by the government, than has usually been allowed for by historians, intent upon the Cardinal's performance. The campaigns of 1620-22 performed the necessary work of capturing their positions in the south-west. Without this preliminary effort the capture of La Rochelle would have been impossible. Yet Richelieu's assessment of the cost of the various policies open to him, his final acceptance of the need for overwhelming force, his personal, single-minded commitment in the face of alarming distractions and the strong temptation to compromise, his sane and even tolerant settlement, all mark his handling of the business as statecraft of an exceptional order, no less by contrast with the subsequent handling of the Huguenots by Louis XIV who managed to create another political problem at a time when the original one had ceased to matter very much.

The Edict of Nantes, signed in April 1598, was a truce in a civil war, which reflected the weariness of both sides rather than the supremacy of one, and secured civil peace at the expense of a surrender of authority on the part of the royal government. Although it took the form of a royal edict it was more like a treaty between two independent powers. It was less sentiment towards his co-religionaries, or the influence of his Huguenot adjutant Sully, or even his own moderate views, than the knowledge that the Huguenots could not be reduced by force that persuaded Henry to give concessions which mocked the whole concept of the unitary state. How had the Huguenots arrived at the point where they could demand such an exceptionally privileged status?

The answer lies partly in the nature of Calvinism, partly in the coincidence of a period of weak royal government with the main impetus of a movement which offered both spiritual and material incentive to resistance. Calvin, a Frenchman, nurtured on law, in his later years an exile in Geneva, had conceived a new sort of polity which embodied the principles of his *Christianae Religionis Institutio* of 1536 and found in the small city state on the border of France the perfect laboratory for its development. He had taken to the furthest limit the doctrine of predestination which, as Jansen and his followers were to maintain, was present in Catholic theology from Augustine, and had recently been restated by Luther. His followers, convinced that they were the elect of God, accepted social and spiritual disciplines which cut across barriers of race and language, aided by the rapid passage of ideas among the academic élite of Europe that characterised the age of humanism. The episcopate was replaced by a hierarchy of consistories and regional colloquies, capped by a national synod. Elected ministers and lay elders shared the government of a body which claimed to control all aspects of the lives of its members: the most ambitious expression of the church-state. Where Lutheranism remained amorphous, subservient everywhere to the secular authority for lack of a viable organisation, as is borne out by the unconvincing record of the Lutheran states in the face of the Habsburg counter-attack, Calvinism faced the Church with a rival plant whose durability came from the cells from which it grew, small groups, tied tightly by family relationships. In Scotland, England, the Netherlands, Germany, France, Calvinists were only a small minority but strong enough to provide a core of resistance or even to take over and direct Church and state. Round the fanatics who were prepared to fight and die for the faith, the Rohans and Guitons, gathered the malcontents, embittered by declining rents or ambitious for a larger stake in society, the restless ranks of the minor noblemen and gentry who were the political activists throughout Europe, the piratical sea-captains of Plymouth, Flushing and La Rochelle, the young gallants who enlisted in the armies of William and Maurice of Nassau, Coligny and Henry of Navarre, who went with the Count Palatine to Bohemia and welcomed the new war as a means of adventure and employment.

There was another element in Huguenotism, the bourgeois: the rigorous logic of Calvinism appealed to the university mind trained to think analytically, and especially to the lawyer. The faith that was nourished by regular reading of the Scriptures, rather than by those symbols and ceremonies which taught traditional theology, was articulate and self-contained. The bourgeois was attracted too by the individual ethics of Calvinism which stressed the merits of work and self-help, and modified Catholic teaching on usury; this class tended anyway to anti-clericalism, in France as elsewhere, critical of the worldly, privileged character of the upper clergy, recruited largely as it was from the aristocracy. It was the *noblesse*, however, who made Huguenotism dangerous to the state; their capital lay in their swords. Leadership came from the great territorial magnates, men like Coligny and Bouillon with interests and connections outside France or Lésdiguières, who treated his provincial governorship as an hereditary fief, and was determined to resist the encroachment of the crown on his control of local troops and patronage. Many Frenchmen envied their brethren in Scotland, England, Scandinavia and large parts of Germany, where Church lands made a rich endowment for leading Protestant magnates. In Calvin's unequivocal affirmation that God was sovereign over all secular powers, bishop and king alike, lay an attractive argument to those who opposed the encroaching centralising state, buttressed in England as in France by the spiritual authority of the Church. Although there were Huguenot communities and families all over France, and a sizeable number in Paris, they were most numerous in the towns which had traditions of autonomy or strong commercial links with other countries, Lyon, Tours, La Rochelle for example. As in the Netherlands the Calvinists came to be concentrated in the north (to exercise there a control out of all proportion to their numbers as a result of the war against Spain and the frontier created by geography and strategy), so in France the religious wars produced a rough division, with Huguenots living predominantly in the southern provinces, the Dauphiné, Languedoc, Guyenne, Saintonge and Gascony. This was the natural outcome of a policy of resistance which was easier to maintain in the remoter provinces.

Calvin himself had inclined towards non-resistance as the ideal, though he told Coligny that revolt might be lawful if it had some established authority like that of Parlement behind it. As was customary with rebels everywhere, the Huguenot leaders maintained the pretence that they were fighting against the bad advisers of the crown. This was intelligible in view of the fact that the crown appeared, at least until the massacre of St Bartholomew's Eve in 1571, to be neutral, the impetus of persecution coming largely from the party of the Guises. That dreadful stroke drove the Huguenots into an avowed revolutionary position, adding bitterness and resolve to the sense of mission with which many Huguenots already saw themselves as members of an international crusade. The author of the *Vindiciae contra tyrannos* claimed that rebellion by the 'magistrates' of a kingdom was lawful in the eyes of God, an argument which was to be used by both sides to justify war and murder, but which clung like a bad smell to Huguenotism in the seventeenth century, reminding their opponents of the traumatic experiences of civil war. By the time the conversion of Henry of Navarre in 1595 made possible a degree of reconciliation, the Huguenots had entrenched themselves. Protestant France was divided into nine areas, with an elected council in each; an assembly, drawn from these, met each year. At Saumur, in 1595, the assembly demanded equal representation of Huguenots and Catholics in every parlement; that of 1596 sent agents to negotiate in London and Amsterdam. They behaved like a sovereign state in order to secure good terms in negotiation. In 1685 the descendants of these war-hardened men were bitterly to regret such arrogance, though each concession of the Edict of Nantes could be defended in the light of previous experience.

Huguenots were allowed public worship in all places where they had enjoyed it for the previous two years (except within five leagues of Paris). Nobles were allowed to worship privately at court. All were granted civil rights, free access to the professions and universities, as well as special privileges. For instance *chambres de l'édit*, in which there had to be Huguenot representatives, were added to the Parlements of Paris, Grenoble and Bordeaux, to try cases involving Huguenots. The system of assemblies was sanctioned and they were allowed to fortify a hundred towns, including such bastions as Montauban and La Rochelle, and the garrisons of these towns were to be maintained at the expense of the state. In all this there was little of toleration, much of impotent jealousy. To the Catholic Pasquier it was *prodige*, monstrous: a normal view among Catholics. Neither side accepted the truce as final. In both camps zealots planned their missionary strategy. Rival congregations sought petty advantages, use of the church bell here, the burial ground there; at all levels there was a war of attrition, fought with texts and lawsuits, in which the only condition of settlement was apathy on one side or the other, or a policy of neutrality on the part of the crown. Henry may have envisaged this for he had grown used to the idea that the crown had to accept special situations and compromise with vested interests. He appointed Huguenots as ministers and tried to draw the two religions together at court. 'We are all French and citizens of the same country' was his version of a *politique* view which Richelieu would not have disavowed.

The crown in this century could not, however, be properly neutral, when nine-tenths of the people were Catholic, when the accepted solution was *cuius regio eius religio* and when it was generally held, as the Protestant Benoît put it, that 'differences of religion disfigure the state'. Everywhere in Europe princes were acting upon this assumption, fighting for power in and outside their states, under religious banners. The Catholic view of the Huguenots should be studied alongside the success of the Calvinist Dutch in achieving independence from Spain. (Few believed that the settlement of 1609 could be reversed.) The

G

Huguenots were accused of wanting to set up a republic, a league of cities after the Netherlandish fashion. One pamphlet of 1622 alleged that the Huguenots' aim to set up *un gouvernement populaire* was opposed to the spiritual monarchy of the Catholic Church. Into this conception Rohan fitted as the French William of Orange. Like Orange, Rohan had the prestige of an independent prince. Before the birth of the dauphin, the future Louis XIII, he had been, through his grandmother Isabella d'Albret, heir-presumptive to the kingdom of Navarre. But the analogy should not be pressed too far. Rohan's party of militants was small: the Huguenots were divided between noblesse and bourgeoisie.

Foremost in the Catholic offensive was the militant body of the Jesuits. Before the end of his reign Henry admitted the Jesuits back into the Sorbonne. Like Louis XIII he had a Jesuit confessor. If, however, the Huguenots were docile they could expect to be left alone at the level of government, even if harried by priests and lawyers, because the first need of the state was calm at home. To some extent Huguenots responded to this opportunity. In the thirty years between the Edict and the fall of La Rochelle, while their numbers remained fairly stable, the leadership slowly changed. The feudal outlook of the nobility was changed, almost imperceptibly, by social and spiritual influences: the new prestige of monarchy and the current of thought towards absolutism, the subtle pressures of fashion, the appeal of a Church in revival. Huguenots were converted, in some cases by plain bribery. Many of the great names remained in the movement, Bouillon, la Trémoille, la Force, Rohan, but leading bourgeois were becoming influential in Huguenot affairs, men like the financiers Laffemas and Tallement, lawyers like the Hérouards who did not care for rebellion. The *prudents*, those who put their trust in loyalty, numbered some traditional resisters, notably Bouillon; the *fermes*, led by the Rohan family, demanding positive action to recover privileges that they believed were being whittled away, were in a minority. They tried to exploit the weakness of the crown, and it was their rashness that created the crisis of 1625-26, wrecked Richelieu's foreign policy and convinced him that he must strike at their stronghold, La Rochelle. They may have believed that Richelieu was looking for a chance to consolidate his place and to placate the *dévôts* by a general assault upon the Huguenots which they therefore sought to anticipate while still strong enough to win. The misfortune of the rising and its timing was that it came at a low point in Protestant fortunes in Europe when Richelieu was considering action against the Habsburgs, to relieve the pressure on the Huguenots' co-religionaries in Germany.

The revolt was occasioned by a reckless act of piracy and supported by a minority only of militant Huguenots. As it turned out it was the last fling, a heroic, desperate epilogue to the religious wars. In the light of Richelieu's firm response and in the international context it may seem to have been misjudged; yet the fourteen months' siege of La Rochelle shows how formidable the revolt could have been if it had been followed by a general rising, or if Richelieu had failed to rise to the occasion. In January 1625 Soubise, Rohan's younger brother, 'infamous Soubise' as Richelieu called him, seized five ships, amongst them the *Vierge*, which had been built in Holland for the Duc de Nevers to lead his crusade against the Turks. He appears to have intended a diversion to distract the Spanish, who were engaged upon the crucial siege of Breda; the action was maladroit, for the Dutch set more value upon the official alliance of France than the enterprise of Huguenot privateers and sent a fleet to assist Richelieu in suppressing the rebels. The Dutch seamen were reluctant to fire upon their fellow-Calvinists until Soubise roused them by attacking their flagship with fireships. The English captains of the squadron originally sent to support the French siege of Genoa also refused 'to shed the blood of Protestants' but Montmorency was able to collect a fleet large enough to defeat Soubise at the isle of Rhé. Soubise collected a few more ships and sailed to Falmouth, whither the French chased him. So Anglo-French relations deteriorated in a familiar sequence of clashes, threats and reprisals. Charles I insisted that the French should respect the terms of the treaty of Montpellier, recalled the English ambassador from Paris and dismissed some of the queen's French courtiers. Henriette smashed a window with her fist, Richelieu was suave and played for time; harmony was briefly restored by the agreeable diplomat, Bassompierre, in the summer of 1626. In November, however, the Duc d'Epernon seized English ships carrying a year's supply of claret in Bordeaux harbour; the English retaliated by an order for the confiscation of all French ships, and in March Pennington collected a string of prizes in the Channel. Encouraged by this success and spurred on by Buckingham, whose vanity was pricked by Richelieu's understandable reluctance to allow him to conduct a personal mission to France, Charles I prepared for war. Buckingham, the spoiled, rash, unpredictable favourite, that 'gadfly, full of extravagance, violent and unrestrained in his passions', Soubise, blood-brother of the sea-beggars of Holland, and d'Epernon, who was bent upon involving Richelieu, fairly represent the forces of disorder and violence. These episodes, and their sequel in English attempts to succour La Rochelle, further illustrate the way in which the designs of statesmen could be prejudiced by the reckless initiative of individuals. No one saw this more plainly than Richelieu, who had now to try to impose his will.

Henri, Duc de Rohan, Sully's son-in-law, is a more appealing figure than his brother Soubise. He was the first duke in his ancient Breton family, whose motto was: 'Roi ne puis, duc ne daigne, Rohan suis'. Small, wiry, harsh-faced, unpretentious in manner, he had the gift of inspiring men and the brains to exploit it. Though most of his life was spent fighting for a lost cause there was a certain integrity about the man; the finer part of his personality was never lost in the toils of conspiracy and war. After the treaty of Montpellier he had retired to his estate at Castres, where a contemporary described him as leading a solitary life in a great château, drinking only water, breaking in his own horses and helping his tenants. If his way of life was by preference simple, his intellect was subtle; as a political philosopher, concerned among other things with the balance of power in Europe, he had some influence on Richelieu. In arms against him he was a formidable opponent. For him, the Huguenot party was not only 'a sacred cause': it provided the rock on which could be maintained the power of the grandees of both religions. He was probably not consulted about Soubise's coup but he determined to turn it into a major challenge, to secure the rights won by the Edict; forthwith he travelled round the towns of Languedoc, the Bible carried before him by a pastor, preaching righteousness and war.

The citizens of La Rochelle were, however, not so certain that war was in their interest. Their town was immensely strong, defended by bastions and half-moons, covered ways and drawbridges; the port was protected by a great chain between two towers. Two islands off-shore guarding the harbour, long tides, marshy ground outside the city and a damp Atlantic climate added formidably to the military problem. The inhabitants of

La Rochelle, firmly Calvinist, well-to-do, sober burghers and daring seamen, had a philosophy of resistance to draw upon. The cautious oligarchy of rich merchants was opposed by a popular party led by some *nouveaux riches* and radical ministers: their bitter feuding was something for the crown to exploit. That the town government hesitated shows maybe that they preferred to keep their independence in peace, that there was an instinctive loyalty to the king and that they sensibly mistrusted the swaggering airs of Gascon adventurers. Their city was, moreover, large and rich. They paid none of the king's taxes, their customs fostered the growth of trade, for duties on exports were less than 2 per cent; goods belonging to Rochellais merchants were free from all duties. Their happy condition illustrates the advantages enjoyed by Huguenot communities and provides one reason for the jaundiced view of their unprivileged rivals. Their hand was forced, however, because Buckingham decided to rescue them before Richelieu had decided upon besieging them. In July 1627 he appeared before La Rochelle with Soubise, a fleet and some soldiers whom he landed on the island of Rhé. Godefroy, mayor of the city, begged Soubise to leave them and a citizen bore a message to the king affirming the loyalty of the city. Richelieu suspected insincerity; he had been forewarned of Buckingham's plan and had planned a muster of troops. The feudal levies, pikemen and musketeers, now converged in bands upon La Rochelle.

Throughout July Richelieu was gnawed by doubt and the sense of facing a critical decision. Louis XIII was ill; he might die and Gaston would be king; this was a recurring nightmare. Luynes had staked his future on the capture of Montauban—could he now succeed with the stronger fortress of La Rochelle where Luynes had failed? Père Joseph's visionary ardour helped to stiffen his resolve and he realised that the operation would serve to postpone the final breach with the *dévôts*. Above all he understood that wars were won by concentrating forces at the vital point; if La Rochelle fell, nothing else would stand out against him for long and success could give him the authority to shape France's policy as he wanted. In the course of the siege Richelieu's will and nerve were tested sorely but he never faltered or paused to reckon the cost. It was his main strength as a statesman that he had the courage to back his judgement and to pursue the consequences to their logical end. Richelieu was not omniscient though his enemies began to suspect it, nor was he above human fears and misgivings. He had, however, the will to succeed in rich measure, and in this siege, one of the greatest ever mounted, he was committed as statesman and as general; he was fighting for his career, for his ideals and for his life.

The king recovered in August and d'Angoulême, who was in charge of the preliminary moves, stopped supplies from entering the city. Buckingham ran into difficulties on his island, storms damaged his siege works and blockading booms, hunger and sickness decimated his men; at home, Charles I was raising money by forced loans too slowly to send effective aid. Buckingham and Toiras, commander of Fort St Martin, exchanged courtesies, melons and scented orange water and waited each for the other to weaken. On 7th October, Beaulieu-Persac relieved the garrison but lost many of the ships laboriously collected by the Cardinal in doing so. The siege meanwhile began in earnest with the king and Cardinal in personal control. A plan to kidnap Richelieu was revealed to Father Joseph and the Huguenot raiders were met by musketeers in the sand dunes. Richelieu realised that La Rochelle would only succumb if blockaded by sea. The island of Rhé must therefore be held. He undertook the relief of St Martin in person. In vile November weather, steel cuirass under his Cardinal's scarlet, with plumed hat and rapier completing a startling effect, he directed the passage of troops to the island. Buckingham attacked the fort on 5th November but his scaling ladders were too short; as his men fell back they were set on by Schomberg. They were forced into the salt marshes and savaged by the French cavalry as they struggled to a disembarkation point. Buckingham sailed back to England with less than half the men he had brought out. Neither inept nor a coward, although casual in an Elizabethan way, he had been defeated by the thoroughness and deadly resolution of Richelieu: 'Your cardinal', he said to his prisoner Beaulieu-Persac, 'is the first man in the world'. Future English efforts were fatally inhibited by this defeat while Richelieu was able to proceed with the siege undisturbed.

Ambrogio Spinola, the celebrated Genoese commander of the Spanish troops in the Netherlands and captor of Breda, visited the siege works in February. Even this connoisseur of the siege must have been struck by what he saw. To form a mole across the roadstead and cut La Rochelle from the sea, Richelieu had

sunk 200 hulks in line, staked them down and filled them with
stone blocks and sand. Once the dyke broke, once it was breached
at high tide by a Captain David with despatches from England,
but it served its purpose. When Denbigh arrived in May, with the
English fleet, he examined the mole, made a show of bombarding
the French encampments, but turned back from the mole and
returned to England. To the famished Rochellais it was a cowardly
betrayal. But Denbigh's ships were mostly converted merchant-
men: their captains, reflecting the unwarlike spirit at home, were
reluctant to take risks and happy to follow a mistaken signal and
head for home. Buckingham was still anxious to help but, after
conferring with Soubise at Portsmouth, on 2nd September he
was stabbed to death by Felton. England rejoiced indecently at
the death of an over-mighty subject; La Rochelle had little cause
to mourn him. For by then the defences were maintained only by
leaders like Mayor Guiton, who had replaced the more conciliatory
Godefroy, and the Duchesse de Rohan. Guiton climbed the
church tower daily to scan the horizon for English sails. The old
Duchesse de Rohan and her household ate the carriage horses,
then the harness. The common people scavenged, suffered, died
or deserted.

The besiegers were organised as if for a permanent camp.
Louis had been sceptical of his minister's power to exert authority
over his generals: 'They are as likely to obey him as to obey the
kitchen-boy'. But the enterprise bears Richelieu's stamp, alike in
its grand conceptions and minute care for detail. The troops were
regularly paid and fed. By the holding of regular services the
troops were reminded of the religious purpose of the siege.
Imaginative schemes cheered their spirits. After reading about
Alexander the Great and the siege of Troy, he built a jetty, facing
La Rochelle, and mounted cannon on it. On the score of reports
from Catholic informers he launched an attack at a point where a
grilled water-gate barred the entrance of a canal leading from the
city to the salt marshes. With Marillac, Richelieu led the expedition down the canal. The assault failed because the party carrying
the petards lost the way. Richelieu blamed Marillac for this and
his mistrust of him may have dated from this incident. The
Cardinal's readiness to lead in person, the way in which he
overcame his usual afflictions, sustained by nervous energy,
restlessly active, braving lashing winds and rain and the dark
night mists, must have impressed his troops, even if they saw

something inappropriate, even ridiculous, in the dress of the soldier-priest.

The English under Lindsay made their last appearance in October and did no more to raise hopes than bombard, experiment with fireships and negotiate so feebly as to convince Richelieu that he held all the cards. When Lindsay sailed away he left a bitter sense of betrayal. It would be fairer to see the whole botched operation in the context of an inconstant, spasmodic, ultimately futile foreign policy. England was hereafter to be a negligible counter in Richelieu's reckoning of policy and commitments, largely irrelevant to the continental scene. The English failed at sea; nor was relief forthcoming by land. Rohan had a disappointing response to his appeals for volunteers and had to content himself with fortifying other positions in the south and west. He was contained by Condé, powerless to move against Richelieu. In his failure we have the clearest indication of the changed mood of the Huguenots; no longer would the peasants turn out obediently at the call of their feudal lords. Many of the nobles too were waiting warily on the results of the siege.

On 28th October the drawbridge fell and twelve sombre figures, an embassy of city fathers in black hats and white collars, emerged to make their submission to the king. Richelieu entered to survey the desolate town; there were corpses everywhere and a hundred men died at once by over-eating from the ration carts. The population before the siege had been 28,000; now it was 5,400 and many of these were to die from exhaustion. On All Saints' Day the king made formal entry and the Cardinal, now priest again, offered the sacraments to the kneeling generals of the king. The behaviour of the royal army witnessed to the firmness and good sense of the king and the respect in which his wishes were held. The siege had been unprecedentedly long and there was a robust tradition that fallen cities should be sacked: three years later Magdeburg was to provide an example of it. In France's own civil wars massacres had been commonplace. Richelieu's impatient temper was only controlled by some effort of will; he was ready to be stern when reasons of state required it, but clemency and moderation were now the order of the day. The food that was brought into the starving but still wealthy town was sold at the same price as in the camp. The walls of the town were razed, the churches given back to the Catholics and the special privileges revoked. The great temple of 1603 was turned into a Catholic cathedral. The Duchesse de Rohan and Mayor Guiton were banished, but the latter went stoutly, protesting his loyalty to the king; he soon took a commission in the army. Richelieu would not, as Bérulle and Marillac wanted, proscribe the Protestant faith; on the contrary, the Huguenot pastors were confirmed in their appointments. Père Joseph refused to be bishop as Richelieu asked; it would have been an interesting appointment.

In the south Condé had been fighting keenly and brutally but pockets of resistance held out. There was a possibility of Spanish intervention; in May, Rohan was offered 300,000 ducats. After the fall of La Rochelle, however, he could not hold the remaining towns together. Richelieu stormed Privas and, being bed-ridden, was unable to prevent the town being sacked. He then made the peace of Montpellier by which the Huguenots agreed to the destruction of all their fortified places. Rohan left to offer his sword to Venice. Montauban held out for another month; with its surrender the submission of the Huguenots was complete, and the peace of Alais in June 1629 ended the religious wars. The Huguenots lost their rights as a separate political entity, their privileged towns, magistracies and law-courts. Religious toleration was, however, assured.

From all this came a widening of the gulf that now separated Richelieu from the *dévôts*. He had indeed no regard for *Messieurs les prétendus réformés* and he yearned for unity within the state; but upon uniformity of belief he could not afford to insist. He expected that he would soon have to fight in Europe with Protestant allies. Moreover the aristocrat in him could appreciate the attitude of the Huguenot leaders, notably Rohan, who had not been disloyal to the king according to his own idea of loyalty. Did he not shout out, when goaded by the behaviour of a Huguenot consistory, 'You are all republicans!'? Monarchist he was then but in an obsolete tradition in that he held that great subjects could negotiate with their king, and with foreign kings. Turenne and d'Enghien later exemplified the same idea and acted upon it, in the Fronde. Richelieu conciliated Rohan by granting toleration enough to ease his conscience and soon afterwards accepted his service as a general.

Ruined churches, the rubble of levelled walls, the sulky acquiescence of the Huguenot towns, taunts, recriminations and outbreaks of violence, confronted the Catholic authorities.

Father Joseph's bare-footed Capuchins, active in this new field
of mission, went everywhere guarded by arquebusiers. Richelieu
was insistent that there should be no duress. There were striking
conversions, however, of pastors, families, even whole communities; some nobles secured pensions in return for their new
allegiance. Cynicism and weariness abounded but also zeal and
faith. Father Joseph was in his element, directing the Capuchins,
reconsecrating churches and founding priories; within months
his friars were established in twenty towns. He deplored the
apparent leniency of the terms of Alais, but Richelieu's judgement
was surely the sounder. He was not in the unassailable position of
Louis XIV in 1685 when he revoked the Edict of Nantes. If he
had to concede freedom of worship, he may also have guessed
that this alone would not strengthen Protestantism in France, but
the reverse; the missionaries might succeed where force would,
at this stage, fail. In the short term he was proved right, for the
difference between earlier civil wars and the Fronde was that,
during the Fronde, the Huguenots were consistently, even demon-
stratively, loyal, as was publicly acknowledged by Louis XIV.
There was no longer an armed republic within the monarchy. An
important step had been taken in the making of the absolute state.

## 9. Critics and Rebels

Throughout his life Richelieu was confronted and challenged by factions and individuals who believed with varying degrees of reason and prejudice that they stood to gain by destroying him. Since opposition was essentially personal, no convincing pattern can be constructed; it is possible none the less to identify some persistent elements. The *dévôts* felt a sense of betrayal at the hands of the churchman who had first made his name as the spokesman of the clerical interest. Marie de Médicis felt this the more sharply as she had regarded Richelieu as her protégé. All those whose sympathies lay towards Spain, notably of course the queen, Anne of Austria, regarded him with disfavour, especially after the affair of the Mantuan Succession. There were those too, like the chancellor Marillac, who were genuinely concerned about the condition of France and believed that his policy would put an intolerable strain upon the economy. In 1629-30, when Marillac and his circle, *dévôts* but responsible politicians as well, with an alternative policy to offer, were actively working against Richelieu opposition had a serious political content. But it was the habitual plotters of court and château who provided, throughout Louis XIII's reign, the intrigues and incidents which make such a rich and diverting tapestry in the hands of Dumas. Nor is the romantic novelist's view of the period so misleading; a study of the noble conspiracies reveals how dangerous they were and how narrowly Richelieu survived. Behind the tragi-comic gestures and manœuvres of Gaston and his accomplices can be discerned a feudal view of society which was incompatible with the growth of the modern state. They believed, even the best of them like Rohan and Montmorency, that they, *les Grands,* lived under a special dispensation; that, given a pretext which might be no more than personal offence, they were entitled by birth and rank to enjoy certain positions and revolt against the crown, to kill men in duels, negotiate with other countries, in short to behave like the sovereign princes which, to all intents and purposes, they had been in the Middle Ages and again in times of royal weakness like the religious wars. Richelieu was convinced that until this attitude was changed, the king could not rely on his armies, the country would remain lawless; taxes would not be raised nor justice done fairly, for the king would not be properly master in his own house. Along with the feuding and brawling there was a growing conflict between two views of society. Richelieu was not, however, opposed to noble privileges as such; he accepted the pre-eminence of the class, admired its courage; he wanted to destroy its political independence, so as to harness its virtues to the service of the state.

In the Chalais conspiracy of 1626 can be seen several distinct motives in a tangle of private interests and ambitions. In that year the Cardinal ordered the razing of private fortresses; a marriage was projected for Gaston of Orléans to Marie de Montpensier which Gaston was reluctant to accept; Anne of Austria was anxious for her own position, for she was childless after ten years of marriage and her position might suffer if the princess were to have children.

Orléans was eighteen and heir-apparent, as he was to remain until he was thirty. If Louis XIII had been more trusting, Gaston more reliable, he might have played a distinguished part. Between rebuffs from the king and recalcitrance from Gaston it is hard to distinguish between cause and effect in the deterioration of Gaston from a popular and agreeable figure to the purposeless rebel. Louis XIII was jealous and suspicious of him: when Gaston went to council to press his claim to command the expedition to La Rochelle, he was told that his proper place was the hunting field. In a situation of prominence without power he was easily tempted. He was ambitious as much for his friends as for himself, but in a crisis his strongest instinct was self-preservation. His agitated manner and disconcerting nervous grimaces, his defensive lying and petulant moods, suggest a personality that was unequal to his rank. His habit of betraying accomplices seems to be contemptible even if set against the impetuous way in which he rushed into further conspiracies to show his feeling for fellow-sufferers from Richelieu's regime. He should not, however, be made the whipping-boy for the faults and strains of a society in painful transition: as the greatest subject he was almost bound to resist, if he could not lead, a process by which the privileges of subjects were being curtailed.

Orléans found Marie de Montpensier unamusing; other princes of the blood, Vendôme and his brother the Grand Prior, illegitimate sons of Henry IV, Condé, Conti and Soissons, the latter a candidate for the princess's hand, were in sympathy with him, and looking for a pretext to revolt. Gaston's tutor, the Maréchal d'Ornano, also claimed to be in love with the princess, who was the richest heiress in France. Another partisan illustrates further the nature of the plot. Mme de Chevreuse, born a Rohan, married to Luynes at 17, a fair, oval-faced beauty with famous eyes, physically desirable, and much loved and gossiped about, was absorbed in exploiting her undoubted hold over a series of men. Her husband now was the Duc de Chevreuse, Grand Chamberlain of France and son of the Duc de Guise of the Catholic League; with him she had gone to England in the train of Henrietta Maria, had a liaison with Buckingham and given birth to a bastard at Hampton Court. She was also the queen's intimate friend and could speak to the restless magnates in her name. She involved Chalais, master of the wardrobe and her current lover, in the plot whose intentions varied with the plotter. Vendôme spoke of putting Gaston on the throne; for himself he wanted Brittany as an independent principality. Others were less specific but it is easy to see what the Rohan family could hope to gain for the Huguenots, and the Duke of Savoy for himself. Richelieu may at first have wanted to stand aside but rumours of assassination forced him to act. In May 1626 d'Ornano was arrested; when his papers were searched they revealed a letter from Vendôme pledging support for Gaston and urging him to 'use menaces and violence against Richelieu'. Chalais, whom Richelieu seems to have used to embroil the Vendôme brothers, gossiped and revealed some further ramifications of the plot. Vendôme and the Grand Prior were arrested, Gaston made one confession and was absolved, only to embark upon another plot at the instigation of Mme de Chevreuse. Again Richelieu was informed, again Gaston confessed. To save Chalais, so he said, he consented to marriage with Mme de Montpensier, which Richelieu performed in person, with haste and scant ceremony, as if he thought that Gaston would bolt again. The marriage was as pathetic as the wedding. Nine months later the bride died in childbirth but the daughter of this vast inheritance lived to be the *Grande Mademoiselle* of a later generation. Chalais underwent intensive investigation from which he emerged a haggard creature, having denounced everybody, none more vehemently than Mme de Chevreuse. Richelieu could not yet afford to offend the houses of Guise and Rohan so Mme de Chevreuse was merely exiled; she went to sin and conspire at the court of Lorraine.

There is some doubt about the nature of Chalais' interrogation and trial by a specially convoked court; for instance, Gaston's testimony is in the writing of Bouthillier, then Marie de Médicis' secretary, but he was not mentioned as being present at the interrogation and it was signed not by him but by Richelieu. Whatever means were employed in the trial, no one believed him to be the principal culprit. His Tudor-style sentence was intended to be an example as much as a punishment: for high treason he was to be decapitated and quartered, and his heirs deprived of nobility. His death was more horrible than Richelieu could have intended. Gaston made the typically futile gesture of bribing the headsman to stay away; two prisoners from Nantes gaol, armed with a cooper's axes, managed to sever the head after more than thirty strokes. The event may have lain heavy on Richelieu's mind, for he explained his reasons at length in his *Mémoires*; it was necessary, he said, to protect the realm from continuance of disorder, a first step in the process of reducing the nobles to obedience.

The years 1629 to 1631, from the peace of Alais to the treaties of Barwälde and Cherasco, can be seen as a decisive period in Richelieu's career; crucial decisions of foreign policy which helped to alter the course of the European war were made against a background of personal insecurity and unease. From his personal crisis he emerged stronger in authority, freer to act. But it was a very near thing. There was a strange mixture in his actions at this time of the boldly incisive and the pent-up hysterical, his strategy cool and forward-looking, but his mood sometimes reflecting the anxieties of a man strained to the limits of endurance by the uncertainties of his position. The strength of his opponents was derived not only from their rank and influence but from serious differences of policy. Marie de Médicis' opposition remained passionate, petty and unforgiving. With her were now ranged the *dévôts*, disappointed by his compromising settlement with the Huguenots and concerned about the implications of his Mantuan policy: hawks at home, doves abroad. The Chalais affair left sour memories and scores to settle. Richelieu's long absences with the troops weakened his grip at court which depended, apart from some loyal subordinates, upon the king alone: he could make him or break him at will. Whatever the machinations of the Cardinal's enemies, all depended in the end upon the mind of Louis XIII; he chose but seldom to reveal his thoughts or play his hand, and Richelieu remained as much in doubt as his enemies. In 1626 the king had told him: 'be assured I shall never change so that, whoever may attack you, I shall support you'. At La Rochelle and in Savoy he had received constant proofs of the Cardinal's resource and courage. Could the relationship forged in stress and danger survive among the rumours and arguments of the court? Richelieu knew that the king was incapable of constancy in his private relations, so how could he feel sure of support in his public capacity? The king was sensitively devout and could be expected to listen thoughtfully to those who alleged that Richelieu was betraying the Church. Accounts of the November crisis have traditionally centred upon Marie de Médicis, and it is true that she provided much of the drama; her vivid personality attracts attention. But since the king detested her and resented her efforts to sway him, it is likely that she damaged her cause more than she promoted it. The greatest danger to Richelieu lay in the *dévôts* and the alternative policy that they put forward.

Cardinal Bérulle's personal following was numerous, his influence was immense. He had helped Richelieu to power and it was to him that Richelieu had turned when he wanted to reform the training of priests in Luçon. There was much in Bérulle's methodical approach to mysticism and in his practical concern for the education and training of Catholics that Richelieu could admire and follow. The ideal of Bérulle and his followers was 'adherence to Christ', a process of active and at the same time self-eliminating exposure of the soul to the object of its adoration: less the divine, imageless Godhead, more the figures of Christ and the Virgin. 'Apostle of the incarnate word', Pope Urban VIII called him when he raised him to the Cardinalate, and put the seal of official approval upon a devotional idea that was new at least in emphasis; the death of true mysticism, as some authorities have held, but a compelling, lively force in ordinary Catholic worship. The Church of seventeenth-century France was above all Bérulle's Church: St Vincent de Paul and St François de Sales were among those who were proud to call themselves his disciples, and his Oratory, founded in 1611, and others founded on the same lines, deepened the spiritual lives of thousands of priests. Bérulle, for all his gentleness and a certain naïvety in worldly affairs, had political antennae; when he was roused, as he was by Richelieu's *politique* inclinations, to the fear that the Church was in danger, he was ready to lend his authority to the group at court who professed to share his concern. Richelieu himself wrote of him that 'he did not know what it was to hate anybody' and knew that there was nothing personal in his opposition, unless sadness at the backslidings of the man who was supremely fitted in abilities and position to give substance to Bérulle's vision of the seamless robe of Christendom. It was all the more embarrassing for Richelieu to have his foreign policy condemned by the founder of the Oratory, his own adviser and benefactor. Bérulle's death in 1629 immensely weakened the *dévôts*, for Marillac's motives of opposition were possibly less altruistic.

Michel de Marillac reached the climax of a brilliant career when he became Keeper of the Seals in 1626 at the age of 63. To some extent he owed his rise to Richelieu for he was made one of the *surintendants* after the disgrace of Vieuville. He was also able to work in sympathy with the Cardinal for as long as the assault upon the Huguenots concealed their basic differences of approach and personality. As President of the *Notables* he demonstrated that he, rather than the Chancellor d'Effiat (whom he tried to replace) was the chief influence in administrative aspects of government. His was the initiative in some of the important edicts of these years and the *Code Michaud* of 1629 was the product of a fruitful collaboration with Richelieu. But he was an ambitious man, authoritarian in temperament, and jealous of Richelieu's ascendancy. When Richelieu parted company with the *dévôts* because of his treatment of the Huguenots after the fall of La Rochelle and his subsequent foreign policy, personal considerations mingled with differences of opinion in a way that the historian cannot hope to disentangle.[1]

It is plain on the one hand that if Richelieu were to be dismissed Marillac could look forward to being first minister in his place. On the other hand the Keeper of the Seals was palpably sincere in his arguments for an alternative policy. He was concerned above all with the evidence which he was receiving in reports from

[1] For the interaction of foreign and domestic policy at this time see pages 90-91.

officials in the provinces that rising taxation was imposing intolerable burdens upon the people. After a sequence of bad harvests local disorders rose to a peak in 1629 and 1630. A phrase from a letter of February 1629 may be taken as typical of his attitude towards government in these conditions: 'it seems to me that the chief glory of good government is to think of the relief of subjects and the good regulation of the state, which can only be achieved by peace'. In July 1630 he wrote in alarmist fashion: 'There is sedition everywhere in France; the Parlements punish nobody. The king has provided judges for these trials and the Parlements obstruct the execution of their judgements. As a result seditions are authorised.' A humane man who deplored the wretchedness of the peasants and a man of law who feared the breakdown of order in society, Marillac was above all a *dévôt*. Brémond[1] puts him among the mystics of the time. He installed the Carmelites in the Convent of Notre Dame des Champs and kept for himself a private cell in the forecourt. He opposed Richelieu's foreign policy in the interests of the Church as well as of the French people. Like Bassompierre, and his own younger brother Louis de Marillac, who had married a cousin of the queen mother and was captain of her guards, he accepted the idea of a Spanish alliance and saw in the Huguenots the enemy to be destroyed. These men were heirs in fact to the policy of the Guises which had been discredited by the breakdown of royal authority at the end of the sixteenth century; now under a stronger monarchy they argued that France would be better served by friendship with Spain than by war in Italy or anywhere else. The course of French history would indeed have been different if this view had prevailed; to say the least it was an open question with risks and advantages in either course.

When Richelieu returned in September 1629 it was to find the whole council 'agitated as though in perplexity about some great design'. Gaston betook himself to the court of Charles of Lorraine, whence he was tempted to return by concessions—the government of Orléans and 200,000 livres to pay his debts. In 1630 he was left virtually in charge of Paris, Marie de Médicis settling down at Lyon, the king and Richelieu campaigning in Savoy. In July the king contracted dysentery; by September his

[1] H. Brémond, *Histoire Litteraire du Sentiment Religieux en France*, Vol. II, *L'Invasion mystique*. Paris, 1916.

H

life was despaired of; all the time he was under relentless pressure from Marie and the anti-Richelieu faction led by the Princesse Conti. The king was given the last sacrament by Richelieu's brother Alphonse, but recovered. Richelieu knew that his enemies had been discussing his fate in the event of Gaston's becoming King of France. He returned to Paris with the court; he was aware that there was now an active plot against him. Marie, Marillac and Madeleine de Fargis, wife of the former ambassador in Madrid, met at the Carmelite convent to draw up an indictment: the main charge was directed against this Mantuan operation. He decided to act first to forestall the event when he heard one day early in November that the king was with Marie at the Luxembourg palace. Accounts of the 'Day of Dupes' vary widely but in essentials it seems that Richelieu walked in upon Louis and his mother, who was making her charges against him; Marie was hysterical, behaving like an Italian woman at a market stall, the king was embarrassed and Richelieu for once lost his nerve. When the Cardinal was allowed to leave he seems to have inferred by the king's silence that he was to be dismissed. So did Marie, who told Marillac that he would take Richelieu's place, and the courtiers, who made their dispositions to exploit the new régime. Richelieu thought of flight to le Havre, the Normandy port of which he was governor, but instead obeyed the king's summons to go to his hunting lodge at Versailles. There the king made a gesture of independence, and cut the remaining ties of family feeling: 'I honour my mother', he said, 'but my obligations to the state are greater than towards her.' Richelieu in turn promised to show the king 'by ever increasing proofs' that he was 'the most devoted subject and most zealous servant that ever king or master had in this world'.

Marillac was promptly arrested and sent to Châteaudun where he died after a few months. Richelieu's danger lay now mainly in the immunity of the royal malcontents. On his urgent plea Marie was rusticated by Louis to Compiègne. To draw the sting of Mme de Chevreuse she was recalled from Nancy to resume her duties at court. Vendôme was released from the Bastille on condition that he left France. Gaston, however, rejected the olive branches offered to him by Cardinal de la Valette and left Orléans in March for Lorraine. Parlement, as so often more concerned with traditional rights than with the safety of the state, refused to register the edict outlawing Gaston's officers, on the grounds that it was no treason to follow their master, and the king summoned their leaders to the Louvre and tore up their remonstrance. Richelieu wanted above all to prevent the opposition from achieving any coherence. His actions appear to be arbitrary, even malevolent, but he could not be aware of the exact extent of the conspiracy against him; his espionage was efficient enough to feed him with scraps of incriminating evidence and these he seized on like a soldier firing at figures as they emerged from a smoke-screen, with more haste than discrimination. Bassompierre, the courtly marshal, who had served the crown well in the Italian campaign, was sent to the Bastille on a scanty pretext and kept there until the end of the reign. Louis de Marillac, the Chancellor's brother, had been appointed to command the army of Italy in November 1630; the day after he heard of it he was informed by Schomberg of his arrest; the Day of Dupes had supervened.

In July 1631 the Baron du Bec, governor of La Capelle, a fortress on the north-eastern border, was called to Paris to explain rumours of treachery. He had indeed planned to hand the place over to Marie but, when she arrived, after a melodramatic escape from Compiègne, she found that she had been forestalled. The gates were barred and she had to ride on to the Spanish Netherlands. She never set foot on French soil again. Meanwhile Marillac's case was provoking a further quarrel between crown and Parlement. The Grand Chambre of Parlement granted him leave to appeal to it, as was the right of a Marshal of France. The crown quashed this by decree; a plenary session of Parlement then declared Richelieu's picked judges to have no competence and forbade them to proceed. The crown turned to the Parlement of Burgundy, which proved more amenable and appointed a commission of two to examine the evidence. Gaston bid for the support of the lawyers by denouncing Richelieu's 'prodigious ambition and frightful audacity' and Parlement forbade any commission to proceed. A special court was then convened and twenty-four hand-picked judges met under the new Keeper of the Seals, Châteauneuf, a loyal functionary, and there was henceforward no doubt about the verdict. The charges of corruption were scarcely relevant to Marillac's punishment. As Richelieu himself admitted, he was sacrificed to the needs of the state, menaced as he thought by a coalition of Spain, the Empire and Lorraine. At the end of 1631, de la Force invaded Lorraine, chased Gaston's troops into Luxembourg and then occupied

Sédan, the seat of the Duc de Bouillon. Isabella, regent of Flanders, sensibly tried to dissuade Olivarez from taking the matter to the point of war, but reports of Olivarez' plans to support Gaston were enough to convince Richelieu that Marillac must die. A large crowd in front of the Hôtel de Ville watched him make a good end. Unless it was Richelieu's object to bring opposition into the open in order to continue his purge, this execution of a man who had never openly committed himself to rebellion cannot be considered wise, for its immediate aftermath was the revolt of the most important nobleman in France. Indignation at Richelieu's high-handed proceedings was one cause of the rising of the Duc de Montmorency.

In 1632 Henri de Montmorency was 37, governor of Languedoc and until lately Admiral of France. His family had produced five Constables of France and claimed for themselves the title of *premier baron chrétien*. He was Condé's brother-in-law, and related to the royal family. 'The great Constable', Anne de Montmorency, a leading protagonist in the religious wars, was Henri's grand-father. Henri himself was more than governor of Languedoc, and Languedoc was no ordinary province. A *pays d'état,* far from Paris, this large province, about the size of Wales, was notorious for its turbulent nobles and its Huguenots: the suppression of the last rising in 1629 had left smouldering resentments. Richelieu had tried to follow his success by altering the system of taxation. Formerly the provincial Estates raised the sum agreed upon after bargaining with Paris according to its own assessment and through its own officers; now he wanted to substitute royal officers and the lawyers of Languedoc were in a ferment. The Parlement of Toulouse quashed the edict creating the new tax offices and Montmorency went to Paris to negotiate on its behalf. A com-promise was reached but in October 1631 Richelieu tried to impose a new system by the appointment of two royal commis-sioners. Their efforts to raise the taxes in 1632 brought the province to the point of open rebellion and Montmorency was urged to lead.

His family's tradition was indeed one of loyal service to the crown, but service essentially in terms of personal relationships in the feudal manner. A Montmorency might be expected to follow a prince in war, to serve him in peace, but on his own terms. If he felt himself or his cause to be slighted, then interests of the state, even if he could discern them plainly, would not be

allowed to stand in his way. In Languedoc he was virtual ruler.
Toulouse was his capital and there, and in châteaux scattered
about the province, he presided over a miniature court. A retinue
of nobles and pages attended him everywhere, he enjoyed a
vast patronage and he was respected by all classes for his generous
and civilised ways. He was a gracious and attractive figure, a
brave soldier who had greatly distinguished himself in Piedmont
at the battle of Avigliana in 1630; for all that, his rising was as
futile as it was foolish. The year was a hard one. As Rohan had
found, five years before, the peasants were reluctant to turn out
against the royal army; however desperate their state it was
better to stay alive. There is some puzzle here, because popular
*jacqueries* were common in France in this century, but they were
never effectively harnessed to any political cause. The rigidity of
class barriers was a stronger factor, seemingly, than local feeling
about leader or cause. The time was past, too, when the bourgeois
could afford to follow the feudal banner even of a Montmorency.

Montmorency was indignant with the Cardinal for depriving
him of the office of Admiral and looked to the higher office of
Constable, the office which Richelieu had suppressed after the
death of Lésdiguières in 1627. It did not need the eloquence of
the bishop of Albi, Elbène, a Florentine and follower of Marie
de Médicis, to suggest how important he would be in France if
the Cardinal were removed and Gaston restored to favour. In
the spring of 1632 Richelieu was informed that Montmorency
was in league with Gaston and Charles of Lorraine. Gaston
forced the issue by an impetuous demonstration, not so much an
invasion as a foray: he entered Lorraine with 2,500 horse which
he had collected at Trier. When Lorraine was invaded by La
Force and Charles made to come to terms which included the
surrender of Clermont to France, he proceeded into France. His
force dwindled through desertions, but his challenge made up in
rhetoric what it lacked in substance. The words of his manifesto
may convey what men of Gaston's class thought of Richelieu.
Frenchmen were urged to overthrow 'Armand-Jean, Cardinal de
Richelieu, disturber of the public peace, enemy of the king,
dissipator of the state, unsurper of all the best offices in the
realm, tyrant and oppressor'. Towns closed their gates on
Gaston's motley force but he managed to find some recruits in the
remote fastnesses of the Auvergne, where the *noblesse* were
notorious for their rough and independent ways. At the end of

July he joined forces with Montmorency. Within a month, however, the affair was over. Schomberg had acted fast and without respect for the rank or property of his opponent. Montmorency was declared a traitor, the duchy was attainted and reunited to the crown, the duke's property was sequestrated. His associates were given fifteen days to leave him or be outlawed. Everything was done to impress the difference between just war and treasonable rebellion, a distinction which had become blurred in the civil wars.

At Castelnaudary the royal troops defeated Montmorency and he was taken prisoner. Much wounded, he had hoped to die on the field, but the surgeons kept him alive to face the tribunal of the Parlement of Toulouse. These lawyers, who had been so concerned about the intrusions of the state upon their province, were now faced by a case of treason and did not shrink from applying the logic of Roman law: *quod principi placet, legis vigorem habet*. Montmorency was sentenced to death and many of his followers after him. He faced trial and death in the Place de Salin in Toulouse, with a composure and fortitude worthy of a hero of Corneille. His widow was exiled to a convent at Moulins, where later she erected a vast monument to her husband; it escaped destruction at the hands of the revolutionaries when someone said that Montmorency had fought against the crown. In his own way he had stood for liberties against the long arm of the state. But neither the idea, so persuasively expressed by Montesquieu in the eighteenth century, that the Estates were a constitutional defence against tyranny, nor the undoubted fact that the inhabitants of the *pays d'état* had to pay less tax, still less the character of Montmorency, a noble figure in his own setting, need blind us to the fact that this was not in an abstract way a revolt about freedom; it was a gesture of defiance, country against Paris, local officers against royal officers, the self-governing feudal estate and household, large in pretension and patronage but answerable only to the head of the family, against the overriding law of the state.

## 10. France Enters the War

After the fall of La Rochelle there was a current rumour that Richelieu would proceed to an invasion of England. Instead, without waiting to suppress the remaining Huguenot resistance in the south, he had marched his army to Italy. England he could afford to ignore and it is doubtful if he thought seriously at all about further action in that direction, but the Spanish presence in northern Italy threatened the precarious balance of power. He was able to intervene with good conscience for he was upholding a legitimate claim; moreover he envisaged the sort of limited war that seemed to be a valid extension of diplomacy, isolating a particular local issue, bringing overwhelming force to bear and imposing a solution before it could be enlarged into a general war.

In December 1627 the last male Gonzaga prince, Vincenzo II, died, depraved and without direct heir. Of possible successors the most serious were the Duke of Guastalla, a remote cousin, and the Duc de Nevers, a nearer cousin. Nevers eludes the usual labels and categories of the historian. Italian by birth but French in interest, an heir among other claims to the Paleologus throne of Byzantium, his life's concern had hitherto been the great crusade. He was made heir by will; then his son, the Duc de Rethel, was married to Marie Gonzaga, Vincenzo's niece, a few hours before the latter's death. This last-minute diplomatic coup did not solve the succession question, however, and for the next three years Mantua was the focus of a keen struggle for power. The juridical questions were complex. The Emperor claimed the right of sequestration and arbitration, since Mantua was an imperial fief; Richelieu opposed this on the ground that a genuine will had been made. Urban VIII looked askance at the prospect of an extension of Spanish sway in northern Italy, and Cordoba, who had a personal grudge against Nevers for sheltering Mansfield in his province of Champagne, confirmed Papal fears by marching upon Mantua. Without waiting for instructions from Madrid he had drawn Charles-Emmanuel into the struggle and the ever-restless duke had seized some fortresses in Montferrat.

In the summer of 1628 Richelieu was tied before La Rochelle while Cordoba sat before Casale, the capital of Mantua. It held out more sternly than had been expected but Cordoba had to carry on with the siege, lightly undertaken but now a challenge to his reputation. As so often in these wars we see how much more depended on the will of the soldier than on the policy of the prince. The Emperor was dismayed by a rash action at a time when he wanted no distraction from his grand and, as he hoped, final stroke in Germany (Wallenstein was besieging Stralsund in 1628 and the Emperor signed the Edict of Restitution in 1629), and his order of sequestration was aimed at both sides impartially. To Richelieu, however, it seemed plain that there was a concerted Habsburg move afoot. He was keenly aware of the strategic value of Mantua and Montferrat, and of Casale, the most formidable fortress in northern Italy, lying in the plain below the Alps, dominating the Upper Po and the road from Genoa to Milan. In fact Spain's design was a strictly limited one, to oust Nevers and to secure military stability in Lombardy; the Emperor was slow to support Spain and, as Wallenstein foresaw, soon regretted his commitment. There was some advantage, too, as Richelieu saw it, in a campaign at this mid-point in the difficult process of realignment: he already had to reckon on the hostility of the *dévôts*, though he went some way to stilling criticism by enlisting the support of the king's confessor. A campaign against Spain for what could be represented as a just and necessary cause would surely unify the realm as it had in the 1590s. Indeed Huguenots like la Force, and Rohan himself, came forward to serve.

Before the fall of La Rochelle scouts were sent forward to survey the Alpine passes. Three movements were planned. One corps was to be shipped to the Ligurian coast, another to enter Piedmont; the main force crossed the Alps from Briançon, through deep snow over the Monte Geneva, where everything had to be dragged on sledges by gangs of mountaineers, and then down the valley. They came to Susa, the complex of forts guarding the entrance of the valley that leads towards Charles-Emmanuel's capital of Turin. Richelieu said mass before the army and gave the sacraments to the king and the generals; then the French infantry, preceded by local guides and led gallantly by Bassompierre, worked their way up the heights above the forts, enveloped them and forced them to surrender. From Spain's hopeful ally, Charles-Emmanuel became France's reluctant host and signed a treaty which allowed the French army to cross Savoy to Montferrat whenever it wished; at the expense of the Mantuans, who had to find 15,000 crowns in rent, he renounced his claim to their city. Cordoba then withdrew from his siege of Casale and Richelieu returned to complete the subjugation of the Huguenots.

The relief of Casale and the rebuff to Cordoba was a direct challenge to Madrid. To evade it would be to risk losing control of northern Italy, upon which depended her position in Flanders and on the Rhine. Philip IV and Olivarez were beginning now to suffer from the obsessive suspicion of Richelieu that was to play such a large part in Spanish policy for the next fateful decade. 'Everywhere', wrote the king, 'the French block me. Frenchmen in Brazil, Frenchmen in Genoa, Frenchmen in the Val Telline, Frenchmen in Breda, Frenchmen on the sea'. The council of state decided upon a display of force in the Milanese and to finance it they ordered the requisitioning of privately owned shipments of gold; to justify this they set up a commission of theologians to satisfy the king's conscience. The arbitrary way in which crucial acts of policy were decided, the strong element of pride and the reckless disregard of the economic facts upon which Spain's future rested, were all truly Spanish, and all to France's advantage.

In the short term, however, the Italian position was critical. Spinola was appointed to command in Italy. Ruffled by the refusal of Nevers to accept the jurisdiction of his commissioner, the Emperor sent an army to enforce the sequestration: 20,000 men marched up the Rhine, into the Grisons and down to Lake Como, and Nevers' men retreated into Mantua to which the Imperialists laid siege. Memories of another imperial invasion a century before, when Lutheran troops had sacked Rome, were too strong for the Pope, who sent a force to the frontier of the duchy. With Spanish troops meanwhile preparing again to attack Casale, Richelieu was faced by the need for a longer campaign and the autumn of 1629 was spent in preparation. At a great fête to celebrate Christmas at the hôtel de Rambouillet which he had recently acquired, he entertained the court and demonstrated to watchful courtiers how well he stood with the king. Then he marched for Italy with the Duc de Montmorency. In February 1630 the old Maréchal de la Force led the difficult passage of the Mont Cenis through driving snow. In March the army by-passed

Turin with a show of force to impress the Duke of Savoy, who was wavering in loyalty as usual, looking for an advantage to exploit. They then captured Pinerolo, which had been French in the Middle Ages and was now intended to be an outpost, an advanced magazine, and a check on Charles-Emmanuel. The Papal envoy, a Sicilian official from the Curia, came to negotiate on behalf of Savoy; he was Guiliano Mazarini, encountering for the first time the statesman whom by extraordinary chances he was destined to succeed, and the strategy that he was to fulfil. While they were negotiating Charles-Emmanuel showed his hand and moved athwart the French line of communications. Richelieu then advised the king to invade Savoy from France.[1] He promptly seized Annecy and Chambéry, the former capital of Savoy, where further parleys were begun. Meanwhile Charles of Lorraine, always open to persuasion and now enslaved to Mme de Chevreuse, had sought imperial aid. In the spring German troops had occupied Vic and Moyenvic and Richelieu's flank was turned.

In this way a limited operation threatened to become the general war which Richelieu had hoped to avoid as being both immoral and unnecessary. Spinola was already in this theatre of war; now Piccolomini came to advertise the Emperor's determination to settle the matter, and to direct his troops. In July 1630 Mantua was stormed and pillaged in the manner to which Germany had become accustomed. Piccolomini joined Spinola before Casale and trenches were advanced right up to the imposing

---

[1] In his important article, 'Autour du Grand Orage. Richelieu et Marillac: deux politiques', Revue Historique no. 179, Jan. 1937, G. Pagès ascribes great importance to Richelieu's advice and the king's decision. Richelieu understood and made plain to Louis that if Pinerolo were kept the war would be extended in length and extent. If it were not, the French might just as well give up their idea of maintaining a presence in North Italy. In view of the subsequent course of the war and France's growing commitment, and also the personal crisis from which Richelieu only emerged victorious in November after agonising delay and uncertainty, Louis' decision was clearly crucial. Richelieu's memorandum to Louis affords us a good example of his method. He rehearsed the arguments for and against with scrupulous fairness but left the king in little doubt as to which course he favoured. He concluded: 'Great undertakings are never without difficulties, and one can do little good in them if one is not on the spot'. It was a clear hint to the king, whose warlike instinct Richelieu understood and shared, to come and lead his army. He came and conquered. For the rôle of Marillac, and the Day of Dupes, see also pages 112-114.

citadel. Within the garrison many were afflicted by fever and famine, but death struck impartially: Spinola died and his troops lost heart. Charles-Emmanuel also died and was succeeded by Victor Amadeus, husband of Louis XIII's sister Christine. Louis fell sick with dysentery at Lyons and Richelieu's position was precarious, for either the king's death or a disaster in Italy would bring an abrupt end to his power and plans. Of his generals he trusted neither Montmorency, who had recently beaten the Savoyards at Avigliana, nor Marillac who, with better reason, he believed to be half-hearted about the war. La Force, doughty veteran, was too weak to raise the siege, the Spaniards too weak to attack. While the armies wilted in the sticky heat of the Italian summer Richelieu worked for a diplomatic solution. He used Mazarin to work for an armistice. First he secured a respite until October: the town was to be held by the imperialists, the citadel by the French. At the Diet of Regensburg, convoked in June 1630 by the Emperor to secure the election of his son as King of the Romans and thus heir in due course to the Empire, France was represented officially by Louis' plenipotentiary Brûlart de Léon, but effectively by Richelieu's personal envoy, Père Joseph; the Capuchin was even armed with credentials signed by Louis XIII. In July, on his way to Regensburg, Père Joseph talked to Wallenstein about the crusade and found him interested, as he always was, by schemes that ranged beyond the accepted limits of political or military action. Brûlart had powers 'to treat of a general peace in Italy' and to bind his government to any treaty he concluded, promising 'the faith and word of the king for whatever he might do, negotiate or conclude'. Between the drafting of these instructions and the conclusion of his mission the situation changed, however. From being primarily concerned with the succession to the Empire, and with thwarting in that matter the King of Hungary, the Emperor's son, Richelieu came to think of Mantua as the crucial issue.

The outcome of Regensburg, and Richelieu's reaction to it, have left a question-mark, to say the least, against the morality of his diplomacy. Clarity and certainty are always hard to achieve in negotiation. The past is littered with the scraps and relics of treaties, broken or disregarded. Often there have been genuine misunderstandings. In the seventeenth century we stand at the beginning of modern diplomacy. When Henry IV came to the throne he found that there was no organised diplomatic service;

his only reliable contacts were with England, Holland, Vienna and Venice. There was some degree of specialisation, with Villeroi in charge of all diplomatic correspondence; after Henry IV's death there was a further period of instability and when Richelieu came to power he had to ask French ambassadors abroad for copies of their most recent instructions—so personal and haphazard was diplomacy. There were physical obstacles to efficient negotiation, notably those of communication: between the couriers of Richelieu's time and the telegrams of today lies a change, not merely of tempo but of method and style in diplomacy.

Grotius had written, in 1625, his masterpiece *De Jure Belli et Pacis*, which was the most ambitious commentary on the 'law of nations' yet achieved. His central assertion was that no balance of power could work effectively unless nations recognised that certain principles higher than mere expediency should govern their acts. In its realism and humanity, his constant effort to distinguish precisely between just and unjust cases and causes, the book points the way towards a system of international law. But it would be a mistake to think that this book or any like it had much direct influence on the political practice of the time. In Richelieu's time there existed little more in the way of international law than a few agreed rules and some understandings between individual states. One such understanding was that 'full powers' to sign committed a prince, whereas powers to negotiate merely left the prince freedom to decide whether to ratify or not. When the Emperor enquired about Brûlart's powers, Père Joseph was evasive: he wanted to retain freedom of manœuvre for the French emissaries. Richelieu's approach was in truth empirical but he was handicapped by being far from the scene; he put great trust in Père Joseph's sense and tact. In return for a favourable settlement in Italy the imperialists demanded the abandonment by France of her allies, Venice, Holland, Denmark and Sweden.

While the French were officially awaiting further instructions from Richelieu, Père Joseph, over-estimating perhaps France's ability to influence events in Germany, devoted himself to persuading the German princes, notably the Archbishop Elector of Trier and Maximilian of Bavaria, to form a third force which should hold the balance between the Habsburgs and the Protestants. The archbishop found himself in a vulnerable position, situated as he was on the line of Spanish advance to Flanders; Maximilian objected to Wallenstein and his influence on the

Emperor. Unfortunately for Père Joseph and his master, the princes resented French patronage. They had already secured the concession, the dismissal of Wallenstein, which they most wanted, and decided none the less not to vote for Ferdinand's son as King of the Romans. Their main interest was in the ending of the war and Père Joseph therefore found himself being pressed by Maximilian to sign a general peace with the Emperor. In this way Père Joseph lost the initiative, for the princes were less abject and resourceless than his master imagined. Addressed as one Catholic by another, he found it hard to resist the attraction of a general peace.

Events beyond the diplomats' control urged them on. The Swedes invaded Pomerania and the Emperor wanted his troops back from Italy. There were now over 50,000 there and their absence had already affected the balance of strength in the Netherlands. Père Joseph was at least as good a Catholic as he was Frenchman and at this moment represented strikingly the dilemma of so many of his countrymen: when faith and fatherland seemed to call with different voices, to which should he listen? There were moral and expedient grounds for making peace before northern Germany was overrun by Lutheran Swedes. Louis XIII lay, by report, near to death and at any moment Père Joseph might be answerable to King Gaston and his entourage of traditionalists and dévôts. He believed furthermore that Casale would fall when the armistice ended, and he had not been informed that Richelieu had sent Schomberg from Champagne to assist la Force in an all-out effort to relieve it. Believing that they already had the crucial concession in the shape of the Emperor's willingness to let Nevers keep Mantua, the French therefore decided to sign: on the 13th October 1630 they affixed their seals to a document that seemed favourable to their cause. In Italy the Spanish were to withdraw from Casale, the imperialists from Mantua. In due course Nevers was to be installed after the Emperor had considered the question of compensation. In return the French would withdraw from all Italy except for Susa and Pinerolo. Further, France would in no way assist the Emperor's enemies. The Duke of Lorraine's being brought into the treaty implied that it was the Emperor's right to supervise matters in the duchy. With the news of the treaty Mazarin halted Schomberg as he advanced upon Casale, just before the opening of a battle, on 26th October, which would have decided the issue there and then. Richelieu was delighted by first news of the treaty, but appalled when he read the full text. It tied his hands at a crucial stage of his German design. Either way he would now be vulnerable: to ratify was to betray his allies, notably Holland and Sweden, upon whom he relied to hold the balance of power in Germany. With the Lorraine question unsettled, with the imperial troops free to pursue further conquests in Germany and the Netherlands, it was by no means certain that he could dispense with these allies. We see here the extent to which his Italian operation was part of a larger design, and the weakness in his notion, if he ever honestly held it, that he could settle the Italian business in isolation. He would have been more optimistic than recent actions of the Habsburgs warranted if he had supposed that peace would come to Germany by the one-sided action now required of him. On the other hand, to refuse to ratify would give not only the Emperor and the king of Spain, but also the *dévôts* at home, mobilised by Michel de Marillac, grounds for the charge of perfidy at a time when his position at home was most uncertain.

Richelieu's reaction was that of a man near the end of his tether and wild statements suggest tension and an ulcerous anxiety. To the Venetian ambassador, an assiduous retailer of such remarks in the best tradition of his post, he declared that he would retire into a monastery. But was he acting a part? To Brûlart he conveyed his extreme displeasure; to his marshals the orders were to carry on. The gap between him and Marillac widened when the Keeper of the Seals suggested he ratify, but with protocols of interpretation. The formal reasons for his refusal to ratify were the vague and unsatisfactory nature of the terms relating to Italy together with the fact that there was no confirmation of the treaty of Monzon; also Brûlart had been authorised to treat only of Italy. The disavowal was explained in despatches sent all over Europe. The Emperor was, however, justifiably indignant. His sense of injury was reinforced when the Swedish soldiers marched south through Germany, subsidised by France. The treaty was to remain the nub of every diplomatic discussion of the next twenty-five years. Already sour enough, the relations of France and the Habsburgs were so poisoned now, that open war came appreciably nearer. However large the area of misconception, however justified he was by the interests of France as he saw them, with Richelieu must lie a share of the responsibility for the opening out of a terrible war at the time when it was

possible that hostilities might end: responsibility that he undoubtedly shares, however, with Olivarez and the author of the Edict of
Restitution.

In Italy he broke his engagement by putting a French garrison
in Casale; he seems to have believed that the Spanish were
planning to surprise the citadel. Then in June 1631 Mazarin
negotiated the treaty of Cherasco. Nevers was to be invested in
his duchy, all armies were to leave his lands, the French were to
give up Susa and Pinerolo. During the summer of 1631 imperial,
Spanish, French and Savoyard commissioners were busy executing
the treaty. Richelieu seems to have thought that a previous agreement made by Savoy, ceding him Pinerolo, justified the use of a
trick to save the town. After the commissioners had completed
their inspection of Pinerolo, the palace was seized again by a
company of French soldiers who had been lying hidden in the
cellars. The Spanish were furious and threatened to stop the
investiture of Nevers. Richelieu announced that the occupation
would only last for six months: meanwhile he could afford to
devote himself to the more pressing problem of Germany.

Mantua had not gone unscathed: her population reduced to a
quarter, her currency ruined, her new duke a recluse in his
ransacked palace until his death in 1636, the city was no longer
worth fighting for. The Emperor had lost all but the formal
recognition of his superior title in Mantua and this had proved
meaningless in practice; for this he had jeopardised his whole
position in Germany. Not without reason has the Mantuan
succession dispute been called the turning-point of the Thirty
Years War. Mantua had forced Spain and Austria together in
tighter partnership than was good for either party. Richelieu saw
that France was threatened on her eastern borderlands and must
depend more upon Sweden for relief. The Pope was confirmed in
his hostility to the Habsburgs and his attitude helped to ease
Richelieu's conscience as he moved towards the logical conclusion
of his policy, open alliance with Sweden.

Gustavus Adolphus of Sweden had been at war ever since he
had come to his throne in 1611; against Denmark, Russia and
recently Sigismund of Poland, who claimed the Swedish throne.
His army was not large but, at this stage, more truly national
than any other. Shaped into a coherent body under his intelligent
and strenuous generalship, taught and toughened by marches,
fights and sieges in the northern plains, it was ready for a more

ambitious part. The king-general was a committed Lutheran in a
straight-forward, undogmatic way; every man was issued with a
prayer book and discipline was reinforced by a solid sense of
purpose. The king's calculations were, however, far from simple.
His style was evangelical but his timing and bargaining were
wary and worldly, as became a man who knew that he was
committing his country to a new and risky course, obsessed and
egotistical, like a gambler who seeks plausible arguments for
what he craves to do. He intended to use his army to serve
Protestantism in Germany but on conditions which promised
profit and reduced the risk. In the short term he was mainly
concerned with ousting Denmark from North Germany and with
sharing, if not securing, control of the Baltic. Of the further
consequences of his intervention in the German war he seems to
have thought little. Like other statesmen who have put their
faith in a military solution, he seems to have thought that early
victories would bring their own solution. Lutheran Gustavus
had been content to see Lutheran Christian IV of Denmark beaten
at Lutter while he pursued his war against Sigismund. His
avowed purpose in crossing into Germany in 1630 was to defend
the liberties of Germany and to restore the lands of ousted princes,
notably the Duke of Mecklenburg; the princes realised, however,
that his overriding concern must be with Sweden's strategic and
economic position, Baltic lands and river tolls, means to his ends
of solvency and expansion, and they were as sceptical of his
promises as they were later to be lukewarm about his victories.

The port of Stralsund had held out in the summer of 1628
against Wallenstein, attached, so Protestants said, 'by chains to
heaven', but aided too by supplies sent in by Gustavus. The Edict
of Restitution in March 1629 threatened to make the Habsburgs
supreme in Europe by the recovery for Rome of the North
German cities, Magdeburg, Bremen, Minden, Halberstadt and
others which had been secularised since 1555. Could the absent,
ineffectual suzerainty of the Habsburgs become a military
empire, directed by Wallenstein and the Spanish-Jesuit party of
Vienna? Wallenstein at least realised the need to reduce the
opposition and began talks with Christian which led to the peace
of Lübeck in May 1629: the battered Dane was content to withdraw.

In December Gustavus came to terms with Sigismund at
Altmark. Richelieu's envoy was Charnacé, a gentleman of means

who had been travelling inconsolably in the eastern countries after the death of his wife; all his skill and local knowledge were needed to overcome the suspicions of the Poles. France's policy towards Poland had been inconsistent, surprisingly since Poland was a natural ally of France: with an eye on Caspian trade France had recently proposed to ally Michael Romanov with Bethlen Gabor against Sigismund of Poland. After making a compromise truce Charnacé sounded out Gustavus and found him disposed to be independent, sending offers of alliance round the Protestant states and making resounding statements of his Protestant fervour. Indeed, the week before the Frenchman arrived in Uppsala, the Swedish royal council had decided on the invasion of Pomerania, whose Duke Bogislaw was old and childless. Charnacé was about to come home when he received a draft treaty from Richelieu and powers to sign; the French were about to march into Italy again and Richelieu needed Swedish intervention to prevent an imperialist offensive from Lorraine. The negotiations that ensued reveal an interesting contrast of motive and personality in the principals. The weakness of Charnacé's brief was that there was a contradiction in Richelieu's whole policy. He wanted to start a short-term diversion from the north but the ally to whom he looked in the longer term was Catholic Bavaria. Gustavus wanted a perpetual alliance and French money to support it, and he proposed to restore Frederick to the Palatinate, whose land and electorate Maximilian of Bavaria now occupied. Both sides had bargaining advantages. When Gustavus shipped half his army over to Pomerania he soon found that he was running short of money. Richelieu could ill afford large subsidies but his whole position was precarious in the summer of 1630; on top of the campaign against him at court and the diplomatic débacle of Regensburg, a military set-back would be the end.

Both men were therefore pushed by circumstances towards a treaty which reflected in its compromising terms their haste and anxiety. At Barwälde in January 1631 Charnacé signed for the Cardinal the treaty of alliance which promised to alter, with a few strokes of the pen, the balance of force in Europe. The explicit objects were defensive: the security of the Baltic and liberty of trade in return for a million livres for five years. Gustavus was to maintain 30,000 foot and 6,000 horse in Germany, but he would respect the law of the Empire concerning religion and he guaranteed freedom of worship to Catholics. This sop to the *dévôts* was

I

meaningless in view of the failure to bind Gustavus to keep his hands off the Palatine. The question of the Electorate was left open and Gustavus consented to respect the integrity and lands of Bavaria and the Catholic League 'only insofar as they sincerely observed neutrality'. Gustavus clearly expected that Bavaria would intervene to preserve Germany, and her own new territories from the Nordic intruder and that this would give him a free hand. With his concern for France's border, and his involvement in Italy, Richelieu accepted an alliance upon securities which were no more than wishful thinking. France's reputation in Germany, her natural rôle of patron of the Catholic princes as against the Emperor, the security which depended upon the equilibrium in Germany—all were jeopardised. The treaty was as much a hasty insurance against an immediate danger as the cool strategic operation with which Richelieu has so long been credited. At best it was a gamble. Richelieu was unfitted by temperament and experience to understand the new force which he had helped to unleash. Thinking always of limited operations with measurable ends, as delicate and subtle in intelligence and manner as Gustavus was direct and robust, he can be excused for failing to anticipate the impact of the Swedish lion upon Protestant Europe. For all his cultivation of mind there was something awkwardly barbaric about the Swede: his assurance of divine mission and his readiness to use the language of faith to inspire and excuse has something Cromwellian about it, repellent self-assurance or heroic simplicity, according to one's viewpoint.

The next year was to bring rude shocks to the Cardinal and a lucky deliverance from an embarrassing ally. Even after Gustavus' death the Swedish alliance continued to draw Richelieu to the point of open intervention. The outcome was favourable to France, at least in military and diplomatic terms, but it was not what Richelieu had intended in 1631.

While Gustavus treated with Saxony and Brandenburg for leave to pass through their lands, Tilly and Pappenheim were besieging Magdeburg, the old Hanse town on the Elbe, claimed by the Emperor in furtherance of his Edict of Restitution. Gustavus failed to reach the city before it fell, at the end of May 1631, to Pappenheim's desperate assault. His troops sacked the city in a horrible fashion and Protestant propagandists made the most of it: 'Magdeburg mercy' as what Germany had to expect from the centralising policy of the Emperor! The Protestant cause assumed for the moment a new clarity of purpose. Saxony, Hesse-Cassel and Saxe-Weimar joined Gustavus as he marched south, and the Margrave of Brandenburg protested but feebly when Gustavus seized his garrisons. At Breitenfeld in Saxony, in September, Gustavus defeated Tilly. Fresh troops, new tactics and superior discipline contributed to a decisive victory which destroyed Ferdinand's position in Germany; but the reaction set in as soon as Gustavus marched south to winter in the Rhineland among the rich and vulnerable electorates of this hitherto unscathed region. It was more than his paymaster had bargained for.

In September, Richelieu's seizure of Pinerolo had shown that he was becoming more concerned with improving his tactical position than with the niceties of diplomacy. He then strengthened his position in the Rhineland by occupying Lorraine. His excuse was the Duke Charles had sent troops to aid the imperial army against Gustavus, but he was also anxious to prevent Gustavus from arriving there first; he wanted to keep his formidable ally away from the border. From this point it is plain that Richelieu was as much concerned with keeping Gustavus within bounds as with hurting the Habsburgs; he wished to avoid war for France, but meanwhile manœuvred to achieve the most favourable positions to fight from, if fight he must. The possession of Vic and Moyenvic in Lorraine was a useful start and worth the protests of the Papal envoy, who voiced the anxiety of his master as the great states moved nearer to open war. Charles submitted to Louis XIII and gave him the right of crossing Lorraine when he pleased. In January 1632, however, the duke's sister Marguérite of Lorraine married Gaston of Orléans.

While Gustavus wintered at Mainz there was anxious speculation as to his next move .The Emperor was urged to withdraw the Edict of Restitution, the Spanish resolved to defend the Palatinate and reinforced Tilly from Italy. Richelieu persuaded Rohan to come back from Venice and put him in charge of an army to hold the Grisons. Charnacé was despatched to persuade Maximilian and Gustavus to declare a mutual non-aggression pact but secured only a temporary truce. When Tilly expelled Horn and his Swedes from Bamberg the gage was down; Bavaria now depended upon the Emperor. In March Gustavus moved on Bavaria, resolved to advertise his Protestantism, defeat the Elector and find himself a base between Austria and the Rhine; the unravaged farmlands of Bavaria would keep his army in food and plunder. Tilly was wounded at the crossing of the river Lech and subsequently died; the Swedes took Augsburg and Munich but their occupation was disturbed by news of Wallenstein's capture of Prague. Fearing that the Saxons would make terms, Gustavus marched north; the summer was spent in manœuvres designed to bring Wallenstein to battle.

Meanwhile Richelieu had been intricately concerned with Gaston, Lorraine and Spain. In July 1632 French troops had again invaded Lorraine; again Charles had submitted. Then the French and Swedes had occupied Trier and Ehrenbreitstein, ousting Spanish garrisons. It was provoking, but Olivarez desisted from declaring war: Austria was against any enlargement of the struggle and after another disaster to the annual plate fleet, the third in one decade, the financial state was worrying. Richelieu still tried to balance his support of Sweden by overtures to Bavaria, whom he subsidised afresh. At Rome he was helped by Cardinal Borgia, the Spanish representative, whose arrogant demands antagonised the Pope. The news of the death of Gustavus in November, on the battlefield of Lutzen, transformed what could have developed into a stalemate. Olivarez was elated and, typically, read more into this lucky chance than the military situation justified. He was obsessed with the need to harry France: 'The more France suffers, the more Christendom will be in repose', he declared before the royal council. For Richelieu, however, lying sick at Bordeaux when he received the news, the death of the Swedish king was not an unmitigated calamity, so long as Sweden could be kept in the war to play a more limited, defensive role. He was better off with the Swedes than was Olivarez with Gaston and Charles.

In July 1633 the Swedes crushed Charles at Pfaffenhofen, and in September the French invaded Lorraine and brought him to terms for the third time. Marguérite was to be kept by Richelieu as a guarantee of the peace, but she escaped to Brussels. Charles abdicated in favour of his son François, a master of intrigue and disguise, indeed on the small scale of these events a worthy antagonist of the Cardinal. Richelieu seized Nancy on the pretext of preserving the right of the Princesses Claude and Nicole, François' cousins, to the duchy of Bar; François promptly married Claude and secured a papal dispensation for doing so. In March 1634 Claude evaded the vigilance of the French governor of Nancy and escaped to Florence and the friendly house of Christine of Lorraine, Grand Duchess of Tuscany and sister-in-law of Marie de Médicis.

The death of the Infanta Isabella in November 1633 removed one of the last restraints upon Olivarez. With the appointment of the new governor, Aytona, came more direct control from Madrid: Ferdinand, the Cardinal-Infant, soon succeeded him, but he was told to follow Aytona's instructions. The Spanish line was hardening for they were convinced that Richelieu was using the German war to annex the Rhineland. He saw equally plainly the design of Olivarez to enmesh him in a conspiracy extending far beyond the pernicious House of Lorraine. Both sides seemed to be concerned more with securing tactical advantages before its outbreak than with preventing the open war that they professed to fear.

In May 1634 Gaston was tied to Spain by a treaty which fell into the hands of a Dutch privateer and thence came to Richelieu. Besides Gaston's commitment to the invasion of France with Spanish troops, the courier carried a document giving power to Aytona to declare war on France if and when it should be necessary. In July a Dutch courier intercepted by the Spanish was found to have a copy of the Franco-Dutch alliance recently renewed by Charnacé, which represented, if not a plan to attack Dunkirk and Gravelines as Olivarez stated, at least Richelieu's determination to keep Holland in the war against Spain at the cost to him of 3 million livres a year. Already Maximilian of Bavaria had committed himself to the Spanish side, since Richelieu had made a defensive alliance with the Protestant League of Heilbronn without exacting any concession from Oxenstierna beyond the clauses of Barwälde that had already proved to be so powerless to restrain the Swedes from attacking Catholic lands. Only the deaths of the Spanish general Feria in January, and then Wallenstein, assassinated in February 1634, checked the Habsburg plans; that they did not alter the general strategy was shown when in the late summer the Cardinal-Infant marched from Italy to the Black Forest. The Emperor's son, Ferdinand, king of Hungary, with Wallenstein's army now once more firmly under imperial control, moved along the Danube to meet him. To save Nördlingen, Bernard of Saxe-Weimar and the Swedish Horn offered battle to the joint forces of Austria and Spain, and there the young Habsburg cousins won a victory that appeared to be decisive: 15,000 Swedish and German dead and 6,000 prisoners,

Horn among them, were the measure of a disaster to the Protestant cause that effectively ended the German war.

The Elector of Saxony soon made his peace with the Emperor;
it was ratified at Prague in June 1635. Of the German princes, only
Bernard refused to submit and he was now in French pay. At
the Battle of the White Mountain the soldiers of Tilly had fought
under banners inscribed 'Sancta Maria'. At Nördlingen the
imperialist device was 'Viva Espana'. There had been a confusion
of motives throughout, but this contrast does mark symbolically
the change that had come over the war, with the encroachment of
France and the closer union of the Habsburgs. At Prague the
Emperor abandoned the Edict of Restitution and with it the
prime German interest in the war. Germany went on providing a
battlefield, however; France and Spain fought a war of the
frontiers in which there was more at stake than French possession
of parts of the Rhineland, nothing less than hegemony of
Europe. The Empire was tied to the policy and strategy of
Spain as under sane and objective leadership she should never
have been. Spain was still involved inextricably in a war with
Holland which it should have been clear she could not win, if
only because of the trends of trade and finance which contemporaries were so slow to assess. Bavaria was bound in interest to the
imperial cause; after suffering so much she would not lightly
abandon her Palatine electorate. Sweden would continue to fight
to secure counters for negotiation; the greater her stake the more
she wanted in compensation.

After Nördlingen Richelieu confronted the king and the leading
counsellors, Bullion, Séguier and Bouthillier, with the necessity
of war. At least the Swedish reverse meant that France could
impose her own terms. In November 1634 in a treaty with the
envoys of Oxenstierna and the Protestant League, France gained
an equal say in the Protestant councils, and the delivery of the
Alsatian towns held by the Swedes. Catholicism was to be
restored in all places where it had enjoyed rights before 1618.
Oxenstierna, realising that Sweden stood to lose control, refused
to ratify, but to give his depleted army a chance to recoup he
had to hand over the Alsace garrisons to la Force. Richelieu came
a step nearer to declaring his hand when the Bavarians and
imperialists laid siege to Heidelberg, for its security was as vital
to France as to the League; at Christmas 1634 la Force relieved
the Electoral capital and marched on up the Neckar. Charles of

Lorraine then promptly crossed the Rhine at Breisach, pushed the French out of Philippsburg and occupied Speyer; the Spaniards advanced to the Moselle and seized Trier, with its unhappy elector, Philip von Sötern. La Force had no option but to retreat. The war had begun in all but formal sense. When, in May 1635, Richelieu sent the herald Gratiollet to Brussels to proclaim the declaration of war with mediaeval pomp, the gesture was irrelevant as well as anachronistic. The cause alleged was the illegal seizure of the Archbishop Elector of Trier, since he was under French protection. It was addressed to Spain only but Richelieu can have been under no illusions about the possibility of confining military action to Spain alone. The operations of the winter had shown how precarious was France's position on the frontiers. The state of the economy and the armed forces was unfavourable to a war in which France must maintain an army of nearly 100,000, besides finding subsidies for her allies.

The first operations of the war exposed those weaknesses in the French army and administration which had made Richelieu so reluctant to commit France to the European war. In experience, cohesion, tactics in the field and movement on campaign, in engineering, discipline and drill, the Spanish and the best imperial soldiers were superior to the French. The system of recruitment and control was being overhauled but the process had not, by 1635, gone far enough. The French army, still in essentials a feudal army, relied upon the skill of individual generals and the martial spirit of its gentleman-officers: professionalism in such vital matters as regular training, systematic promotion and accepted standards of discipline was unknown. The rapid recruitment of new regiments only worsened the situation. An English mercenary and veteran campaigner commented on the difference between the French army at the start of the first season of war—the cavalry gay with feathered crests and resplendent in scarlet and silver lace—and the ragged deserters who slunk away, officers and men, before the end of the year. Brézé's northern army clattered into Flanders, aiming for Brussels, looting churches and alienating the Belgians. They were checked at Louvain, and outflanked by an imperial thrust through the Ardennes. As Brézé's force disintegrated, the main part with its commander had to join the Dutch at Nijmegen; so easily was France's northern frontier laid open. At the same time Charles of Lorraine recovered his duchy and the imperial general Gallas forced la Valette to retreat to Metz after a ding-dong struggle.

In Alsace before the year was out the French were on the verge of mutiny: the aged la Force was able to do little. Gallas' troops had learned in the German war to let no considerations of humanity deflect them from tactical advantage; their scorched earth tactics posed a severe problem of supply. The king insisted, against Richelieu's advice, upon going to the frontier to see things for himself, and derived little comfort from the sight of his demoralised army. The governors of the two forts taken by the Spaniards in the Iles de Lérins off Nice were tried by Parlement for cowardice but acquitted. When in the next year the governors of La Capelle and Le Câtelet, towns lying in the path of the Spanish army of Flanders, surrendered without a fight, they were burnt in effigy; but they had taken the precaution of leaving the country. Richelieu learned, moreover, that his alliance needed success to maintain it. Holland and Sweden both dragged their heels, perhaps not reluctant to let France bear the brunt of the fighting for a time, and when Créqui's Franco-Savoyard drive on Milan came to nothing, Victor Amadeus, as unreliable as his father, threatened to defect. At home a new dimension was added to Richelieu's difficulties when Parlement objected to edicts creating new offices.

1636 was the year of crisis, the 'year of Corbie', when Richelieu's worst fears about the fallibility of French arms were realised, when he came near to despair, and when, as can be seen in retrospect, the Spanish had their last chance of winning the war outright. A Spanish army under the Cardinal-Infant invaded northern France from Flanders in July. Soissons fell back to the Somme, outnumbered and unaided: both Condé, forced to give up his siege of Dôlé, and la Valette were occupied by attacks on their own fronts; the latter was threatened by the offensive of Charles of Lorraine and Gallas through the Zabern gap in the Vosges. The gravest danger lay in the possibility of a general collapse before Bernard of Saxe-Weimar could stage an effective diversion. In Paris there was consternation when it was learned early in August that Corbie, near Amiens, less than eighty miles away, had fallen to the Spanish and that the Croatian squadrons of the Bavarian general Werth had thrust on to Compiègne, but two days' ride away. It was to prove the furthest point of the advance. In Richelieu's concern for the defence of Paris there may have been some personal qualms. Was this to be the outcome of a decade of patient and expensive diplomacy? He had himself destroyed part of the walls to make the garden of the Palais Cardinal and had taken no steps to prevent new housing from screening the walls that guarded the bastions of St. Honoré and Montmartre; placards now appeared, condemning him for his short-sightedness.

With refugees in the streets of Paris adding their woes to the general consternation, Richelieu at one point advised evacuating the city, but his resolve was stiffened by Father Joseph and the example of the king. Commenting on 'the slackness and carelessness' of his troops, Louis XIII defied his advisers and rode off to join his army at Senlis. Men rushed to join the army which la Force was raising to defend the capital and armourers enjoyed an unprecedented business; Parlement voted subsidies with alacrity and the Cardinal recovered his nerve. In the Guyenne, some rebel peasants laid down their arms so as to release troops to defend the capital.

Logistics counted more than gestures. Like all armies of the time the Spanish found that their difficulties increased with every mile they added to their line of communications. When Bernard of Saxe-Weimar moved along Gallas' flank and compelled him to retire, the Cardinal-Infant decided to call off his offensive. Werth was then recalled by Maximilian and the Spanish gave way before a series of counter-attacks in which Gaston of Orléans played a spirited part. Before winter the country round the Somme had been cleared and Corbie, a name that the French would not soon forget, recaptured. Gaston withdrew in pique when he was superseded by the king; he had been party to yet another plot to assassinate Richelieu at the height of the crisis. Richelieu had reason to be relieved, though not reassured, by the year's work. He put an inscription on two fountains at his country house, boasting that as they shed water he would shed Spanish blood. His *Gazette* puffed the smallest French success. Such gestures could not, however, conceal the ease with which France could be invaded through Picardy or Champagne. The French were reminded of the proximity of Paris to the frontier, some hundred miles of as easy going as any in Europe, which the modern traveller who speeds from Lille to Paris will discover. The crisis of Corbie confronted Richelieu with the urgent necessity of re-forming his armies and strengthening his grip upon the administration.

## 11. The 'Croquants' and the 'Nu-pieds'

The year of Corbie was also the year of the most extensive peasant revolt since the *jacquerie* of the fourteenth century. Risings in Angoumois and Saintonge spread into Poitou, Périgord and Guyenne. At one time or another, in 1636 and 1637, the whole country from the Loire to the Garonne was affected, more than a quarter of France. Coming at a critical stage of the war the risings posed an alarming challenge to the government. Neither the war effort, nor fiscal policy, nor the ceaseless work of administration that was building piece by piece the structure of absolute government, can be fairly judged without reference to what was happening in the deep countryside of France. Like the other spectacular insurrection of Richelieu's time, that of the *nu-pieds* of Normandy in 1639, this was only a larger, more violent and concentrated form of the protests and disturbances that everywhere met the advances of royal government. These revolts should not therefore be seen as blind, wild swipes at authority, unconnected with contemporary events and trends. The violence was undoubtedly engendered by hunger and fear. Sublet de Noyers wrote to Séguier in January 1636 about 'the extreme misery of this people and the strange commotion that is being excited in people's minds'. But not even the most wretched village, the remotest hovel in the fastnesses of the Dordogne or the Auvergne, was insulated from news of the great world. If accounts were garbled, ideas embroidered by superstition and the fantasies of ignorance the impact was all the greater; for rumour is more potent than truth in peasant communities and memories of the past or even apocalyptic visions of the future may weigh more than the facts of present time.

On the roads there were numerous beggars, unemployed peasants, the maimed or derelict outcasts of society, and now, in wartime, a growing band of deserters. The *curé*, perhaps the only literate man in the village, might be driven to protest out of concern for the squalor of his flock. There were many parishes as

wretched as Châtillon-des-Dombes, in the Landes, where Vincent
de Paul first worked, but few men were able like him to move on
to a wider field. In loneliness and despair the *curé* might brood
upon drastic or visionary solutions. The radical rôle of the clerical
proletariat of countryside and country towns requires more
examination; from individual examples it seems to be important.
From one source or another, in church, market place or tavern,
in a chance encounter perhaps with an old soldier in a country
lane, the peasant could learn of the storms that rocked the state: the
great debate about Richelieu's policy, the campaign of the *dévôts*
against his alliance with heretics, the opposition of Parlements
the conspiracies and revolts of *les grands* and, of course, in the
provinces where reform had taken a strong hold, the war against
the Huguenots. If he lived on one of the main routes or near a
large town it is likely that one or other of these matters had made a
personal impact; the passage of troops never went unnoticed and
billeting was the keenest grievance of any province that endured it.
The government's attempts to impose the *arrière-ban* antagonised
many of the poorer nobles. Every challenge to Richelieu was
accompanied by a flood of propaganda of a conservative sort
which appealed to local feeling and idealised the past, directing
attention always upon the sinister figure of the Cardinal and his
creatures, combining in one charge his reckless war policy, higher
taxes, the creation of new officers; working thus on the ever
combustible feeling of country against court. The assumption that
the king was being misled and his name exploited by his officers
wrapped the idea of resistance in the comforting illusion that it
was not treason but the honest service of loyal subjects.

A number of incidents started in towns upon the news that the
king was going to create new tax officers, *élus*, or increase the
indirect taxes. The creation of new offices lowered the value of
existing ones and moreover, since the more important offices
carried with them exemption from tax, it increased the burden on
the ordinary bourgeois. An indirect tax was one levied on articles
of current use and consumption, like wine; it was held to be
'extraordinary', a *gabelle*. There was a strong feeling that taxes
should be 'customary'. The *taille* had acquired this character,
though there persisted the idea that increases should pass some
form of local consent. At Dijon in February 1630, a rumour that
the government was going to establish a new tax on wine led to
riots in the town. There was some sacking and looting before

order was restored and effigies of the king and Cardinal were burned. At Aix-en-Provence in autumn of the same year, there was more serious trouble. The king's intention of appointing *élus* was a breach of the province's privileges as *pays d'état*; the local Parlement was angered by the appointment of an *intendant* and delay in confirming their offices. The populace was inflamed by a rise in the cost of living and in November there was a concerted march upon Aix from the surrounding villages. A demagogic group in Parlement, the *Cascavéoux*, with the insignia of a bell on white ribbon, sought to use this alliance of agricultural and urban workers to further their power. This brought a reaction from more conservative rivals and Condé had little trouble in restoring order, with some summary executions; the *élus* were abandoned, however, the *paulette* restored. Here the governor, the Duc de Guise, actually encouraged the rebels. In Languedoc, too, the notorious discontents of the Duc de Montmorency encouraged the resistance of the local Parlement to royal centralisation; here feeling was exacerbated by the recent Huguenot revolt and the subsequent reprisals. Montmorency's rising, in 1632 misjudged or at least mistimed, jeopardised the cause of the Parlement and his defeat was its defeat as well.

Peasants and artisans usually played a subordinate part in these urban affairs. They could be dangerous allies. In 1630 there were bread riots in Poitiers; shops were looted and towns attacked by a hungry mob. In 1632 there was another unwelcome intrusion when the regiment of St Hilaire was stationed in Haut Poitou and 2,000 refugees crowded into the city. In Bordeaux in 1635 a *gabelle* on barrels and wine provoked uproar among coopers and innkeepers which was at first welcomed by many office-holders and *parlementaires*; but a general rising of local peasants brought about a reaction and the Duc d'Epernon was able to repress the peasants with the help of solid citizens.

At Rennes in September 1636 the Estates made difficulties about paying their tax and there was a furious commotion for three days. The Breton mob shouted 'Vive le Roi et M. le duc de Brissac [governor] sans gabelle, nous aurons chacun un morceau de commissaire'. The *commissaire,* d'Estampes de Valençay, justifiably agitated, ascribed the trouble to the deliberate alliance of the local Parlement and the mob. Because in the last resort the bourgeois feared the common people—*le menu peuple*—more than the royal authorities and because the government was usually ready to compromise, urban revolts were less critical than inconvenient, incidents in the ceaseless struggle of the Crown to secure more control over the urban oligarchies, to exact a more realistic contribution to the revenues. The more privileged the towns, the less likely they were to push the struggle *à l'outrance*. Compromise was the order of the day. It was a different matter, however, when the unprivileged peasants took and kept the initiative, as did the *croquants* and the *nu-pieds*.

The provinces affected by the revolts of the *croquants* were remote, inaccessible and backward: country where seigneurs, small town officials and peasants alike prided themselves on being immune from the influence of Paris in manners, controls and taxes and resented 'foreign' intrusion, whether of the king's troops or his *intendant*. Much of the land was thickly wooded, hills were steep, roads bad, ideal terrain for resistance; it was easy to evade the royal seneschals with their bands of archers. When the peasants of Saintonge and Angoumois took up arms in the spring of 1636 they were able to organise themselves without much interference. In June an army assembled at Blanzac, 7,000, half of them armed with arquebuses and pikes. With them were a number of old soldiers and they were no rabble but used passwords and marched in formation, led by fifes and fiddles.[1] Some village sections were led by their *curé*; parishes formed communes and chose deputies to plead with the king, of whom several were nobles or leading bourgeois. The total number under arms in one place or another in 1636 has been estimated at 40,000. The revolts spread unevenly, however, and lack of an overall organisation embracing the different provinces made it less effective than the map would suggest. Moreover, many of those who marched may have been under some constraint and men came and went as the harvest or their womenfolk required.

A popular movement of this sort always faces the problem of objectives. Its grievances were plain: direct taxes had been increased and a new tax on wine hit farmers and merchants alike. The methods of collectors were objectionable, especially the seizure of

[1] These incidents are vividly described by la Force in his letters of June 1636 to Séguier. In a phrase which must have chilled the reader he pin-pointed the danger: 'dans le grand désordre de ceste canaille il y a quelque dangereux ordre'. He advised the use of force but he was 'touché d'une très grande compassion en voyant les pauvretés extraordinaires des peuples'.

goods and stock to defray the expenses of collection. But what strategy could the rebels pursue? Without rapid movement upon a desirable target, the common purpose which alone could bind this force together would evaporate. Isolated acts of violence satisfied some, and no doubt some old scores were settled. At St Savinien a tax collector was cut up alive and his parts distributed to be nailed up on people's doors, but the movement did not degenerate into aimless violence. Certain towns were blockaded, Cognac and Angoulême among them. From the Saintonge emissaries were sent out to incite the neighbouring provinces. A programme was drafted which is interesting as much for what it left out as for what it contained. There was no demand for any innovations, regular States-Generals for example, or control of the administration by such a body. There is little trace of concern about inequalities, even about the *seigneurial* rights, which may reflect a lack of genuine peasant leadership but also suggests a degree of common interest between seigneur, *curé* and peasant: all was aimed at the hated outsider. Some of the nobles undoubtedly consented to take the lead or voice popular demands to save their own skins, but again it is notable that there was little looting of the châteaux. Here was a genuine upsurge on a wide front, and the explicit target was the government, 'the creatures of that man who governs the state'—the predatory agents of the faceless men of Paris, not the king who was badly advised. In all the tone was loyal and conservative. The king should live as before, for the *taille* and the old rights ought to be enough. They had to revolt in order to ensure that their grievances reached the ear of the king, but they would not aid the Spanish or rebellious nobles against the king.

In Poitou the organisation of the insurgents was more advanced. In some places regulations for the fair distribution of the *taille* were drawn up in the presence of the *curé*. The idea was mooted that the *curé* should be an official, appointed by the inhabitants, and acting for them; the surplus from his tithe, over and above what was required for his salary, was to go to the poor, and to repair the parish church. Here we have a glimpse of the people in arms, and the gentry and the priests, sometimes no doubt under constraint, supporting and voicing the common interest. Their plan for the Church would have struck at non-residents and reduced the power of bishops but given new status to the resident priest. The example of the Huguenots is plain to see in this. But the Poitevin peasants seem to have been concerned only with their own village and there was no plan for a hierarchy of democratic assemblies.

The rising in Périgord was potentially more dangerous to the Crown. The Sieur de la Mothe la Forest afterwards claimed that he had led the movement only out of fear for his château and his family; if so his organisation was remarkably ambitious and efficient. At least one other leader, the Marquis d'Aubeterre, had already been active in the Saintonge. The town of Bergerac was seized and made a base, despite the reluctance of its inhabitants; it was an unhappy place, its walls razed after the treaty of Alais and its population reduced to half by a recent plague. Under the direction of a commune the peasant army was tightly disciplined: there was to be no immorality, no looting. By the time it was assembled, however, the other provinces had been subdued. By a judicious mixture of concession and firmness the Comte de Brassac, the *intendant* Villemontée and Richelieu's special emissary, la Force, persuaded the rebels to disperse, when they pledged abolition of the hated wine duties. Périgord was isolated and could therefore be treated more brusquely. On the 1st of June, 1637, at La Sauvetat, la Valette, who was commander of the royal troops in Guienne, beat a larger *croquant* force and killed a thousand of them. The action was decisive. De la Mothe saw his force wavering, his peasants drift away to the harvest. He offered to disband his army in return for a general pardon. One Magot, leader of the artisans of Bergerac, denounced his 'treachery' and tried to take over the leadership. De la Mothe then forced his way into Bergerac, Magot was killed in the fighting, and the town was handed over to the king's troops. The amnesty did not stretch to the ringleaders, who were executed. This example and the prompt action of the royal commanders were sufficient to quell the revolt despite its good discipline and purposeful leadership. There were sporadic outbreaks of resistance, taxes went unpaid here and there and this part of the country was never really quiet during the next decade. But the greatest danger to the government was an *entente* between the peasants and the upper classes. This came near to happening in Normandy.

The revolt of the *nu-pieds* in 1639 affords a striking picture of the distress of a province when the exactions of government were piled upon natural disasters. In the years before the revolt there had been severe epidemics of plague; in some parishes two-thirds of the inhabitants perished. In the country around Caen,

Avranches, Rouen and Coûtances, fields lay unploughed, unsown; trade declined, so the taxes weighed the more heavily on the survivors. The Estates were an anachronism in this province and had not been called since 1635; the *taille* was exceptionally heavy and a clumsy system of assessment made insufficient allowance for sudden mortality. Prices rose in town and country. In 1636 and succeeding years regiments were billeted in Normandy—dread imposition; furthermore the province had to support levies of troops, every parish having to arm and clothe three or four soldiers. These burdens and provocations were all felt in one part or other of France; in Normandy they came together to bring the province to the point of combustion. The nobles were required by the *arrière-ban* to go to the war or pay for a deputy. Office-holders had their pay withheld; some offices were devalued by the creation of new ones, while for the reversion to others an exorbitant charge was made; so the Parlement of Rouen was sullen, slow to register edicts, actively encouraging defiance on the part of the officials. Lawyers and lords made common cause against the outsiders, the new office-holders and the agents of the central government. *Parlementaires* could gain an easy popularity by standing up for tanners and wine merchants against the new taxes and their collectors. Finally the torch was lit when the rumour spread that Lower Normandy was to become *pays de la grande gabelle*.

Most of Normandy was already within this system, paying salt tax at the full rate. Some districts, however, paid at a lower rate and the difference sustained a thriving business in smuggling. A new *commis-général*, Dorneau, who was zealous or foolish enough to grapple with this smuggling, was one of the first victims of the revolt of Caen. A change in the system would have affected the living of some 12,000 peasants who lived by the production and distribution of salt, and also the landowners whose woodlands supplied the fuel for the salt pans.

The revolt began on 16th July in Avranches on market day with the lynching of an official, Poupinal, who had, as it happened, nothing to do with salt. The rebels took the name of *nu-pieds* after the salt-panners who walked barefoot on the sands. The identity of the leaders is obscure but there are signs of intelligent direction. Their appeal for support did not confine itself to mere sectional interests, but invoked an ancient patriotism against the foreigner; in one crude verse manifesto *la patrie* is not France but Normandy, the province whose attitude towards Paris had for so long been

affected by its close relationship with England. Normandy claimed
what it had once received, special treatment at the hands of the
crown, and even cited the charter granted by Louis X in 1315,
with its vital provision that 'there should be no extraordinary levy,
except in emergency'. In this admittedly sentimental appeal there
are the makings of a lively autonomist movement; the Fronde was
later to show the dangers of such a movement when led by an
ambitious magnate, in that case the Duc de Longueville. Directed
against the development of the absolute state, it was a retrograde
affair, essentially negative; its targets were mostly officers of
finance.

A number of towns followed the example of Avranches. At
Agen the mob was particularly violent. It was usually the towns
that took the lead, the peasants acting as auxiliaries. In some cases,
however, there were spontaneous outbreaks in the countryside,
where there was a natural alliance between the peasant who felt
himself to be exploited by the tax collector, and the seigneur who
wanted to keep his share of the peasant's dues secure from the
government's increasing demands. 'Mort aux gabeliers' was a cry
that appealed to both. One of these *gabeliers* may be taken as
exemplifying what so many hated. Jean Fortin, Sieur de Beaupré,
was a *trésorier de France*, a pluralist office-holder and a leading
figure in a local syndicate which was exploiting the office market,
buying a block to sell piecemeal. Such a man had a natural interest
in increasing the number of offices, and with them the extension
of the *élections*, the *aides* and the *gabelle*. He now went in alarm to the
king to implore the revocation of the *Grande Gabelle* in Lower
Normandy. He secured it, but local officers made no attempt to
spread the news; professional jealousy of the small man for the big
operator was an important factor.

The revolt was curiously patchy in extent. In the *élection* of
Avranches, *bocage* country of small farms and poor soil, where
without salt panning and fishing the peasants would be hard put
to it to survive, out of ninety-seven parishes, twenty-seven only
participated and some of these probably under threats. Most
refused to budge. Perhaps the Norman is less volatile than the
southerner; whatever the reason, the revolt was rendered ineffective by lack of concerted action. The nearest to large-scale
organisation was to be found in the army which gathered in mid-
July around Avranches. Its organisation into districts suggests
prior planning and one seigneur at least had been drilling his men

K

since the previous autumn. The peasants, under the standard of John the Baptist, received orders from 'Jacques Nu-Pieds'. Who was he? Possibilities include the Sieur de Ponthébert, reputedly in league with bigger men outside the country, and Jean Morel, *vicaire* of Saint-Saturnin. Most likely he was a collective personality, the directing council of four priests, one of whom was Morel. The men they led included a smattering of gentry; one such, the Vicomte de Coûtances, subsequently indicted for spreading false rumours, was the son of an old Leaguer. There were some lawyers, men mostly on the lower rungs of the new feudalism of office, and a handful of tradesmen and artisans. The majority were salters and foresters, rough men fighting for their livelihood. Notably absent were the leading men from any level of society; there were no upper clergy or respected nobles and among the peasants few independent proprietors; it was a revolt of the under-dogs, the resentful and dispossessed.

Once the government reasserted its authority there could be no doubt about the result. A detachment of troops under Gassion occupied Caen in November. He then went on to Avranches, surprising the rebels by his speed, and they were beaten before they could concentrate; had the result been different the whole province might have come out. As it was, all was over except for the inquest and reprisals. Chancellor Séguier arrived in person, embodying the affronted majesty of France. He took over the authority of the Parlement of Rouen and suspended its members from their offices. Responsibility for the rising was thus laid squarely on the local officials, high and low. He struck at the most vulnerable point, for no peasants' rising could succeed without the complicity and leadership of the bourgeois of the towns. The government needed the cooperation of local officers, but in the last resort the officers, too, needed the mandate and security that the crown alone could give. For fiscal reasons the government had jeopardised this relationship, but so long as it commanded sufficient military force it could bring the office-holders to heel. The Fronde was later to show what must already have been obvious to many, that the government's interference might be inconvenient but civil war, bringing out as it did the violent and radical elements in every class, was worse. 'Offices', wrote Richelieu, 'are a disorder that is part of the order of the state.' He knew that the crown could safely stake its future on this defensive alliance of mutually dependent interests.

There were numerous executions. Coûtances in particular was
made a special example. One man was broken on the wheel in the
market square and others were hanged. Some had fled to the
Channel Islands or elsewhere and their houses were demolished.
Of the villages, one, Cérance, was ordered to be demolished
because of a persistent record of rebellion. There was nothing in
these stern but discriminating punishments to assuage the people's
hatred of Paris, but much to discourage future revolts. Parlement,
once reinstated, continued to be recalcitrant, certain parishes went
on being awkward about their taxes. There was no further open
revolt, but the peasantry were encouraged not to pay their taxes.
The seigneur of Montbrun in Guyenne, in a letter of April 1643 to
the Chancellor, after referring to 'the great wretchedness which
passes belief' and to an incident in which the *intendant* in the
province, de la Ferrière, was compelled by a large armed band to
accede to their demands, went on: 'Monseigneur, since then this
band or collection of soldiery and armed individuals has greatly
increased in size'. From all around the people were flocking to
Villefranche to join in the disturbance. 'They are protesting that
because of their extreme poverty they want to pay the tax-farmer
precisely what they owe to the king and nothing more.' The
letters of the *intendants* refer constantly to the problem. Du Boulay
Favier, in January 1645, writing from Alençon, was explicit:
'Whole *élections* could very well pay the taxes imposed on them if
the protection of the gentry did not incite them to rebellion'.
Until the government could tame the rural gentry, there would be
no lasting peace in the countryside.[1]

[1] The causes of popular revolts are also discussed in the broader
European context on pages 186-91, and in relation to the economic
problems of France on pages 256-60.

## 12. Partners in Power

By 1633 Richelieu's personal ascendancy was assured. In February of that year Châteauneuf, Keeper of the Seals, was dismissed and gaoled. He was unpopular with Parlement because of his part in the trials by special court of Marillac and Montmorency, and latterly with Père Joseph and Richelieu who suspected that his notorious affair with Mme de Chevreuse, the *femme fatale* once more, had political implications. His successor Séguier was able but pliable; the circle of loyalty was now complete and henceforward the ministers worked together, outwardly at least, in so harmonious a fashion that it is hard to say who took all the decisions. That Richelieu was in charge is beyond doubt. The emergencies of war only consolidated a position which, since the execution of Montmorency, few had cared to challenge. Richelieu was upheld by the king, respected, if grudgingly, by the court and supported closely by the select group of ministers and officials who knew that their prospects depended on him. He was director, instigator and co-ordinator of policy. At all levels of government, in matters of state and in the small, arbitrary decisions which could affect the lives of remote peasants or keep a man immured for years in the Bastille upon mere suspicion, he was answerable only to a king who seldom chose to cross him, and to his own conscience, a sensitive but supple thing. It is misleading, however, to call Richelieu a dictator. The word has modern overtones which suggest the thorough and far-reaching machinery of the totalitarian state. Furthermore Richelieu was always at heart more of a diplomat than an administrator and had some of the aristocrat's disdain for the mechanics of government; he did not want to monopolise the whole range of decision. So while he did not pursue a conscious policy of refining and extending the administration, his long period of dominance was marked by a steady advance in the powers of the state, not merely in their negative aspects, coercion and the justice that was doled out in the light of *raison d'état*, but also in positive ways that anticipated the mature development of the bureaucratic state under the great ministers of Louis XIV. The traditional view of Richelieu as omnipotent dictator needs to be modified in two ways. He did not bend the will or exploit the name of a royal puppet, but attracted the conscious support of a sane and earnest king by policies that appealed to Louis' patriotic sense of what was right for France. So far, moreover, from governing through servile instruments, Richelieu encouraged a measure of initiative in ministers who relied on him for their position; it is a measure of his authority and confidence that he could trust them to extend their own specialised empires of office.

Louis XIII's was not an endearing personality but he has been treated by historians more perfunctorily than he deserves. Unlucky in occupying a place between two men of mark, Henry IV and Louis XIV, assured and resourceful, legend-makers in their own right, he has been unlucky too in the 'court' tradition of historical writing which dwells excessively, perhaps, upon superficial traits of character as they were exposed in the restricted sphere of palace life; so he has remained obscurely in the background behind the Cardinal Minister who dominates our image of the reign. This is not altogether surprising. In this age, half-way between the feudal monarchies in which effective action largely depended upon the lead and impact of the king, and the more impersonal, bureaucratic governments of later times, it was still desirable for the king to cut a figure and impress his courtiers. Judgement was none the less more important than grace of person and manner, even in the heyday of the Renaissance kings: a comparison between Louis XI and Francis I, among earlier kings, bears out this point. Louis XIV was to prove supremely well fitted to play the part of king, and an able, conscientious ruler as well; unfortunately the more competent the performance, the greater the scope for mis-judgements and this greatest of French reigns ended in the greatest calamities. Louis XIII's failings were but too plain. He was prone to emotionally exacting friendships; in two of these, his boyhood devotion to Luynes and his passionately possessive cultivation of Cinq Mars, he revealed his inadequacy, seeming to invite and even to relish humiliation and mockery. He enjoyed for a time a level and satisfactory relationship with his equerry, the Duc de St Simon, father of the famous diarist. St Simon served the king in a loyal and apparently disinterested way until 1636 when he was dismissed from his post for giving a warning to a friend who was about to be arrested for treason.

All his life Louis was subject to periods of depression, when normal business was impossible. The ordeal of an upbringing that had been at different times lax and oppressive, stimulating and frustrating, everything but stable, had marked his character for life. Inhibited, resentfully shy, especially in the presence of his wife and mother, more at home in the saddle than in the salon, suspicious in manner, abrupt in speech, he was an odd, dull, rather sad man if we judge him only as a private person. Yet he has some claim to be called a great French king, and this not only because he had the courage and sense to uphold Richelieu against all pressures in court and family.

The very contradictions in Louis' character are important. The chronic invalid who was an old man at forty was also an intrepid horseman, never happier than when following hounds or relaxing afterwards in his hunting lodge at Versailles, or supervising the operations of his troops, at least so long as they were on the move. The man who shrank from his wife and grovelled before Cinq Mars was also firm, consistent and impressive in public pronouncements and meetings of council. He was patient in application to business rather than quick-witted, and he had been deplorably educated, but he had a good head for the details of government. Ministers might not like him but they learned to respect his constant zeal, his occasional insights and, not least, his rasping tongue. The king was often separated for long periods from his ministers; long and formal letters were at such times the main instrument of government. The king insisted upon being properly informed: he might only write 'bon' or 'il le fault' in the margin against one of the state alternatives, but he played a regular part in policy-making even if he but rarely initiated it. He kept all under constant review and though his gaze might be distorted at times when he was ill or depressed it was usually keen enough to keep his ministers alert. They prepared their despatches carefully since they knew that they would be called on to explain and justify instructions that did not please the king. He understood, and demonstrated several times before councillors of Parlement, the value of a show of terrifying majesty, backed as it could be by summary dismissal, the Bastille or the block. His idea of the *métier du roi* was, however, serious, paternal and dutiful. He was called 'just', not only because of the arbitrary justice dealt out to

rebels and malcontents but also because of his concern for the
rights and interests of his subjects. What he perceived plainly he
held to doggedly. His patriotic awareness was limited; he never
understood the intricacies of finance but in his approach to war
and diplomacy he took more heed than Richelieu of the human
and material cost. He was an upright man and treated all as being
under God, with whom he had that sense of special relationship
that we see again in a less humble form in his son, Louis XIV, and
which he expressed as follows: 'He has made me king only to obey
Him, so as to give an example to my subjects and make all those
whom He has made subject to me obey Him'.

He supported Richelieu with growing respect and feeling,
though less from any personal affection than from a sense of mutual
dependence. He was naturally drawn to robust, healthy, outgoing
men and the Cardinal was the reverse of this: the pale face and
tense, perhaps unconsciously dramatised manner of a man who
was never really fit, cannot have appealed to him; but he appreciated Richelieu's 'courage and fidelity' and relied on him for the
intelligent and sympathetic spirit of direction that made a coherent
policy out of the various decisions required of him. Richelieu left
to him what he was best fitted to do, ordering and scrutinising
matters of detail. In return, he left his minister scope not only to
shape a foreign policy but also to transform the nature of royal
government. Richelieu dominated the other ministers and made
them a unified body. They knew that it was by his influence that
they were appointed and through his favour that they remained in
office.

By his deliberate choice of men who would conform to his
methods of government and accept his authority, and by thorough
use of the patronage which he dispensed, either in the king's name
or on his own account, Richelieu created an instrument of government more compact, united and specialised than any before. The
*créatures* (the word implies dependants and is in no other sense
derogatory) supported him since their offices depended on it. At
the same time Richelieu was content to see them enlarge their
own spheres of authority since he felt assured of their loyalty and
knew that he could insist upon conformity in matters of general
policy.

As in England and Spain the office of secretary developed from
that of confidential clerk into that of a minister with an autonomous sphere of action. It followed naturally from the extension of

the king's authority that those who enjoyed his confidence shared in his power. The Valois kings had established the tradition of dividing responsibility for the provinces among the four secretaries The *règlement* of Henry III, in 1588, had reserved the right to rotate these departments every year; being unsure of his own position, that king wished to prevent the establishment of blocs of political interests. This system persisted even after the growth of specialisation, reflecting the condition of the state as it emerged from the Middle Ages when the king ruled by treating with individuals and provinces, when there was no machinery of central government in the provinces and the king's will was expressed mainly in letters. The disadvantage was that the wires could be crossed: the control of troops as they moved from one province to another was an obvious difficulty. In Richelieu's time troops in the field came under the Secretary for War, but garrison troops were under the authority of whichever secretary controlled the province they occupied. Such geographical divisions did not make for efficiency but Richelieu accepted the system, seeing in it the advantage that the secretary gained first-hand knowledge of the conditions of his province through his contacts with the governor, prominent churchmen and officials. At council meetings he could produce the accurate evidence of local conditions that was such an important factor in the advance of central government.

The framework within which the secretaries worked was less rigid than it sounds if described on paper. A great deal of the business of government was done by individuals, by discussion and decision outside the formal meeting of councils; from this it follows that it was not so much the shape and official composition of the councils that mattered, as the men who regularly sat in them, the professionals in the business of government. The trend in the form of the councils was towards smaller groups acting in a more specialised way. As government had become more compli- cated the feudal council had proliferated; alongside the traditional pretensions of *les grands* to share in counsel, and the undisputed right of members of the royal family to attend with the king went a steady increase in professional *conseilleurs du roi*. Out of sessions held for special purposes arose specialised divisions of the council. At the end of the sixteenth century there were four sections of the council, though the fiction that it was one council was preserved. The *conseil d'affaires* under Henry IV, and under Richelieu, handled important matters of general policy. The *conseil d'état* dealt primarily with matters of internal administration; the *conseil de finances* conducted most of the financial business, but in a number of matters, appeals and disputes arising out of taxes, for example, its functions overlapped with the *conseil d'état*; finally there was the *conseil privé* or *des parties* which was the domain of the lawyers, the *conseilleurs d'état*, who constituted a court of judgement and appeal—*privé*, because they represented the king's own justice as opposed to that of Parlement, and *des parties* because of their rôle as mediators in judicial disputes. The powers of the *conseil privé* were defined in 1624. Peers retained their right to sit in this council, but the permanent *conseilleurs* attached to the council did most of its work.

The main changes of the years 1600 to 1642 were what would be expected from the more effective assertion of the king's will and, in the latter half, the success of Richelieu in creating a closer group of ministers whose importance consisted less in the office they possessed than in the hierarchy of favour and confidence established by the Cardinal, a confidence which enabled them to become executives as well as advisers. The series of regulations that followed the death of Luynes, from 1622 to 1630, reflect the authoritarian temper of the young king and Marillac's zeal for regularity as well as Richelieu's desire to make the existing system work better. The competence of the *conseil d'en haut*, as the *conseil d'affaires* came to be called, was enlarged to include internal affairs and financial control. The *conseil des finances* continued to perform its specialised business. The *règlement* of 1630 carried further the process of specialisation by delineating the work of the *conseil des dépêches* which was to handle all internal affairs, judicial, ecclesiastical and administrative matters not important enough to receive the attention of the *conseil d'en haut*.

The flexibility of the system is shown by the use made of *commissions* for the specific purposes of absolute government. In 1627 the *grand règlement* of Paris instituted ten of these, each with five or more councillors: for ecclesiastical matters, finance (two *commissions*: for disputes arising out of taxes, and dealings with the *traitants*), police and public assistance, war, justice, the affairs of the *religion prétendu réformé* (the RPR of state documents), foreign affairs, *cahiers* from the *pays d'état*; and finally marine and commerce which Richelieu kept for himself. As well as these departments there were also special commissions, the most notorious of which was the *chambre de l'arsenal*. In 1628 a register was opened for financial documents, the first attempt to provide the records which are such a vital element in government. State papers remained, however, the property of the secretary concerned, or of the Chancellor; there was no central archive. After 1628 the Chancellor would only admit holders of the royal brevet. There was a retreat during the minority of Louis XIV, but firm precedent had been established for the exclusion of *les grands* from the council, which was final after 1661. So at the start of Louis XIV's personal reign, in place of the earlier conception of a group of courts, limbs of the Curia Regia, performing different functions under the surveillance of the sovereign, assisted by some trusty confidants and occupied especially with war and foreign affairs, we find a council with many duties, political, administrative, fiscal and judicial, superior to all the courts, divided into numerous sections and well organised for the work of centralised government.

How did Richelieu work within this system? When the king and his ministers were in the same place, or at least within range, Richelieu and Louis exchanged views, sometimes personally, often by way of comments on memoranda. The Cardinal was careful to secure the approval of the king for his actions; Louis for his part was usually ready to accept advice and to endorse his minister's policy. For much of the reign Louis lived at his palace of St Germain, Richelieu nearby at his château at Rueil. When the two men were separated for any length of time, as when on military expeditions, Richelieu saw to it that his interests were represented by one of his *créatures*. Otherwise he worked largely through the *conseil des affaires,* where might also be found Père Joseph and those ministers who enjoyed Richelieu's special confidence, also one or two of those who could assert their right to be consulted, notably the queen, queen mother and Gaston. In the second part of the reign, not only did the group of Richelieu and his *créatures* grow closer, but the council met more frequently without the king.

Hitherto the king's ministers had tended to form parties in competition for prestige and power. From the outside they still seemed to function independently and to have a direct relationship with the king (as his secretaries). Their importance came to depend, however, not on the office they possessed, but on their position in the hierarchy of favour and confidence established by the Cardinal. Two Secretaries of State, Loménie and Phélypeaux, loyal and punctilious in the execution of their secretarial duties, were of minor importance in the government because they were not thus favoured by the Cardinal and were not allowed an executive rôle. Two others, by contrast, Chavigny and Sublet de Noyers, specialised in the fields of foreign affairs and war respectively in a way that anticipates the great ministers of Louis XIV's reign.

Léon de Bouthillier, Comte de Chavigny, was the son of Claude Bouthillier, whose own father had been a clerk in the law office of Richelieu's grandfather, François de la Porte, and subsequently taken over the practice. Claude had been made Secretary of State in 1628 but became in 1632 the joint *surintendant des finances* with Bullion. Léon was then only twenty-four but was entrusted by Richelieu with vital tasks. He prepared despatches, received and briefed ambassadors, negotiated with Gaston of Orléans (whose Chancellor he was), toured battlefields, supervised the royal household and toiled incessantly on the Cardinal's behalf. Reporting daily to Richelieu on the king's moods and views, he became an essential intermediary. Counting too much on Gaston's support, he made the fatal mistake of opposing Mazarin after Richelieu's death; he was soon dismissed, and died when he was 44. Jealous, submissive to Richelieu, but haughty with underlings, he was deservedly unpopular but he left his mark. In his time the foreign minister's boundaries of action were fixed.

Sublet de Noyers, a distant relation of Richelieu's mother, succeeded Servien as Secretary for War in 1636. Servien had worked hard and loyally and was unlucky to be dismissed after falling out with Bullion and Chavigny; at that critical juncture Richelieu was concerned above all with harmony amongst his *créatures*. In the seven years up till the death of Richelieu, Sublet laid the foundations for the more far-reaching military revolution associated with the names of the Le Telliers. A *dévôt* whose purposeful faith pervades his work and writing, essentially an austere man, Sublet was, however, no philistine. He patronised Poussin and saved the palace of Fontainebleau by a timely restoration when it would otherwise have fallen into ruin. Much of his work was hurried and piece-meal for he took over in an emergency and he was chronically short of money. He was however a resourceful administrator and a glutton for work.

Sublet has been described[1] as 'a Colbert in a minor key' and in

[1] C. Michaud writes interestingly about Sublet's work as artistic director in 'Francois Sublet de Noyers, Superintendant des Bâtiments de France', *Revue Historique*, no. 241, April 1969.

one respect he justifies this description. He believed that the presence round the king of France of a cortège of artists known for their virtue and intelligence would contribute as much as victory in war to the grandeur of the monarchy. He took enormous pains to get Poussin to come to France but he patronised him only on the understanding that he would 'paint for no one without my leave, for I have made you come for the king and not for private citizens'. Artistic mercantilism indeed! In other respects he was different from Louis XIV's great minister, who would not have approved Sublet's large religious benefactions. No one was more immersed than he in the world of the *dévôts*. Of six maternal uncles four were religious: there was a Carthusian, a Capuchin, and a commander of the order of St Denis among them; two sisters were nuns and his own father ended as a Carthusian.

With Bullion, the genial but strong-willed *surintendant* who became a key figure in the war years, Richelieu enjoyed a close and fairly amicable relationship; yet Bullion remained fairly independent. He was a veteran from the time of Concini, a natural survivor. His ways of raising money were reviewed neither by the council nor by the king. The *surintendants* had vast powers: they fixed assignations, contracts with tax farmers, the interest on loans and the issue of offices. Bullion was not an outstanding manager. When he died in 1640 he left administrative confusion and a set of financial arrangements which invited the reform they were eventually to receive at the hands of Colbert. He had himself grown very rich in office and he left a fortune of some 8 million livres. He had served Richelieu loyally in his bluff, rather cynical way; in a letter to Chavigny, thanking him for a good turn, he wrote revealingly of the Cardinal, 'I prefer his good graces to all the wealth in the world. You know the decision that we have made together to live and die in fidelity and obedience to his Eminence.'

The elder Bouthillier, Claude, was of all the ministers perhaps nearest to Richelieu. In a letter to the secretary, as he then was, Richelieu subscribed himself in terms of rare affection, 'me croyez de cœur et d'affection vostre très affectionné à vous servir'. He was also fond of Bouthillier's wife, born Marie de Bragelonne, the daughter of a Norman landowner: their son, we have seen, received rapid promotion. With two members of the family in key positions after 1632 the Bouthilliers were in an unusually strong position in the latter part of Richelieu's ministry. They depended entirely on Richelieu, but he also depended greatly on them.

Bouthillier might serve as a model for the virtues of the *petit noblesse* and the civil servant when, as in him, they were happily combined. His was not a very subtle intelligence but he was hard-working and methodical. There is a strain of naïveté in the way he expressed his views about thrift and loyalty, but they sound sincere: he was by nature, inclination and interest a king's man. Richelieu relied on him sometimes to see that his orders were carried out if he had reason to think that Bullion might have other plans. He also left Bouthillier increasingly free to formulate his fiscal policies, surely a sign of confidence rather than of indifference. He entrusted him with diplomatic business, sometimes of a personal nature, as for instance the negotiations for the marriage between Richelieu's niece, Clair-Clémence de Maillé, and the Duc d'Enghien. A vital part of his duties was to represent the interests of the Cardinal at court and with the royal family, the king in particular. He looked out for plots, studied the barometer of royal moods and kept Richelieu briefed, thus enabling him to adapt his advice and tactics to the current situation. He was nothing if not versatile: at one time he worked on the decoding of Marie's correspondence, at another he handled Richelieu's interest in the matter of the appointment of wet-nurses for the Dauphin. He was not a great *surintendant,* though he was more conscientious than Bullion. But the part he and his son Chavigny played in preserving and strengthening the relationship between king and first minister was of the greatest importance.

The other minister of importance was Séguier. Keeper of the Seals in 1633, Chancellor from 1635 to 1672, Pierre Séguier played a central part in French history for forty years. The office of Chancellor was second to none in dignity and prestige. He was a sort of viceroy. When the king died, the Chancellor alone, as personifying his authority, did not go into mourning. On many occasions he acted for the king, at the opening of a States-General for example, or concluding a treaty. As supreme justiciar he presided over councils other than the *conseil d'affaires.* At a *lit de justice* he sat immediately below the royal throne. In his function of sealing royal edicts he possessed a powerful means of altering or rejecting anything he deemed prejudicial to the interests of France. According to his character he could be a mere bureaucrat with a decorative rôle as well, a docile executor of royal policy, or he could secure a share in power. Pierre Séguier came from a family of able lawyers. Two of his brothers and four cousins were leading *parlementaires.* His grandfather had been *président à mortier* (next in seniority after the Chancellor and *premier président*). His father, Jean Séguier, was one of the *fidèles* of Henry IV and was rewarded by being made *lieutenant-civil* of Paris. Pierre himself had the sort of legal career that a man might expect if his family were very rich, influential and already entrenched in Parlement. He became in succession *conseilleur, maître des requètes, président à mortier,* and then *garde des sceaux* at the age of forty-five. Humanist, scholar, assiduous collector of letters and documents,[1] patron of the Academy, Séguier did not aspire to dominate, like Marillac, but supported Richelieu, as he later supported Mazarin, intelligently and consistently. Since neither king nor Cardinal attended council meetings at all regularly, Séguier had ample opportunity for influencing decisions at ground level. He was firm but cautious; and he certainly had staying power. He seems to have been authoritarian by temperament and to have been content to see the powers of the state advance so long as the interests of the judiciary were preserved; and there the rôle of Parlement was crucial.

[1] Historians have reason to be grateful for Séguier's assiduity in preserving correspondence. An important part of the Séguier papers is now in Leningrad, whither they found their way at the time of the French Revolution. From the rest R. Mousnier has edited a selection in two volumes (Paris, 1964) which provides valuable evidence for the extent and nature of the local disorders of the period, as described in the letters of commissaries and *intendants*. See also pages 141 and 289.

## 13. The King Above the Law

With a jurisdiction extending over a third of the country, the Parlement of Paris was the most important of the parlements. From its beginnings at the end of the thirteenth century, as a branch of the Curia Regis, it had become a cluster of courts, the highest in the land, with administrative and political functions as well. The right of registering royal edicts had been developed into the right of examination, and hence of approval; defence of the Gallican liberties against the Pope had also enhanced its prestige and bred notions of a political rôle. It enjoyed the right of remonstrance, by which the magistrates could point out to the king faults in a law, something which clashed with precedent or which was harmful to the state. The right did not extend beyond objection and if the king wished the edict to become law, Parlement could do little but delay registration. It was from this right, however, more than from theories based upon the notion of a contract between the ruler and the people, that the pretensions of Parlement in the seventeenth century were derived. Furthermore the feeling of being at the centre of affairs, of belonging to a privileged and exclusive club entrusted with the care of the traditional rights and usages of the realm, was fostered by the practice of passing on offices from father to son. Once they found themselves in possession of this considerable investment in a very limited market, *parlementaires* saw to it that their own rights and the future of their families were secure. This body was therefore essentially a conservative oligarchy, in sympathy with the crown in its basic task of maintaining the order and security of the realm but tenacious of its own privileges, which inevitably conflicted at times with the demands of the monarchy.

The Valois kings, the authoritarian Francis I especially, had succeeded in establishing the principle that Parlement owed obedience to the king. In the words of Francis' Chancellor Duprat in 1518, 'It is not for us to question his commands'. In the religious wars Parlement had opposed the disruptive principle of the League, that hereditary right must yield before religious orthodoxy; when the Pope intervened, depriving Henry of Navarre of his right to the throne, and touched maladroitly on the sensitive Gallican nerve, it affirmed the existing law of succession to be immutable. After 1588, however, the loyalty of Parlement was put to an unfair test. Harlay, Premier Président of the time, declared that, since it was established by the king, Parlement could only function in his service, but for a time after the assassinations of Guise and Henry III the lawyers were split between supporters of the League and those of Henry IV.

The extremism of the *Seize*, the revolutionary government in Paris, and the intransigence of the Pope, and finally the fact that there was no credible substitute for Henry IV, restored unity and the traditional position. Henry sometimes found them obstructive —did they think, he asked, that they could stop the Spaniard with red gowns?—but appreciated their moderate conservatism. They accepted the Edict of Nantes, despite its separate courts, because they were even more concerned about the spread of ultramontane views, the introduction of the decrees of the Council of Trent and recognition of the Jesuits. Henry respected their vision of the *patrie* and its fundamental laws, their opposition to the alienation of crown land and to the excessive sale of offices. He also found that they could be left to function in the margin of political life. Professional pride and legal expertise were no substitute for the wider views and knowledge of the king and his ministers; nor were the leisurely procedures and technical arguments of the law courts a training for political maturity.

In the strong monarchy of Henry IV Parlement was unable, therefore, to become an effective check upon the executive. The regency of Marie de Médicis was a different matter. At the outset they took the lead in deciding that the queen mother should be regent: no mere formality since precedents were ambiguous. She began with an obligation to Parlement, which set out to secure its position, in superiority to the States-General, as unique guardian of the rights of subjects. Roused to defend the principle of sale of office, which had been condemned by the three orders of the States-General of 1614-15, they produced in 1616, and in fuller form in 1618, remonstrances which went so far beyond the original issue as to represent a general attack. They asserted their right to play a part in public affairs, and denounced the introduction of favourites into the royal administration, encroachment upon the proper courts and sovereign authorities, the spread of gambling and duelling; and they required that the liberties of the Gallican Church be respected. Sweeping though these pronouncements were, more like the *cahiers* of a States-General than the judgements of a law court, they were not truly radical. Parlement wanted strong kingship under the restraints of the fundamental laws; the right to advise and to reprove, rather than to share in the running of affairs. Only a minority wanted what Parlement in 1648 was to try, an alliance with *les grands*, to put pressure on the crown. Though Marie responded with a decree forbidding the intrusion of Parlement into political affairs, the dispute was not so easily covered up. It was unrealistic to separate judicial and political business in this way. Not all *parlementaires* went so far as to claim, as did de la Roche-Flavin in 1617, that without Parlement's free registration no royal enactments could be held valid; but the conduct, if not the theory, of royal government, under Richelieu no less than in the regency, ran so contrary to the desire of most *parlementaires* to preserve their authority, that a clash was inevitable.

In 1597 Parlement had submitted to the king a list of names from which it suggested that he should choose his council; it was a belated and futile protest against the evolution of the royal administration. Its decisions, as representing the will of the crown in day-to-day matters, ignored or flouted the authority of Parlement; furthermore traditional councillors, princes of the blood, great officers of state, had been largely replaced by professional bureaucrats, new men who were not over-particular about the claims of Parlement and were impatient when that body put legality before *raison d'état*. Villeroy, the great secretary who served four kings in turn and played an important part in the reconstruction of France after the religious wars, was such a man. Richelieu, of course, epitomised the new spirit: he was autocratic as none had been able to be before, and unwilling to compromise when the needs of the state clashed with traditional liberties. He did not hesitate to set up special courts. In 1624, he created one to try administrators accused of financial offences; he also used it to try political enemies. In 1631 he established the *Chambre de l'Arsenal*, an extraordinary commission, ostensibly to judge crimes involving the security of the state: forgery, the removal of money from the country, but also again political offenders; the very vagueness of its jurisdiction was its strength. Parlement refused to register the edict creating the new court but it met and judged all the same. There was no logical argument which the lawyers could produce against the right of a king who was the source of justice to set up his own court. Parlement's freedom of action had already been restricted by the *Code Michaud*.

The *Code Michaud* scarcely deserves the name of *code* and it is quite different from the later *codes* of Colbert's time, which were attempts to rationalise distinct areas of law and custom. It was a great ordinance of 461 articles concerning a wide range of subjects: justice, universities, military discipline and arrangements, hospitals, taxes; in short, an attempt to institute reforms in all areas where reforms were held to be necessary and to give them the sanction and authority of a single pronouncement. Its inspiration may be looked for in the complaints made at the States-General of 1614; the ordinance was introduced as the answer of the crown to these complaints. It was the product of the cooperation of Richelieu and Marillac, the Keeper of the Seals who lent his first name, Michel, to the title. In that most of its provisions were ignored, it must be deemed a failure, though it also provided a useful lesson to later administrators, if not as a model, at least as a study in the snags that beset the reformer of institutions. Its failure is not hard to understand. Too many of the provisions reflected the current concerns of the government, with censorship, for example, duelling and fortifications. The scope of the enactment was so wide that those whose interest it was to oppose it could easily find ground for doing so. Parlement refused to register it because they saw in Richelieu's proposal to let the lesser nobility into certain administrative positions, in colonial affairs for example, an attack upon their privileged position. A *lit de justice* was arranged to make the *Code* law. Several provincial parlements refused to register it or did so only with modifications. But Parlement's wings were trimmed by the article in the *Code* in which it was stated that remonstrances had to be made within two months of the publication of an edict, after which its registration was automatic.

Both by council decree and in a harangue delivered by Châteauneuf in person, the magistrates were forbidden to deliberate upon political matters. Then in January 1632, in response to remonstrances against the *Chambre de l'Arsenal* and to the perhaps reasonable but typical demand that its members should be drawn from its own body, Louis XIII summoned Premier Président le

Jay and a deputation of magistrates to Metz to hear his mind. When le Jay was rash enough to compare the king's behaviour with that of Louis XI, he was told: 'You exist for no other reason than to judge disputes between Master Peter and Master John . . . and if you continue to venture beyond this, I will cut your nails to the quick'.

There existed always the danger, substantiated by the Fronde, that leaders of Parlement would make common cause with a faction of nobles; it must have occurred to Richelieu. But the magistrates could not draw, as could the leaders of opposition in the English parliament, upon the idea of representation; nor upon the tradition that the king, like his subjects, was under the law. Parlement was the prisoner, when it came to political action, of the laws that it guarded and enforced; its very privileges were its weakness. A sharp thrust against these privileges by a determined government was always enough to make the *parlementaires* bow their heads. The *lit de justice* could be used as a last resort; ceremonious but arbitrary, it epitomises the relationship of king and Parlement. In 1635 the king held such a session for the registration of edicts creating new offices, twenty-four of them in Parlement; some outspoken councillors, outraged by an action which devalued their own offices, protested over the heads of the compliant Premier Président. They were arrested and exiled, whereupon the court of the *Enquêtes* staged a strike and refused to dispense justice. They were not unsuccessful, for their colleagues were restored and the number of offices was reduced from twenty-four to seventeen.

In 1640 there was another tussle over new creations, then further exiles and imprisonments. The issue was balanced in equity: on the government's side, necessity of state in a time of war, on that of Parlement, the injustice of arbitrary interference in a field traditionally regarded as its own. That there was something superficial about this quarrel may be judged from the crown's next action. A *lit de justice* of February 1642 limited Parlement to judicial matters. The preliminary lecture dwelt upon the disorders of the League, the restitution of royal authority under Henry IV when France became 'the perfect model for accomplished monarchies', the lapses of the minority when Parlement presumed too much, and the subsequent elevation of the crown in the person of Louis XIII: so went Richelieu's version of recent history. The moral was that it was only when royal power was fully recognised that 'France recovered her true strength'. But after all the thunder it was only a mouse that emerged, for Parlement was allowed to keep its right of remonstrance about matters of finance 'if they find any difficulty in verifying them', though they could not use the phrases 'we cannot' or 'we ought not', which were derogatory to the prince. Even after the edict had been registered, further representations were allowed. So the gate was left open to the later militants of the Fronde, presumably because the king and his minister did not fear that any danger would come of it. They needed Parlement's authority in matters of succession and the fundamental law of the realm. A few months after the Cardinal's death the king requested it to register a declaration naming the queen mother as regent in the event of his early death; a second declaration pardoned five *parlementaires* who had been exiled the previous year, and restored their offices.

Uniformity and centralisation are the major themes in the progress of royal government in the seventeenth century. This progress was less even and less confident (and contemporaries may have been less aware of it) than the result would suggest; moreover, even Louis XIV's monarchy at the height of its powers was not so effective in the provinces as might be imagined from the apologists of absolute monarchy. Up to the Revolution there persisted enclaves of independence and local differences of law and custom. Several of the *pays d'états* survived into the eighteenth century, examples of the particularism and the liberties that were extolled by liberals from Fenélon to de Toqueville. Provinces which kept their Estates, of which the most notable were Languedoc and Brittany, amounted altogether to more than a quarter of France in area and wealth, but paid a relatively small proportion of the *taille*. This fact was the central reason for clashes between the Estates and the central government in this century. Richelieu is unlikely to have seen any grave deformity in the mere existence of these Estates and their separate system of taxation. Men of his time envisaged their country in a way that is hard for us to understand, inured as we are to the precise calculations of the modern administrator. For them the constitution was not a mechanism but a body, whose shape reflected the stages of its growth; untidy, ill-proportioned, certainly, but integral in its varieties, a living organism operating according to the laws of its being, not to be reduced to the formulae and patterns of geometricians. The slow accretion of provinces had left a patchwork of conflicting customs, and royal authority had to be enforced through whatever agencies were available.

The States-General was a futile body, an occasional meeting and sounding-board for the interests and differences of the classes. It had developed no machinery by which pressure could be mounted against the executive; it was a babble of voices which the crown could safely ignore. The provincial Estates sat regularly, voiced the spirit and concerns of the province and represented its needs in the vital matter of finance. Here alone there could have developed a genuine constitutional opposition and it was this that later attracted the gaze of the *philosophes,* and those who became disenchanted with the absolute state before and after the Revolution. Their picture of the Estates as bastions of liberty should be treated sceptically. They were essentially oligarchic institutions, representative only in the narrowest sense; the same conservatism which we see in parlements went inevitably with a narrowly parochial view. On balance the peasants were probably better off, in a *pays d'état,* as Locke found in his travels later in the century, but there is also evidence of maladministration and unfair assessment of taxes in these provinces.

Finance apart, Richelieu's prime concern with provincial estates was the threat to security when they took up a local cause. He would have preferred to see them abolished, but he could take a more benevolent view. As governor of Brittany he wrote to his cousin La Meilleraye, the king's representative, that he was to restore the Estates to their former liberty 'allowing each man who has the right of attending to come freely and vote without any obstacle'. He took action only when there was a favourable opportunity or grave provocation. Empirical in domestic matters as in his foreign policy, he was content, like later statesmen of the *ancien régime,* to see these archaic institutions atrophy through lack of interest; there was less danger in this than in a headlong conflict. Hatred of Paris and its officers was one of the strongest forces in the life of a province, especially in one which cherished a tradition of independence, like Normandy, Brittany or Languedoc.

The Estates of the Dauphiné were suppressed in 1628 in the aftermath of the Huguenot revolt, which gave Richelieu the chance to impose *élections* upon the province. When in 1630 he tried to impose *élections* upon Burgundy, however, there was trouble. The Estates of this province were particularly futile; they met with great pomp and spent time in matters of etiquette, but shrank from the pressing problems of local government which they were happy to leave to Paris. Dijon prided itself much upon its municipal liberties, providing its own militia and artillery, an elective town government and magistracy. It was the capital of Burgundy and the centre of its flourishing wine trade; its wealthy merchants were also extensive landowners in the countryside around. They revolted at the prospect of more direct royal government but were quelled by the arrival of troops. The liberties of the town were reduced but in the following year the *élections* were quashed in return for a gift of 400,000 livres. A similar process occurred in Provence, where the Estates were allowed to continue in their custom of violent debate, without interference by royal spokesmen. Even in Languedoc it appeared that the Cardinal's main objective in proposing the *élections* was to obtain money in return for their abandonment. An attempt after the peace of Alais to impose a *bureau d'élection* in each of the twenty-two dioceses of the province was one of the main reasons for the decision of its governor, Montmorency, to join the revolt of Gaston of Orléans. He got little support from the province and after his defeat the government secured a big increase in the contributions of the province. Normandy's Estates petered out in 1635; the four others remained to provide Montesquieu with object lessons in the virtues of representative government.[1]

[1] In his article 'Henry and Guyenne: a study concerning the origins of royal absolutism', *French Historical Studies,* vol. IV, no. 4, 1966, Russell Major argues that Henry IV and Sully pursued an absolutist policy that represented an important departure from the 'Renaissance' tradition of decentralised government with a large measure of concession to local institutions and an element of consent. Russell Major's view of the sixteenth century is controversial. The more generally accepted theory is that of Pagès (*La Monarchie d' Ancien Régime en France,* Paris, 1946) that 'it was at the beginning of the sixteenth century that the absolute monarchy triumphed'. Whether or not Francis I was 'absolute' (I would incline to say he was) there is no doubt that in imposing the *paulette* and the *élus* Sully was seeking to take on from where Francis had left off. The motives behind the *paulette,* as Sully told Richelieu, were primarily political—to break the client power of the Guise faction—and the sustained attempt to impose *élus* on Guyenne, eventually successful after bitter debate and resistance, was to have been the prelude to the reduction of the whole of France to a single tax system. Sully overcame the resistance of Bellièvre (for this see R. Mousnier, 'Sully et le Conseil d'Etat et des Finances, La Lutte entre Bellièvre et Sully', *Revue Historique,* 192, 1941) but his premature disgrace led to the reversal of his policy by Villeroi, Jeannin and Sillery

Richelieu's dealings with the Estates should be viewed in the light of his constant concern about the activities of the more lawless nobles and the danger of an eruption in which all the elements of opposition might fuse into one general insurrection. The plots and revolts of the magnates were made more dangerous, we have seen, by special factors: the reckless conduct of the Duc d'Orléans, the traumatic effect of Richelieu's foreign policy upon the *dévôts*, and the social distress produced by war taxation. That any of these outbreaks could have started a civil war, without firmness, dexterity and some luck, can be seen from the subsequent history of the Fronde. The condition of society in general, and of the *noblesse* in particular, was such that some features of a revolutionary situation were present throughout this period. The provincial revolts reveal a greater degree of complicity among the social classes than might have been expected. It is perhaps less surprising that these revolts occurred than that they did not grow into something bigger than mere *jacqueries*. At this time a rising population was apparently pressing against a ceiling of productivity so that famine was endemic. Moreover, there was a dangerous discrepancy, if not as the Marxist would say, contradiction, in the survival of forms of society which had evolved in feudal conditions alongside the dynamic new forces of a capitalist economy. The state meanwhile was encroaching as never before upon ground long held by the privileged classes. Efforts to strengthen royal government brought reactions from Parlement, but they bore hardest upon the nobility, who were still feudal in outlook and manners and thought in terms of personal allegiance to immediate overlords, within the limits of class, estates or province, rather than of civic responsibility to the state (a remote conception at best) or even of loyalty to the crown, which was easily obscured when a proud ecclesiastic stood between them and the king, their ultimate feudal superior. The following of a great noble could still be a world within a world. The governor of St Antonin, summoned to open up his fortress to the officers of the king, replied simply that he belonged to the Duc de Rohan rather than to the king.

However, attitudes were changing, along with the composition of the class. The feudal nobility was being steadily diluted by

---

in 1611. In 1621 the elections were again imposed on Guyenne. Major believes that it was Marillac who was responsible for the further attack of the *pays d'états*, and Richelieu who was now prepared to be 'realistic' and accept money in return for political rights.

important civic and legal functionaries, army officers, financiers and merchants who bought titles of nobility; it was not a closed caste. In 1636 usurpers of nobility were punished; they had to pay a large fine as well as back-payments of the *taille*. One may suspect a financial motive in the crown's zeal for the integrity of the class, for in 1643, to celebrate the accession of Louis XIV, nobility was conferred on two men in each generality on payment of 4,000 livres.

Richelieu was fitted by birth, as well as by experience, to identify the problem. His own family history offered two ways of life, opposed, though not incompatible. He had grown up in the straitened circumstances of the country gentleman but his father was a successful example of the courtier and his life was determined as much by that example as by the family bishopric which was the beginning of his official career. The nobles were caught between the conventions of their class and the effects of the price rise which, to take one central example, had increased fivefold the price of wheat in the last hundred years. It was held to be derogatory to take part in business or to do anything involving manual labour. Richelieu himself held that the army was the proper career for a nobleman and that, except for war, 'the nobility were a charge upon the state'. A few took advantage of the view, reinforced by a royal edict, that it was permissible to take part in maritime trade; some gave up their status in order to trade or enter a profession; many served in the army and thus fulfilled the rôle which in theory justified their privileged position. The church provided relief for a member or two of most noble families. The court offered an uncertain opening for the ambitious, and others attached themselves to some magnate on the same principle. Land sales to rising bourgeois and peasants illumine the decline of many owners of small estates who failed to find any way of furthering their fortune except their rents, which had fallen behind by comparison with prices, and their feudal dues and perquisites. The decline of ancient families to the condition of peasants, failures in the scramble for patronage, posts and pensions, chronic indebtedness were familiar enough to the Cardinal. He showed none of the bourgeois prejudices of the great ministers of Louis XIV's reign; he struck at individual rebels but he was no leveller.[1] He was

[1] It is likely however that many nobles saw Richelieu as their oppressor rather than as their friend. In his article 'A propos des Rapports entre la Noblesse française et la Monarchie absolue pendant

prejudiced rather against the financiers high and low who seemed to flourish on the fiscal needs of the state. He listened sympathetically to the requests of the Assembly of Notables for measures to reinstate their class. He realised the disadvantage of the presence of *les grands* in council. He wished, however, to found an academy for the education of the sons of impoverished nobles and he recommended the king to curtail the extravagance of court life, where so many were ruined by the competitive spirit in dress and entertainment, by the tyranny of fashion.

The nobles, in Richelieu's view, should be devoted, loyal, ready to serve the king. Their natural bravery should go to fighting for the crown abroad; at home they should obey the laws and live peaceably on their estates. He could argue that the disorders of the civil wars had not benefited the mass of the nobles though it had brought temporary gains to some. Privilege in return for acceptance of the new order—here we can see forecast the future of the nobility under Louis XIV. That it was to become privilege without responsibility he may not have foreseen exactly, though it was implicit in the parallel development of an administration from which the nobility was largely excluded. Richelieu did not shrink from the logic of his beliefs: if obedience was essential to

---

la première moitié du XVII siècle', *Revue Historique,* 231, April 1964, P. Deyon analyses particular aspects of their discontent in the face of government attempts to limit fiscal privilege, which were for a start opposed by local proprietors who were not entitled to claim noble status and immunity: checks on titles of nobility were the cause of bitter clashes. In the provinces of the perimeter the government's efforts to enforce the principle that nobles paid *taille* on land that was *roturière,* such as the edict of 1639 enforcing the principle in the Dauphiné, where the nobles had formerly been free from tax, were resented. It was mainly in the *pays réelle* that the nobility associated themselves closely with the interests of the common people. They also grumbled about the indirect taxes, the imposition of the *ban* and *arrière-ban* (which became a regular contribution rather than a feudal levy of men so that in 1639 offers to serve in person were actually rejected). Their anger was focused on the *traitants* who stood between them and the paternal benevolence of the king! Another bogy was the *rentier,* the unproductive parasite who chased nobles and peasants alike from their lands. But not the least of their complaints was that tax levies made it hard for them to collect their seigneurial dues! It was convenient for propaganda purposes to talk about nobleman and peasant as 'twin pillars of the state'. But they were far from disinterested in their defence of the peasants. (See also pages 53-5 and 138ff.)

the well-being of the state and of the nobles, then disobedience
must be punished, and 'in judging crimes against the state it is
essential to banish pity'. He was not afraid to apply his maxim to
the highest in the land.

The feudal tradition of independence and the danger of separatism in the provinces were combined in the Provincial Governors;
it is remarkable how successful Richelieu was in curbing the
power of these men and thereby altering the nature of the institution. He outlined the problem in his *Testament*. The gigantic
expenditure entailed in this office, whose occupant had to maintain
a miniature court and government in his province, meant that it
had to be given to a great landowner; such a man did not accept a
governorship for altruistic reasons alone but for the power that it
conferred. He may have intended to serve the king, but in his own
way and on his own terms. The command of troops in the name of
the king, patronage and influence that he enjoyed in the towns,
parlements or Estates, helped to preserve the idea that he could
remain a law unto himself. From this state of prestige and immunity, political defiance was but a short step. It was plain to
Richelieu that there would be no security against civil war until
the king had the means of enforcing the law through his own
officials. The governorships did not have to be abolished, but they
could be passed by so that they declined into decorative obsoles-
cence. This was the pattern of future development, though a
resourceful governor of strong personality might be important
locally even in the eighteenth century.[1]

---

[1] It is important not to exaggerate the change in Richelieu's time in
the situation of the governors: according to personality and circumstances they could be figureheads or local potentates. Theirs was an
office of a sort, given by royal letters of appointment, normally tenable
for life, still often passed from father to son: for instance Schomberg
was succeeded by his son in Languedoc in 1644. An active governor
would find himself dealing with the Huguenots in his province,
enforcing royal edicts, taking action against rebels, negotiating with
merchants over emergency corn supplies, in contact with the Chancellor
over all matters of order and security—and taking the initiative in
emergencies. The *intendant* was often regarded as an ally in government,
his prime function being judicial; it was not till the reign of Louis XIV
that he moved decisively into the field of administration though this
was implicit from the start. Where the governor was much absent, or
under suspicion at court, the *intendant* might take over; it was also a
deliberate policy to give all new responsibilities and functions, as they
arose, to the *intendant*. In his article, 'Rapports entre les gouverneurs de

Meanwhile *les grands* had to be taught that defiance did not pay. In 1614 there were sixteen local governorships. At Richelieu's death only four of the original sixteen governors survived. Vendôme had exchanged Brittany for the Bastille after the Chalais plot. Soissons had already lost the important province of the Dauphiné before he ended his life of intrigue on the battlefield of Marfée. Guise was dismissed for encouraging revolts in Provence. Any grandee who resisted the authority of one of the king's officials could expect punishment. The Duc d'Epernon, governor of Guyenne, quarrelled with Henri de Sourdis, Archbishop of Bordeaux and Richelieu's commander of the local naval forces, and was forgiven only after the most public humiliation. De Vitry, governor of Provence, later fell foul of de Sourdis and struck him with a cane. Again Richelieu upheld the provocative prelate and de Vitry went to the Bastille. Richelieu gave some provinces to men whom he knew to be loyal or safe, like Chevreuse, for example; Brittany he actually took for himself. Other provinces he left vacant or entrusted to loyal lieutenants-general such as the Comte de Praslin or the Marquis de Montespan.

In Richelieu's words, 'To make a law and not to see it carried out is to authorise what you yourself have forbidden'. In February 1626, a royal edict forbade the duel under penalty of death. Montmorency-Bouteville, a notorious dueller, soon afterwards fought a duel under the Cardinal's window in the Place Royale. He was arrested and sentenced but awaited the king's pardon: was not duelling acceptable in a gentleman? The king received a flood of appeals, for the dueller was a Montmorency and a close friend of Gaston of Orléans. Richelieu advised him to maintain his law: 'Do you wish', he asked, 'to make an end of duelling or of your own power?' In June 1627 Montmorency-Bouteville was executed. The incident is more important than the reckless

---

provinces et les intendants dans la première moitié du XVII siècle', *Revue Historique,* 128, October 1962, R. Mousnier gives a number of illustrations of governors and *intendants* working harmoniously together. In 1640 a governor, the Comte de St Geran, wrote asking urgently for an *intendant* to help deal with rebels imprisoned by him, since the local magistrates were refusing to sit in judgement! In general the picture is one of gradual development, with more of compromise, of empirical handling of situations, than is conveyed by retrospective judgements made from the position established by *intendants* in Louis XIV's reign.

hoodlum who occasioned it and who had already killed twenty-two men in duels. Richelieu may have had some personal feeling, for his eldest brother had been killed in a duel. According to Savaron, few of the noble families of France escaped casualties of this sort; indeed few contemporaries saw the duel as a sporting contest, though the view that gentlemen should defend their honour was received with indulgence. It was also defended on the grounds that it helped the status of the ordinary gentleman to be equal with the greatest in the land in respect of this obligation to fight. The crown alone was above this obligation and had good reason to enforce the old formula: 'le Roi seul a droit du glaive', for duelling was a vicious and anti-social practice. Professional swordsmen, adventurers, hangers-on, picked quarrels in taverns and brothels, then fought to kill, not only with the rapier but also with the more deadly short sword, and often with professional seconds. The Montmorency-Bouteville case did not, of course, end duelling in France, but the weight of the crown, the church and therefore of fashion was henceforward firmly against it. The judicial element in the duel, as a means of settling insoluble quarrels, persisted. The edicts of both Louis XIII and Louis XIV provided for a special court, the *tribunal de maréchaux*, to deal with such quarrels. This did not conflict with Richelieu's determination that there was only one law, the king's, which all must obey. In Louis XIV's reign it was generally thought that France was one of the two countries (the other was Holland) where duelling had been effectively brought under control.[1]

The main instrument of the crown in combating disorder and enforcing the law was to be the *intendant*, who during Colbert's administration in the reign of Louis XIV was established as a permanent, resident official, responsible only to the crown. There is some ground for the view that Richelieu made too little effort to remodel the institutions of France, that he thought primarily in

[1] In his interesting article on this subject, 'Honor versus Absolutism, Richelieu's fight against Duelling', *Journal of Modern History*, 27, 1955, Richard Heer stresses Louis XIII's deep feelings about the subject, suggests that duelling reached epidemic proportions in the first two decades of the seventeenth century, and points out that the originality of Richelieu lay not so much in his attempts to stop the practice as in his new penalties: the Cardinal saw that to men who took life so lightly banishment or deprivation of office, land and status might be a greater deterrent than execution. In the *Testament* he virtually admitted his failure to stamp out the practice.

military and diplomatic terms, and lacked administrative originality. He did not however start, like Louis XIV and his ministers in
1661, from an assured position. For only half of his eighteen years
was he able to work through a group of men in the council on
whom he could wholly rely, under a king who he knew would
support him. This, moreover, was wartime and there were military
and financial emergencies. In these years Richelieu began to make
extensive use of the *intendants de justice et police*. Under more
settled conditions, or if he had lived longer, he might well have
come to use these men in a more regular way and given them
resident status.

France was familiar with the *intendant* before Richelieu. Henry
IV sent out officials, usually to oversee the movements of an army
in a province and to help overcome the problems of liaison
between soldiers and civilians in foraging, billeting, recruitment
and pay. A complaint before the *notables* in 1626 reflects the extent
to which *intendants* were hated by the sovereign courts, and also
the use being made of them to discover and check negligence and
corruption in the courts. Abel Servien, *intendant* in Guyenne in
1628, found himself violently opposed by the parlement of
Bordeaux, whose representatives were then summoned to appear
before the king. When Premier Président de Gourges stood before
the king, Louis seized him by the collar and said, 'On your knees,
little man, before your master'. In the *Code Michaud* the work of the
*intendants* was formally defined. Richelieu made increasing use of
them as war and higher taxation added to administrative problems
and created new opportunities for local corruption. To *trésoriers-
généraux* and parlements these men stood for the unwarranted
intrusion of Paris in local affairs; to Richelieu they were useful
instruments of sound and honest government. His *intendants* were,
however, essentially *commissaires*; their instructions were specific
and their commissions were temporary. They were given powers
of inquest and supervision but they were not properly executive
officers of the crown. They might have widespread powers.
Barentin, *intendant* with the army commanded by the Comte de
Soissons in Saintonge, Aunis, Poitou and the surrounding
provinces, was not confined to the surveillance of the army but
necessarily occupied with the relations of the army and the civilian
populations. There were special situations in which the *intendant*
was bound to take great responsibiltiy on himself: at La Rochelle
after 1628, for instance, or in the provinces affected by revolts.

The withdrawal of the *intendants* was prominent among the demands of *avocat-général* Omer Talon at the outbreak of the Fronde. He told Parlement that it was fifteen years since they were ordained, 'and for eleven whole years they have been in the provinces'. It seems that he was referring to their more extended use, for otherwise his dates are of doubtful validity. Even so they were doing enough to arouse noisy opposition and their future was plain. In the more stable conditions of the 1660's and 1670's the *intendant* would indeed be 'the king in the province', the essential agent of the administrative revolution, the most efficient instrument of government in Europe.

## 14. Army and Navy

The French had not been engaged in a major war since the peace of Vervins at the end of the sixteenth century. Largely untouched by the 'military revolution', the work of the great innovators, Maurice of Nassau, Wallenstein and Gustavus Adolphus, they were also unused to the large scale of operations which had been advancing the science of war since 1618; nor had they learned in the relatively short campaigns in Savoy and Italy the discipline required by armies like the Spanish and Swedish which had to fight far from home. The troops which marched to the frontier in 1635, freshly equipped and mounted, through peaceful Champagne and Burgundy, made a fine showing by contrast with the polyglot veterans of the Habsburg armies, Spaniards and Belgians, Germans, Italians and Croats, under the direction of disillusioned professionals. They acquired their experience soon enough in defeat and the demoralising shambles of retreat, the wretchedness of disease, dysentery, plague and syphilis. The frontier lands felt the breath of war at once: burned crops and deserted villages, atrocity, famine and dereliction. In the so-called war of the two Burgundies, the nobility and peasantry of the Spanish provinces joined with Gallas' Spaniards and Croats in pillaging their French neighbours. Richelieu was soon raising Swiss from the Val Telline and Germans, Scots and Irish to stiffen the ranks of the native armies. That they could be brave was beyond doubt; their discipline was, however, atrocious.

Feudal in spirit and tradition, mercenary in composition, the army displayed the bad features of both systems. The government licensed officers to raise troops. Many of these were noblemen for whom war was a way of life and as proper and natural a way of spending a summer as was hunting in the winter. They brought as much science, discipline and spirit to the battle as they would to the chase. They did not, however, regard regular attendance, attention to petty administrative detail or the dull slogging of a war of siege and manœuvre as part of their obligation to the crown.

After a troop had been raised it could be sold as personal property and this could be a profitable speculation. Grants of commissions came not from the king, but from independent officials, the Colonel-Generals of Infantry and Cavalry. Like a tax farm or a holding in the *rentes*, an officer's commission was an investment whose value rose and fell with demand: in the expansive years of war, before rumours of negotiations affected the price, a company of Guards might cost up to 80,000 livres. Not until after 1661, when Louis XIV himself assumed the post of Colonel-General, was there any radical reform of this corrupt and inefficient system. Louis XIII's army was not then effectively his at all, but a motley of armed levies for whom the king was only one of many contractors, the biggest of the shareholders in an unwieldy enterprise. He enjoyed the traditional right of leading in the field but he had little administrative control. His Secretary for War had less, and his main anxiety was often to keep the army occupied, away from the metropolitan provinces where they might cause a revolt by their exactions. Billeting and foraging arrangements were usually casual; at worst they could reduce a French province to the condition of an occupied territory.

The state which could not control its armies was impotent when it came to the test. The mutinies of the Spanish army in Flanders in the 1570s had provided evidence for this which was the more telling in that the Spanish armies were generally thought to be the best in discipline and fire-power. As during the great European war one army after another—the Emperor's, Maximilian's, Louis XIII's, Oxenstierna's—experienced the demoralising effects of continuous campaigning, it became apparent that the prizes would go to the state which could afford to keep a standing army in action for long enough to gain professional expertise, while at the same time preserving control over its commanders. Holland, with the war on its doorstep, and Spain, by confident professionalism and good training, were relatively successful in this endeavour—Spain at least until the deterioration of her economy in the late thirties. General Monk, who ended the participation of English armies in politics when he negotiated the restoration of Charles II, pointed to the strength of the Dutch army, where 'soldiers received and observed commands but gave none'. The Great Elector of Brandenburg was soon to show what could be done. By virtue of his disciplined army he acquired a leading position among the German princes and laid the foundations of the Prussian state.

For France, with her large population and growing revenues, there was a rich prospect, if the *fureur française* could be contained within a disciplined framework. The armies of Richelieu's time lacked certain elements which are assumed today in the very word 'army': uniforms, systematic promotion and barracks, for example. They were also very small. Spain never had more than 60,000 on her muster rolls and these never marched as one force. The army of the Empire existed mainly on paper; it was the weakness of the Emperor, finally decisive in the German war, that he fought through allies or mercenaries bound to him by costly and precarious bargains. Nowhere, unless we count Poland, did the feudal spirit, proud, anarchic, casual, weaken the state so much as in France. Everything that Richelieu and his fellow-ministers contended with in French society was to be found in the army; their work of reform was therefore crucial, not merely in providing France with a means of implementing her foreign policy, but in building absolute monarchy. Michel le Tellier, *intendant de l'armée* and later war minister under Mazarin and Louis XIV, wrote of the army at this time as 'a republic, composed of as many provinces as there are lieutenant-generals'. With his son Louvois who shared and then took over his office, he was largely responsible for the reforms which created the immense force which made Louis XIV for a time master of Europe. He was helped by his long tenure of office and latterly by an ample revenue. At the outset it was in his interest to belittle the work of his predecessor Sublet de Noyers, which deserves more attention than it has received.

Appointed Secretary of State for War in 1630, with Richelieu's backing, Abel Servien supervised the preparations for war. He was dismissed at the end of 1635, not for any proven incapacity, though the armies were in disarray, but because of a concerted effort on the part of the other ministers to get rid of him. The affair is somewhat obscure but it seems that Chavigny was jealous of him and anxious to promote the self-effacing Sublet, and that Bullion was at loggerheads with Servien over military expenditure. François Sublet de Noyers earned promotion on his merits, however, for he was single-minded, a beaver for work but also resourceful and original in administration. He had experience of financial affairs and he had recently been *intendant* with the armies in Picardy and Champagne. Like the other secretaries he continued to prepare letters concerning all aspects of royal government, for specialisation was not complete, but military affairs predominated

M

and he showed enough talent to enlarge the independence and scope of his department. The 18,000 letters and despatches which have survived testify to his ceaseless activity and indicate the weight of his responsibility. As the middleman between his officers' demands for more money and the *surintendants'* demands for economy he was much occupied with finance. Military and fiscal maladministration, false musters, default of pay, mutiny and desertion, thwarted his efforts in the field, while the *surintendants* struggled to find him about forty million livres a year. Ceaseless negotiation was the war minister's lot, bargains rather than orders, contracts for munitions and artillery, weapons, clothing and food —and rich pickings for the contractors. Richelieu himself had estimated that the siege of Montauban in 1621, which cost fifteen million livres, should have cost two million, and every military operation saw wastage on a comparable scale. The Cardinal often intervened in Sublet's field and sometimes carried on his own transactions.

The calling up of the nobility was done by the feudal *ban*; the *arrière-ban* or general summons to service, three months in France or forty days beyond the frontiers, was proclaimed in 1635; apart from the acquisition of a number of reluctant and ill-trained country squires or the substitutes that they were allowed to send, there was little gained from this archaic exercise and it was carried out by all four secretaries of state acting for their respective departments! The transmitting of money to the troops, and its distribution by officers who were often negligent if not downright dishonest, provides further examples of Sublet's problems. Once in 1640 he went in person with the supply carts. Since there was no trained staff either at headquarters or in the field, he attended to the smallest details: the provision of pikes, plans for fortification, the provenance of flour and cheese. He commended himself to Richelieu by the pious, fervent spirit in which he tackled his work and by his readiness to fit in with the first minister's requirements. In 1638 he was given the additional office of *surintendant des bâtiments,* which he undertook with typical seriousness. His unquestioning loyalty to Richelieu encouraged the latter to increase his field of action and responsibility. He had his own favourites too: Guébriant became general-in-chief of the army with his backing. 'It seems to me', Sublet wrote, 'that I have contributed to all the honour and fortune that has befallen you', and he expected a return in the shape of total loyalty, so that 'the king, having paid for an army, should be the absolute master of it'. This was what was required of 'a monarchical order which binds all into one'. Precise in its demands and confident in its assumptions, this is the authentic language of absolutism.

What was achieved by all this activity? The *contrôles*, or muster-lists, were calculated more exactly and with them the army's requirements in pay and supplies. The practice of posting *intendants* to the armies was regularly adopted. They were, of course, unpopular but at least one of the generals asked for one, recognising his value as an aide. Men like le Tellier in Italy and Grémonville in Champagne, kept Sublet informed and took over some of the local administration; even at their least effective they represented the concern of the king to maintain control over local commanders. Again, though there was nothing comparable with the later work of Louvois, 'the great victualler', a start was made in matters of equipment and commissariat: clothes and weapons were provided for any soldier who had served for a season (pay was docked accordingly). Large carts, copied from those used in imperial armies, were constructed for the transportation of supplies. Though Gustavus had shown already what could be achieved with sequence-firing by musketeers, the future lay with the army which could improve upon the existing weapons, the arquebus, musket and pike—and how slow progress was then by comparison with the escalating technical advances of our century! *Fusil* and bayonet were yet to be invented. Money was spent on the improvement of artillery, but there was no administrative department for the provision of weapons, no arms-making factory. Still more surprising is the fact that there was no regular drill or training in manœuvres until Louvois. If France's effort is compared with that of Sweden under Gustavus it may seem unambitious. But in Sweden the authority of the king was personal, direct and assured. In France the crucial issue was still that of authority. A start had been made, however, in the long struggle against the multitude of individual rights and corporate traditions that prevented the crown from having complete control of the army, and the goal had at least been established, the unification of the whole military establishment under the king. In the shorter term the heroic efforts of Sublet de Noyers were rewarded by the victory of Rocroy in 1643, only a few months after the death of Richelieu and his own dismissal.

No less serious, in Richelieu's view, than the shortcomings of the army was France's weakness at sea, for commercial as well as for strategic reasons. At the assembly of the *notables* in 1626 Richelieu won support for his plans for building a strong navy when he revealed the extent of the damage the country was suffering from this weakness. Spain's maritime blockade of Holland affected French trade with the northern ports. Ships were being forced into Dunkirk and, so Richelieu alleged, sailors being bribed to say that they were carrying goods for Holland: ships and cargo were then forfeit. A privileged company at Seville, under Spanish protection but composed of Flemish and Hanse merchants sent ships in convoy with naval protection; beyond the legitimate aim of ruining Dutch trade, they were empowered to search the ships and confiscate the cargoes of other nations. 'This nation,' said Richelieu of Spain, 'proposes to usurp sovereign authority over the sea, allowing no freedom to trade, not even to other nations among themselves.' During his years at Luçon, near the Atlantic coast, he must often have thought about sea-power and the opportunities that were being wasted by disorder and negligence. From Isaac de Razilly, Knight of Malta and an enterprising adventurer who knew the world from Morocco to Canada, he received trenchant advice. Razilly's memorandum to Richelieu in 1626 was an essay on sea-power, based on the example of the Dutch and smaller states such as Venice, whose influence rested on their ships. At a time when 200,000 French sailors were employed on foreign ships (we may allow that Razilly exaggerated) the French were unable to deal even with their rebellious subjects without turning to foreigners for naval aid. The first ships commissioned by Richelieu were indeed built in Holland. By contrast, Razilly went on, 'Look at the king of Spain; since he took arms at sea he has conquered so many kingdoms that the sun never sets on his lands'. When the fortune of Spain literally depended on the safe arrival of the annual plate fleet it was likely that the outcome of the war between Spain and the United Provinces would be decided at sea: if the Dutch could strike effectively at the *flota* they would eventually win the war. If the Spanish could maintain their convoys intact, they could at least maintain the struggle and give their generals a chance. Meanwhile France had no ships capable of surviving in combat with Dutch or Spanish ships, or English for that matter. When, therefore, Richelieu laid before the king his plans for the construction of thirty ships to save the goods and liberty of Frenchmen, he was tackling an urgent matter of national security.

Sully had tried to establish an adequate Mediterranean fleet of galleys and to restore the fortifications of Provence. There was a galley fleet by the end of Henry IV's reign; if Sully had continued longer in power he might also have grappled with the more difficult problems of constructing an Atlantic fleet, for we know from the remark of Sir George Carew, the English ambassador, that he was 'ever hammering for building a navy for the sea'. The subject was much aired and Richelieu was not original in his ideas, any more than he was in the broader sphere of economic policy. His methods, however, bore the distinctive mark of his personal philosophy and style.

The actual provision of ships was the least difficult part of the operation. The creation of good ports, the manning of the ships and the control of naval operations raised more complex questions. Again we see that behind the material business of supply and administration was the fundamental issue of authority. The crown had few ships; moreover it had virtually no coastline, as the reports of Richelieu's agents reveal. Leroux d'Imfreville visited the coast from Calais to Bayonne and found ports mostly in ruinous condition. At Cherbourg French sailors were engaging in piracy under Spanish commissions. Most of the beaches and harbours were private franchises, bartered away to nobles and churchmen who exploited their privileges and obstructed reform. The Duc de Nevers, for example, laid a tax on every ship built in his port of Saint Valéry. Off the coast of Brittany *curés* were demanding the value of one fish for every twenty caught. The authority of the Admiral of France did not run in any coastal province except Normandy and Picardy; elsewhere the governors would be admirals in their provinces, if there were any ships to command. The Mediterranean coast was in no better shape. In 1633 Henri de Séguiran reported that the port of Toulon was defenceless: its amiable governor commanded 'a garrison consisting of no more than his wife and servants'. Everywhere the coast was vulnerable to the Barbary corsairs, and the experience of the young Vincent de Paul, seized by a slaver when voyaging along this coast, was not unusual.

Richelieu attacked the privileged positions which obstructed the state. He bought the rank of Admiral of France from Mont-morency; it was one of the grievances that induced that splendid

nobleman to revolt in 1632. From Gondi he bought the command
of the galleys. He became himself *surintendant-général de la navigation
et commerce de France* and filled other top posts with members of his
family. Amador de la Porte he made Admiral of Galleys, Pontcourlay's eldest son he put in charge of the *conseil de la marine*. The
special naval privileges of the governors were abolished; his
*ordonnance de la marine* did away with all private coast-line rights.
He began the creation of a fleet by ordering five ships from
Holland. Every port was required to build one ship for royal
service. To man these vessels, some built hastily or so badly that
they were 'open to the sea', needed violence or bribery since there
was no tradition of royal service at sea and young nobles mostly
preferred to fight on land or to enlist as Knights of Malta and
sail against pirates and Turks. Colbert was later to devise a form
of conscription; Richelieu merely ordered all French seamen who
had settled abroad to return home, on pain of death if they were
taken in foreign service.

Before his death the new navy had won victories. Henri de
Sourdis, Archbishop of Bordeaux and admiral, strenuous and
combative in both rôles, soon justified his appointment: in 1637 he
recaptured the Lérin islands from which the Spanish threatened
the southern coast, and in August 1638 he defeated the Spanish
when they were trying to escape from the blockade of the
Pyrenean fortress of Fuentarabia; they lost fourteen ships.
Richelieu's nephew Maillé-Brézé, general of the galleys at twenty,
won three remarkable victories, at Cadiz, July 1640, Barcelona,
July 1642, and Cap de Gata, September 1643. Audacious, brave
and an excellent tactician, Maillé-Brézé was to succeed his uncle as
*grand maître et surintendant*; four years later, still only 27, he died in
action, a severe blow to the young navy. A different sort of seaman
was the Chevalier Paul, son of a washerwoman, who learned
seamanship on a barque travelling between Marseilles and the
Château d'If and subsequently served with the Knights of Malta.
He fought under Sourdis and Brézé, and then enjoyed an independent command in the Mediterranean operating against Turkish
pirates. The exploits of these men show what an instrument of
power the navy could have been. Its promise was not fulfilled at
once. In the upheavals of the minority, without vigilance or
money, Richelieu's navy of sixty ships decayed rapidly, so that
Colbert had almost to begin again in 1661.

## 15. *Economic Depression: the Debate*

The advent of Richelieu to power is often regarded as marking a clean break with the immediate past, in policy as well as in the personnel of government. His political skill and excellent propaganda encourage such simplification: la Vieuville and the Brûlarts slip unnoticed into the wings as the Cardinal commands the stage. So the period from 1624 to 1631 is a time of beginnings, as if the conduct of the *guerre couverte* against Spain, the struggle against the Huguenots and the establishment of his own position at home represented an immediate departure from the inconsequential policies of the preceding years, and a deliberate choice of priorities by the Cardinal which was justified by the outcome. Like most attempts to impose patterns upon events to fit in with the career of an individual, this view is misleading. The Huguenot question, for instance, was seen by Richelieu as a permanent conspiracy against the state which was essentially the same in 1626 as it had been in 1620, and he dealt with it in the way indicated by the efforts and the partial success of his predecessors. Moreover Richelieu could not and did not confine his attentions exclusively to these political objectives. The early years of his administration were rich in plans for a variety of reforms in all fields, conceived in a purposeful and coordinated way. That some of these plans were no more novel than the problems they were designed to solve does not detract from his accomplishment; if anything, it is enhanced by being set alongside the work of Sully, the 'greybeards', Luynes and la Vieuville before him.

Like Richelieu, Sully belonged to the *noblesse d'épée* and was torn between the claims of privilege and the subordination that the state required. They thought alike on the place of the nobles and sought to accomplish their ends by the same means: drawing them into the apparatus of court and office, providing scope in the army, navy and diplomacy for royal service in an honourable but also manageable form, and at the same time striking at their castles and fiefs, terrorising rebels and dissidents. With a centralised

183

administrative structure, Sully reformed the finances to a point at
which the budget was balanced and a reserve created, set up a
directorate for communications, for the artillery and the fortifications. As *surintendant des bâtiments* he directed or encouraged a
building programme which made Paris a modern city and one of
the most beautiful in the world, witness in its new streets and
squares and improved palaces, the Louvre and the Place des
Vosges, to the sophisticated pride of an urban patriciate and to
the rôle of the city as the administrative centre of the state.

Even during the period from the death of Henry IV to the
battle of the Ponts de Cé there had been some constructive purpose
in the operations of the government. There were lavish distribu-
tions to the grandees, a feeble and wasteful policy of appeasement;
but at the same time attempts were made to secure a measure of
agreement for a programme of reform by means of Estates-
General, to reduce the *taille* in a humane and realistic way, and to
keep France out of war on the simple view that the country could
not afford it. There were also some initiatives of a constructive
sort, as for instance in 1616, at the request of the merchants, the
setting up of a *chambre générale du commerce*. Luynes introduced in
1617 a general retrenchment in government finance, and the
*paulette* was abolished (a short-lived measure). After 1619 more
purposeful military action was possible and the campaigns against
the Huguenots represent not only the right choice of priorities, as
we have seen, but also a sustained effort which made Richelieu's
subsequent task much easier.

After Luynes there had ensued a bitter struggle for power
between the Brûlarts (Chancellor Sillery and his son Secretary of
State Puisieux) and Charles la Vieuville. The career of the latter is
of particular interest as he was Richelieu's most formidable rival
at the outset. If he had not encountered the relentless opposition
of the Cardinal, he would undoubtedly have played a larger part in
French history. As it is, we can only guess what he would have
done. His father had risen in the service, first of the Duc de Nevers,
and then of Henry IV who made him Grand Falconer and then
lieutenant-general in Champagne. In 1612 Charles inherited his
father's military position and supported the government in the
years of civil war. He was made captain of the king's bodyguard in
1620 and it was in this capacity that he arrested the Cardinal de
Guise in the following year. Trusted by the king, proved by events
in the civil war, he was strengthened also by his contacts with an

influential group of financiers through his marriage to the daughter of Beaumarchais, a leading financier. Like Sully and Schomberg, the *surintendant* immediately before him, he combined military functions with financial administration; ties were commonly forming between the new plutocracy and politically ambitious members of the nobility. The intrusion of high finance into politics shows how indispensable the tax farmers, bankers and *rentiers* were becoming in the absence of a properly developed system of state credit. But it is most likely that in the case of la Vieuville, the king, with war imminent in Italy, considered it useful to have a military man in the top financial post. Even so, he was lucky to be promoted; the first choice, but for his death in 1622, would have been another soldier, Senecey, governor of Auxerre. La Vieuville's tactics in angling for the *surintendance* were similar to those by which he was later removed. He discredited Schomberg by exposing the parlous state of the revenues and he emphasised the *surintendant's* close connection with the ever-suspect Condé. La Vieuville came into office in 1623 with a firm undertaking to put the finances into good order. He was at first aided by the Brûlarts, who were confident in their control of key positions. Their successful diplomacy in northern Italy (the alliance between France, Venice and Savoy) and in the Rhineland, where they helped to secure Bavaria's electorate, postponed war and gave la Vieuville a chance to balance the budget. He reduced the size of the army and some pensions and salaries, secured more money from the financiers by threat of closer inspection, slightly raised the *taille* and made some new offices for sale. Far from favouring the financiers with whom he was supposed to be in league, he actually increased the price of certain tax farms. These measures were enacted amidst public controversy engendered by a flurry of pamphlets in some of which the hand of Richelieu has been seen. That he was actively concerned is certain; the most notable of his supporters was Fancan, who hammered away at the failings of the ministry in foreign affairs and at home. In *La Voix Publique au Roi* la Vieuville was accused of corrupt practices. Pamphlet writing provided a vehicle for individuals to influence policy; it also indicates an educated public capable of understanding political issues. Familiar themes were resumption of the war against the Huguenots, concern for the sorry state of the ordinary people, the reform of conditions of pay, discipline and, above all, billeting in the army and the reduction of the nobles' pensions.

La Vieuville not only acted in a way that showed sympathy with proposals for reform; he also went some way along his chosen path of economy. His downfall came because, like other finance ministers, he found that his plans for fiscal economy involved him in the consideration of foreign policy and he began to interfere in this field. His opposition to the Brûlarts went deeper than disagreement about means and ends; la Vieuville was undoubtedly ambitious to oust them. He was younger, and his activity and confidence had made some mark on the king. Both in the Val Telline and in Germany affairs seemed to demand French intervention if allies were to be maintained in good heart and strategic interests protected; the Brûlarts discovered that it was hard to have an effective foreign policy without adequate funds behind it. With the Spanish once more in the Val Telline the king was easily persuaded that the Brûlarts must go and in January Sillery was made to hand over the Seals, without which the Chancellor had no real power; they were given to a puppet. In February the Brûlarts were dismissed. But the problems remained, and now there was only one target for criticism, la Vieuville himself. By thus undermining his fellow-ministers, he exposed himself to Richelieu's determined thrust and, as we have seen, he lasted but a few months.

From this backward glance to the years before Richelieu came to power, we see something of the nature of the problems that faced him. He did not begin from an assured position to implement clearly defined objectives, but rather proceeded tentatively to meet the difficulties that had teased his predecessors. Nor on the other hand is it the case, as is so often asserted, that he had no understanding of economic problems. He was a man of his time in treating the needs of the state as a whole rather than as belonging to separate compartments, financial, diplomatic, military, and so on; he was also intelligent enough to base his planning on measures to increase his country's wealth. He was well aware of the fact that the country which was so amply endowed by nature, with fertile land, established manufactures, a long coastline and good harbours, was lagging behind both England and Holland in industrial production.

It is fashionable today to talk about a 'general crisis' as affecting in some degree all the countries of Europe, and as a common source for the interpretation of all the political and social struggles of the middle of the seventeenth century. Recent research, concentrating upon social and economic causes, has contributed to this idea from several angles. In one view[1] it is essentially a crisis of demand, the culmination of difficulties inherent in the pre-industrial economy from the fourteenth century. This crisis varied in intensity in different parts of Europe, being most severe in the Mediterranean countries, the Hanse towns and Germany, least so in the Netherlands, Sweden, Russia and England, France occupying an intermediate position. Decline or stagnation of population in most countries, the decline in output of certain industries, notably textiles, rapid falling-off in the years 1620-50 of the Baltic and Levant trades and shrinking of the Spanish and Portuguese empires, are called to witness to the extent of this crisis; further evidence is gleaned from the coincidence of social revolts: the English civil war, the Fronde, the Catalan, Neapolitan and Portuguese risings, the Ukrainian revolution of 1648-54, the Kurucz movements in Hungary, the Irish troubles in 1641 and Stenka Razin's rising in the Ukraine in 1672, not to mention recurring revolts in the provinces of France. This was therefore a crisis not merely of advanced capitalist economies but of the relatively backward ones as well. The causes lie in the social structure of a feudal, basically agrarian society, in obstacles in the way of conquering and maintaining overseas markets and in the narrowness of the home market. There was no way of ensuring the steady growth in effective demand which is the necessary condition of the investment required to promote and sustain capitalist production.

Another view (Mousnier's[2]) is grounded on the contrast between the 'boom' epoch of the sixteenth century and the sustained depression of the seventeenth century. Of prime importance is the disparity between the growth of population and the resources available for feeding it. To periodic famines must be added sharp fluctuations in prices, but with a persistent downward trend. The connection between economic conditions which were little better than catastrophic and the political and social trends of the time was direct: everywhere in Europe social antagonisms became more acute. In France chronic instability discouraged

[1] As notably presented by E. J. Hobsbawm, 'The General Crisis of the European Economy in the Seventeenth Century', *Past & Present*, vol. 5, 1954.

[2] As in vol. 4 of *Histoire Générale des Civilisations* (1953) and in 'Discussion of H. R. Trevor-Roper: The General Crisis of the Seventeenth Century', *Past & Present*, vol. 18, 1960.

investment and compelled capitalists to turn to making loans to the state: the social importance of the financiers and of financial and judicial officers increased, the sale of office grew, the 'official' class was consolidated in power. Merchant manufacturers, buying land, acquiring offices, participating in the business of government, grew in strength. Social antagonisms grew out of the advance in political power of the larger landowner, the new plutocrat, the monopolist, the courtier. The conditions of a class struggle can be seen in the revolts of 1630-59 but rebels were opposed as much to the officers of government, notably tax-farmers who embodied the alliance of authority and capitalism, as to the possessors of property and wealth.

In a few lines it is impossible to convey the range, depth and originality of these arguments; in detail they lie beyond the scope of this study but the questions they raise are relevant to our study of Richelieu. A very wide variety of interpretations is open to historians who try to find common causes and a comprehensive framework for the historical development of different countries. In trying to escape from the old faults of separate national histories with their narrowly political outlook, their insularity and blindness to the economic and social factors in a common culture, they run new risks. If an argument is based upon study of the available economic evidence, most of which is still unexplored, then the whole argument may be upset by a relatively minor piece of research. When one considers the way in which economic analysts can derive widely different conclusions from agreed data, it is not surprising that historians will differ fundamentally, even if they share a common method and viewpoint, when the evidence is uncertain.[1]

An example of the difficulties that the historian faces when trying to assess different interpretations is provided by the researches and views of Mousnier and the Marxist historian Porchnev[2] who was the first to use extensively the Séguier papers in Leningrad. Marxist economic analysis and the evidence provided by the correspondence of the Chancellor who was a central figure

[1] Thus the Russian historian Lublinskaya, tackling Hobsbawm on his own ground, rejects his conclusions, along with others, largely because of her reading of evidence that at least half Europe was exempt from the 'crisis' phenomena.

[2] B. Porchnev. *Les soulèvements populaires en France de 1623 à 1648.* Paris, 1961. (Original Russian ed. 1948.)

through the period from the *croquants* to the Fronde combine to form a view which is too dogmatic to be entirely convincing: Porchnev sees the French absolutist state as the instrument by which the dominant and privileged economic class exploited the masses. The Marxist dialectic of class struggle is provided in this instance by two opposed forces: the people against the machinery of the state. The weakness of Marxist historians, and their fellow-travellers, is that they impose too rigid a pattern and over-simplify in order to sustain it. Porchnev, for instance, fails to make allowances for the ramifications of his dominant class and its often divergent interests: local officials opposed to the central government, *intendants*, the administrators, opposed to *traitants,* whose interest was primarily financial. Naturally Mousnier, uninhibited by dogma and with a wider range of evidence to draw upon, is critical of Porchnev's thesis.[1] His study of the evidence leads him to conclude that the 'dominant class' idea is meaningless: the nobility itself was engaged in a struggle against increasing state-interference. The office-holders were, however, by and large agents of the central government. The latter statement is open to criticism. There was a continuous movement from the ranks of the upper office-holding bourgeoisie into the nobility: in 1644 all the magistrates in Parlement were granted hereditary noble status. Were they still bourgeois at heart? Does their opposition, for example, to the *intendants* suggest that they were in accord with the central government?

The rôle of Parlement is also an awkward piece in the fascinating pattern constructed by Trevor-Roper. It is immensely stimulating to read him on the general crisis.[2] He draws attention usefully to the weaknesses of the term 'absolutism' as applied to the political systems of the period and substitutes for it 'Renaissance State' in which political power is implemented by a monarch with a bureaucratic machine. It was against this state, swollen, un-manageable, with structural defects that invited opposition, that

---

[1] R. Mousnier. 'Recherches sur les soulèvements populaires en France avant la Fronde', in *Revue d'histoire moderne et contemporaine*, vol. V, 1958.
[2] H. Trevor-Roper, 'The General Crisis of the Seventeenth Century', *Past & Present*, vol. 16, 1959. The article was followed by a symposium on the General Crisis, *Past & Present*, vol. 18, 1960, which has been reprinted in book form as *Crisis in Europe, 1560-1660*, ed. T. Aston, London, 1965.

the revolutions of the seventeenth century were directed, revolutions which prepared the way for the states characteristic of the age of 'enlightened despotism'. One weakness of this argument lies in the way in which it is developed through a key concept, that of 'puritanism', which covers all expressions of protest against the extravagance of the Renaissance court, no longer after about 1620 sustained by the riches of an advancing economy. So far as French history goes, the idea of a revolt of the country against the court and the machinery of the state is simply not sustained by the facts. The popular risings were not primarily, as we have seen, revolts against court and bourgeoisie, unless one defines bourgeoisie as that small section of the office-holders who were directly serving the government. Seigneurs, officials, peasants joined hands against the commissaries sent out by the government: the struggle was between the old bureaucracy, allied with local interests, and the new agents of the government, whom local officials, and Parlement too in the Fronde, conceived to be damaging their vital interests.

The widespread criticism that Trevor-Roper's scheme has provoked testifies to its value as a contribution to debate, but serves also as a reminder of the danger of using terms derived essentially from the experience of one country to interpret the history of other countries; more generally, perhaps, the danger of creating any sort of scheme into which the facts have to be fitted: servant then becomes master in history's Liberty Hall. Historians should not be mesmerised by the coincidence of revolts into exaggerating their significance in every case. The first half of the century should be seen in the context of the centuries before and after it, not merely in relation to the spectacular events of the middle period.

The government, unpopular as it evidently was, weakened by the fact that the king was a minor, reasserted its authority with surprising speed after 1652. Short-term causes can be detected in the major revolts of Richelieu's time, as later in the Fronde: new measures provoked the opposition of the conservatives, the resentment of tax-payers. Peasant revolts were nothing new, but a traditional and natural exercise of local resentments in a very large and unwieldy country. There were few signs of the revolutionary outlook which might be expected in a 'general crisis'. Neither king nor church came into the various categories of complaint. This was a society in which men were prepared to stand up for their interests and rights. It was not fundamentally an unstable society.

An all-embracing interpretation of society may lead to unsatisfactory or contradictory answers; a further danger is that the wrong questions are asked. The questions we have to ask are these: how did Richelieu see the problems that he inherited—at just the time when all historians are agreed, though of course it would not be at once plain to contemporaries, that there was beginning that decline in prices which ushered in a prolonged depression of demand? And what was available to him in the way of opinion and analysis; what ideas were current? For evidence we have a large body of contemporary writing, usually labelled mercantilist, about the wealth, trade and the state, and the important meetings of the *notables* in 1626.

Of the writers who expressed the aspirations of the moneyed community in these years when religious and political struggles were beginning to lose some of their interest for educated Frenchmen, and *politique*, *bon français* attitudes were becoming widespread, Laffemas and Montchrétien were most important. Barthélemy Laffemas had been a useful man at Henry IV's court in Navarre and was eager to adapt his ideas to the larger scale of national policy when his master give him the chance. Henry made him president of an 'assembly of commerce' which contained seventeen of the most prominent experts at court, held 176 sessions between 1602 and 1604 and gave a thorough airing, not merely to the ideas of Laffemas but also to the more moderate ones of the assembly of *notables* which had met in 1597. Laffemas believed that new industries should be encouraged at all costs, by protecting them against foreign competition, by giving them monopolies at home, by letting raw materials into the country duty free, and by learning new methods from foreigners who were to be encouraged to work in France with French apprentices. He further wanted taxes on home-produced goods to be dropped or, as was eventually done, simplified into one fixed tax on all of them. He urged uniform weights and measures and a system of guilds to cover the whole country. 'Simplify and centralise' was his sensible theme and he lived to see some of his ideas implemented.

The power of the guilds was extended by an edict of 1597 putting new crafts on the same footing as the old ones. The crown soon gained control of the guilds, through *intendants*, royal courts specially set up for guild cases and using Roman law procedure, and in 1626, the institution of officials whose job it was to supervise particular industries. Certain industries were directly run by the state, like gunpowder manufacture, which, under Sully, was in the hands of royal contractors, and mines, which were brought effectively under national administration by a series of important edicts. Production in the gold, silver, copper, lead and tin mines was encouraged by the state: the workers were allowed to be exempt from the *taille* and nobles were urged to start mining on their own account, without, however, much response. The state was entitled by Roman law to the royalties. Acting on this principle the salt industry was massively exploited and a large administrative staff was created to collect the *gabelle* or salt tax, as well as to prevent the smuggling which grew as the inevitable result of an unnatural market situation. Laffemas was given many chances to experiment. In the grand gallery of the Louvre a school for fine arts and crafts was set up; money was lent to the leading workers, clock and instrument makers, silversmiths, cutlers, perfumiers, the *élite* of France's craftsmen, and they were encouraged to pass on discoveries to their pupils. These men were exempt from the guild organisation but elsewhere it was restrictive. There is a crucial paradox here, in the expansive aims of the state and the restrictive means it adopted to achieve them, for the guilds were inevitably concerned with preserving the profitable *status quo*.

Significant as Laffemas was, it is to Antoine de Montchrétien that we turn for a fuller understanding of 'political economy', to use a term which first appeared as the title of his famous treatise, written for the king's ministers in 1614 and published in 1615. A Norman, born in 1575, enriched by marriage to a wealthy widow, killed in 1621 while recruiting soldiers for the Huguenots, Montchrétien tackled in his writing the problem which was as important for France then as it is for 'under-developed' economies today: that of creating the conditions for advance where natural resources existed in abundance but capital and trained skills were lacking, and foreign enterprise therefore played a disproportionate part, keeping the French out of lucrative markets and providing goods and services which the French should have been providing themselves. Largely responsible for this state of affairs was the long duration of the religious wars, during which time the English and Dutch gained, as the French lost, in commercial strength. The English were challenging French merchants in the Levant and the Dutch were establishing themselves in the Mediterranean, and were edging their rivals out of Senegal and Guinea and were appearing in Canada. In Henry IV's reign there was a revival of French trade but after his death a relapse, as it seems, to the position in the seventies and eighties; when the government was bullied at home it could not maintain its rights abroad. The state of the currency underlined the need for reform. After Henry IV had established a sound gold and silver coinage, this good money was being smuggled out of the country while bad flowed in. Montchrétien alleged that Flemish exchangers operating in France were making large profits out of their transactions. France could suffer the fate of Spain, where there had been a similar flight of good money.

Essentially Montchrétien was an industrialist rather than a 'mercantilist' in that he was interested in increase in manufactures before foreign trade, navigation and colonies. Believing that everything depended on the workers' skills and therefore on their training, he laid down an exact sequence for industrial development, starting with metal and proceeding with textiles and leather, printing and glass, all industries which could be made cheaper by technical improvements. He wanted the state not so much to organise the whole economy or to concern itself with trade (both essential to Colbert's more ambitious plans) as to direct the economic development of the country at certain selected points. At the same time it was the duty of the state to hold the ring: to protect against foreign competition, to ensure domestic peace, to tax fairly. In due course it should create a strong merchant marine and found trading companies on the model of the East India Company to reap the rewards of industrial enterprise. Montchrétien owned an ironworks; he had also visited England and Holland, and his ideas reflect his experience and his practical interest in economic development. As the voice of *le populaire,* the Third Estate, which he regarded as the most important part, *le premier fondement* of society, his ideas help to correct impressions of the age formed mainly by the doings of the administration and the nobility: with Montchrétien we are in that other France, of solid bourgeois, who were building themselves the tall, solid mansions in the formal style which provides many French towns today with their characteristic centre; they bought offices and sometimes land, patronised the theatre and frequented *salons* and, if they had social ambitions, secured titles for themselves, impoverished noblemen for their daughters and army commissions or Church preferment for their sons. At the top of the pyramid there were tycoons,

N

financiers, merchants, lawyers who might feel they had some
weight in the state, but the social and political influence of the
class as a whole was negligible compared to their wealth and
worth. In Italy and England, according to Montchrétien, merchants were highly regarded, in Holland they were dominant. The
Dutch, combining the business ability, *ménagerie*, of the English
with the industriousness of the French, were leading the world in
trade and their country was growing richer than Spain, but in
France the monarchy which could brush off the protests of
Parlements, the pleas of merchants, presided over a court and
culture which remained aristocratic in tone even while it reduced
the political independence of the aristocracy. At the same time,
bourgeois wealth played an inadequate part in the economic life
of the country. Investment and initiative in manufacture, without
which France could not realise her potential, came second to 'safe'
investment in land, offices and funds: in 1614, according to one
estimate, the bourgeois derived an income of 6 million livres a
year from land alone. These defects were deep rooted in French
society and the forms of government it had produced. That they
persisted in the seventeenth century, despite the efforts of successive ministers, notably Sully, Richelieu and Colbert, is well known.
All the same, Montchrétien's imaginative ideas indicate that they
were not past curing.

Montchrétien believed that France's failure to create wealth
commensurate with the numbers and talents of her people was due
primarily to the lack of scope for people to use these talents to
advantage. So French workmen found employment abroad, in
Spain, Flanders and Germany. Amongst the remedies he suggested were technical training, with facilities in every province,
provided by the government; compulsory labour for vagabonds
and beggars; the division of labour in factories in accordance with
the experience and capacity of the workers; curtailment of the
privileges of foreigners; a new tax system based upon an income
tax to be paid by all and accompanied by a detailed statistical
survey which could be used also for recruitment and for planning
in other fields; colonies as outlets for the products of the mother
country. Although specially interested in metal working, Montchrétien began his enumeration of industries, in the order in which
they benefited the state, with agriculture. He analyses it with more
insight than most of his contemporaries, singling out as special
evils the facts that landowners did not manage their own estates

but leased them out, that peasants owning little land themselves were not inclined to work hard and improve the land, that the soil was exhausted by too much cropping for quick profits, that taxes were too high and weighed most heavily upon the peasant.

In the trade that he knew best he produced figures which reveal in the microcosm of a craft that employed half a million, 'like salamanders in the fire', the weakness of the country as a whole: since French-made scythes and sickles were twice as expensive as German, because the French insisted on high quality metal and there were no iron-masters who would spend money on *engins* and improved processes, over 800,000 livres were spent yearly on foreign tools. He wanted to abolish quality controls so that French scythes could meet the needs of the peasant market: with an assured market would come progress in methods of production. 'Nothing brings cheapness so much as plenty, plenty comes from the work of many men, and there can be no shortage of work for them if the goods they produce sell well.' Dealing with the textile industry he finds evidence for the need for protection and does not shrink from its consequences. The French, he said, made the best linen and canvas and exported it, so that Spanish ships were rigged with French sails, but the French were losing their secrets to foreign rivals; the Dutch in particular were setting up factories in France, being more willing to invest than their French counter-parts, while the English were being allowed to flood the country with cloth that was inferior in texture and dyes. Though the French were capable of weaving their own silk, this was largely imported (on stockings alone, 3 million livres a year were spent) and the French were therefore failing to exploit the growing demand for fine silks amongst the rich and fashionable. Colbert was later, with some success, to make the silk industry a prime target in his commercial planning. From leather work, printing and paper manufacture, Montchrétien drew similar conclusions. The government must therefore act positively and come to the aid of businessmen. 'Have courage then, Most Christian Majesties, and carry through this great task, making glorious your reign thereby.'

This appeal was made in 1614, the year of the States-General, when the ministers of the boy king, harassed by the demands of the magnates and alarmed by the danger of embroilment with foreign powers, were pursuing a policy of cautious appeasement. France's need to maintain her political alliances was being exploited by England, Spain and Holland, who, so it seemed to French merchants, were shamelessly violating the rights granted to French merchants by the commercial treaties of Henry IV. Montchrétien provides evidence for the way in which French goods and merchants were being discriminated against; clearly the political and economic problems of France merge at this point. Not until Richelieu had achieved real power, had dealt with the Huguenots, had shown *les grands* that the king was master of his own house, could he set about putting his house in order. That he was determined to do so may be seen by the proposals and measures of his early years.

From the instructions of deputies to the States-General in 1614 and the burgeoning pamphlet literature of the time we find that Montchrétien was exceptional only in the range and force of his ideas and writing. There appears to have been a consensus in bourgeois circles, at least about the nature of the problem if not about specific remedies. The composite mandate of the *Tiers Etât* dealing with trade and urging further protection might have been written by Montchrétien. Richelieu must have been influenced not only by the public debate but by the propaganda that accompanied it. He would be familiar with the general problem that France was falling behind in the intense competition in the markets of Europe and also with the special local difficulties: for example, the quarrels between towns and provinces which made it so hard to decide on a common policy. The merchants of Marseilles had become so used to looking after themselves through their own trading organisation that they were unwilling to subscribe to a national policy which meant sharing their privileges. The towns of Brittany and Normandy were always at loggerheads; Catholics were jealously aware that the Huguenots had secured privileges and profits out of proportion to their numbers. Essentially, of course, the mercantile community of France were as ready to work and venture as their Dutch and English rivals. But before they would invest in trading companies or join in corporate efforts they had to be persuaded that such companies could operate profitably. They looked to the state to provide the framework and support for their efforts, and petitions and proposals were showered upon the king and council.

Nor was the government inactive in the years after the death of Henry IV. In 1616 a *Chambre Générale du Commerce* was set up at the request of the merchants. Plans were drawn up for the creation of new maritime orders of chivalry, with their own fleets to hunt down pirates and protect French ships. The main effect of such plans was to convince Richelieu that the state must have its own fleet. Some large trading companies were formed: the *Compagnie de Montmorency pour les Indes Orientales* in 1611 and the *Compagnie de Montmorency pour la Nouvelle-France* (1620). Their name came from the Admiral of France at that time, the capital was raised by shareholders who were mainly merchants and shipowners, and they were managed by a *Collège des Directeurs* and an *intendant* appointed by the Admiral. For a number of reasons these companies floundered. Ship-building was more costly in France than in Holland or England. French ports were mostly shallow, the ships therefore had to be of small tonnage, about 200 tons as against the 1,000-2,000 ton vessels which could show big returns on oceanic voyages. The seamanship was good but the discipline casual, not least because so many foreign sailors were used. Protectionist measures in Spain in the 1620s closed the Spanish and American markets to all French goods other than grain, linen and haberdashery. The acute deflation of prices in Spain also told against the French, who had long enjoyed an advantage in the disparity of prices between the two countries. The competition was ruthless everywhere but just as damaging were the rivalries at home, where import firms with established connections were threatened by the new concerns with their monopoly rights.

The measures taken by Spain to protect her crumbling position antagonised French merchants. So far from supporting the government's attempts at appeasement they favoured war (the Huguenot element in the western ports always saw Spain as the natural enemy) and their mood undoubtedly influenced Richelieu in his foreign policy. Some reacted by seeking new markets, in the Baltic, Russia, in the Near and Far East, North Africa and America. There were voyages of Norman and Breton merchants to Java and Sumatra in 1620-3, a group of Norman merchants formed to trade in Senegal, French Capuchin missionaries co-operated with merchants in the Near East; there was a growing interest in colonies. The memorandum of Isaac de Razilly, submitted to Richelieu in 1626, provides evidence of this activity and also, since Razilly was well known to Richelieu and was to become one of his intimate advisers, points to Richelieu's direct interest in this subject. Razilly's arguments may have impressed the Cardinal particularly because of the particular danger he was facing at the time, as he contemplated the reduction of La Rochelle without proper naval resources. But Razilly ranged beyond considerations of security and profit and his imaginative speculations accorded well with Richelieu's passionate nationalism, his taste for heroic enterprise. What Razilly wanted was a decided shift of emphasis from military to naval expenditure; he proposed, for instance, the disbandment of fortresses other than those on the frontier. He looked for a flow of money into colonising enterprise from courtiers, financiers and cities, with the king and Richelieu taking the lead. The French should trade with the west coast of Africa, where the Portuguese presented little effective opposition, and with Persia, avoiding Turkey by an ocean voyage round Africa and up the Persian gulf. His greatest enthusiasm was reserved for the eastern shore of South America where he believed that strong colonies could establish themselves to exploit its fabled wealth. This would be a tolerable substitute for the plundering which had enriched Spain, Holland and England but which relied upon a power at sea greater than France possessed.

## 16. Economic Depression: Colonies and Commerce

The meeting of the States-General in 1614 was the last before 1789. In 1626 an assembly of *notables* met at Fontainebleau, again the last before 1787, when they were summoned to consider the bankruptcy of the Bourbon monarchy. The constitutional history of this assembly is obscure and also confused by association with the States-General. In origin in the thirteenth century the *notables* were simply prominent persons invited by the king to consider matters on which he needed extra advice; such meetings were rare in the fourteenth and fifteenth centuries but in 1558 the idea took a new lease of life with the summoning of individuals to what was called a States-General but at which representatives of the officials met alongside selected members of the three Estates. Upon this model, though on a smaller scale, meetings were held occasionally; the last had been at Rouen in 1617. They were comparatively small, about fifty attending: bishops, court nobles and leading law officers. They came by invitation and therefore without local mandate, though no doubt they were open to lobbying. In session they debated and answered specific questions put to them by the government. They voted by counting heads, which gave the officials a small majority over court and episcopal elements combined. Whereas nobles and churchmen did not represent their estates, the officials did represent their own courts, which were therefore bound to carry out decisions of the *notables*. Indeed, an important reason for the summoning of the *notables* was the wish of the government to bind Parlements to register fiscal edicts which should follow the assembly: in 1617 the main one enacted the abolition of the *paulette*, in 1626 Richelieu had more extensive proposals of financial reform.

Sully had begun the arduous operation of redeeming the royal demesne, providing for a period of sixteen years, by the end of which the crown's land and offices should be returned, free of debt, by the financiers to whom the operation was entrusted; meanwhile they had the right to use the revenues. In 1615, however, the partly redeemed offices and lands were mortgaged once more. Richelieu now wanted a more drastic redemption over a six-year period, and money to start the process. He intended to buy back some of the demesne and use the proceeds progressively to redeem the rest. The assembly met in Paris in December 1626. Keeper of the Seals Marillac opened the proceedings with a discourse upon the state of France, Schomberg spoke of the army and Richelieu about finance. Marillac and Richelieu seem to have been working upon agreed lines and Richelieu left it to his Keeper of the Seals to explain the financial problem. Because of special payments, notably the campaign against the Huguenots and the Italian war, expenses, at 40 million, were more than double receipts at 16 million. Yet the government had not increased the *taille* or reduced official salaries or interest rates on *rentes*. Despite projected savings on court upkeep, army and certain offices, notably those of Constable and Admiral which Richelieu was to take over without remuneration (pursuing his political design in the process of financial reform), the revenue must be increased or the people must suffer. Using material provided by Richelieu, Marillac dwelt hopefully on the results of the upsurge of trade that would follow the government's measures: new trading companies, new canals and other projects which the *notables* were invited to consider. Richelieu in turn stressed that more direct taxation was unthinkable for 'les peuples ne scauroient plus porter'. Redemption of the demesne would, however, bring eventually another 20 million livres' revenue with all the confidence that would accrue from such good management. The crown could exact better terms from tax-farmers, and Parlements would not be called on to register new edicts.

It was a golden age indeed to which Richelieu invited the *notables* to look—but they were not enchanted. Procedural difficulties bedevilled the early sessions as the officials objected to the crown's proposal that voting should be by estate. They yielded reluctantly. The army plan, with measures to regulate recruitment and pay and improve discipline and training, was largely approved. The main debate was, however, about finance. The nobles attacked the office-holders, while the officials called for a reduction of pensions. Richelieu tried to shake them out of their class concerns and compel them to think about the critical state of the nation. D'Effiat, recently appointed *surintendant* and a close ally, gave some alarming figures. He had found on coming to office that there had been an annual deficit since 1610 of over 5 million livres, that some short-term loans had recently been accepted at rates of interest as high as 30 per cent, that confusion if not corruption arose from the fact that in some cases the royal treasurers were lending money on their own account. Of 19 million livres collected as *taille*, only about 6 million reached the Treasury after passing through the hands of 22,000 local collectors, 160 regional collectors and 21 collectors-general. Of the 7,400,000 livres of *gabelle* collected, only 1,100,000 reached the Treasury, and the rest was mortgaged. Revenue for the first quarter was already spent and some regiments had been waiting for their pay for up to a year. The situation called for urgent, sacrificial remedy. Without war the budget might be balanced; any sort of war would at once upset the equilibrium. This certainty was the master-factor in all planning. While war provided the obvious, if not always the only, solution to the state's political problems, the state lacked the resources to make war effectively. Was Richelieu, knowing that a major campaign must be mounted against the Huguenots and that the European war was likely to continue for some time with the growing danger that France would become involved, simply deceiving himself when he advanced his proposals for reform? There were two main conditions of success: a prolonged period of peace and cooperation from the *notables*; as neither of these materialised the question remains open.

Richelieu presented to the *notables*, in the king's name, certain propositions which amounted, with his own explanatory comments, to a comprehensive programme of reform. They reveal the workings of his mind at a time when several options were apparently open to him, before he was carried along by the logic of events to a point at which his foreign policy meant expensive commitment and his domestic policy became a succession of expedients. Representing the political intentions of the ablest servant of the Bourbon kings, a man who perfectly understood that politics was the art of the possible, these propositions are more valuable even than his *Testament*, where art took a hand and the precise formulations were composed with an eye to posterity.

They can be grouped in two parts: those which were concerned with the order of the realm in general and those which were more specifically financial. The *notables* were invited to draw up lists of fortresses which could be abolished and to decide upon the size of garrison to be maintained in those which survived: a realistic approach to the Huguenot question. The provinces were to undertake the payment of these garrisons and to accept the charge of maintaining a proportion of the army. The avowed object of this was to save the Treasury the cost of these garrisons and the people from the depredations of the soldiers. Another advantage would be that there could be a useful reduction in the financial establishment. Many collectors of the *taille* would become redundant. So far from putting more power into the hands of local officials and Parlements, the government would be strengthened in the provinces through the *intendants*, whom Richelieu already envisaged using more generally. The various actions that constituted *lèse majesté* were precisely defined: unauthorised recruitment of soldiers, acquisition of guns and munitions, pacts with foreign ambassadors, fortifying cities and *châteaux*, assemblies, publication of political pamphlets, and other components of rebellion. Resistance to the king's will, *désobéissance*, was to be punished not by *peine capitale*, which was usually rescinded, but by forfeiture of offices and appointments, on the assumption that the certainty of loss of status would be a greater deterrent for most nobles than the possibility of death. A strong loyalist element was already coming to the fore: the crown's sane attitudes encouraged moderate, patriotic men to serve the state. The levies of private individuals were condemned; as Richelieu said, 'Whoever has money can find as many soldiers in France as he wants', and certain grandees were powerful enough to collect money in their own districts. These proposals should be seen in the context of the suppression of the offices of Admiral and Constable and Richelieu's whole drive against the provincial governors. On a constructive note, the crown proposed to introduce into council certain *sages gentilhommes* to train them in state affairs, which reminds us of Richelieu's constant concern about the divorce between the aristocracy and administration; he wanted the aristocracy to give the sort of political service that he and his father before him gave. A travelling assize such as was sent out to the Auvergne in the 1660s, the *Chambre des Grands Jours*, was envisaged to hear complaints against powerful officials and lords: Richelieu explained tactfully that this was specially needed in provinces where there was no Parlement. *Sergents*, petty local officials, should be reduced, for they were a 'menace to the people'.

The *taille* came first, of course, in the financial proposals: the *notables* were asked to consider seriously the question of exemptions, with a view to reducing the load on the poorer peasants. The theme of relief of poverty running through these proposals appears again in the crown's request to *premiers présidents* to advise from their local experience on the best means of controlling grain prices and preventing speculation. The assembly were asked finally to involve themselves in the main business of state finance, by reviewing the budget, considering where priorities lay and where economies could be made. With an eye not only on increasing the revenue but finding the means of reducing the *taille* at once (it was reduced by 600,000 livres in 1627), the *notables* were asked not merely to approve the redemption of the demesne but to find funds for this purpose. The Cardinal dwelt on this scheme in a way which suggests the importance he attached to it. He asked for a new effort to raise 'un fonds extra-ordinaire qui en engendre un autre qui soit ordinaire et qui dure toujours' and he went out of his way to assure his no doubt sceptical audience that such a fund would be used exclusively for the purpose of redemption and pledged his honour to the carrying through of this 'si glorieux dessein'.

So the *notables* were left with carefully loaded alternatives: they could search for some other means of helping the people and increasing the revenue—but there were no such other means; they could accept the present position, but this would be unworthy. There was careful calculation in this approach: it was generally accepted that redemption of the demesne was the soundest way of restoring the fortunes of the crown. Since, however, Richelieu is usually portrayed as an entirely heartless intellectual, condemned out of his own mouth by those maxims of his which suggest a pitiless and cynical view of the ordinary Frenchman, it is well to record that when he was talking the language of practical politics rather than diverting himself with maxims for the *salons*, even allowing for his tactical need to talk in terms of 'the people' and the rhetorical touches appropriate to his subject, he appears conscious of the need to avoid war and to create the conditions for a fairer society. Just because he appreciated the difficulties of carrying out a policy of fiscal and social improvement, he is not therefore to be judged incapable in economic matters. Nor was he, one suspects, so objective in appraisal as those found who met him only on formal occasions. He suffered from nervous and intestinal disorders which tried his will to breaking point. His position was painfully lonely, despite the growing number of loyal associates, and at this time it was also precarious. In these days, when he was making every effort of intelligence and will to secure a favourable response from the country's leaders, he used metaphors of sickness in a way that suggests his own pains and worries. The grudging response of the *notables* was a tragedy for France and it left its mark on Richelieu, on body and mind; hopes were blighted and plans modified and in the process of reassessment he learned to limit his aims, to expect little from mere human agency.

The proceedings of the assembly were business-like. On Richelieu's suggestion, separate commissions were formed for army and financial affairs. The Estates then discussed the resolutions prepared by these commissions. A serious quarrel arose, predictably, over the Gallican question: was the nuncio an ambassador and was he therefore to be included in the prohibition of dealings with foreign ambassadors? The officials displeased the king and clergy by insisting that he was. The *notables* drew up a list of fortresses to be razed, accepted the proposals concerning the inclusion of members of the lower nobility in Council, the regulation of the grain trade and price of bread, and the collection of the *taille,* but rejected the extra proposal to extend the *taille réelle* to all the provinces of France. They also rejected the idea of *Grands Jours.* Concerning the abolition of minor offices they decided that compensation should be paid in full and at once, rather than in *rentes* at $6\frac{1}{4}$ per cent until the capital of the debt which the government wished to redeem should be paid: they thus rejected the working fund Richelieu asked for. Furthermore they accepted billeting of the army in the provinces only if two-thirds of the upkeep were paid for by the state. They agreed to the government's estimate for naval building and the plan for forming trading companies, so long as edicts instituting the latter were registered by Parlement. About the need for a strong navy there was general agreement (but it will be noticed that here there were relatively few special interests to defend). A deputation of the *notables* led by the Bishop of Chartres accepted the crown's proposals for trade and navy and declared that Cardinal Richelieu was the right man for the office of *Grand Maître et Surintendant du Commerce et de la Navigation.* This was timely support for Richelieu, who was facing concerted opposition by the Parlements to the registration of the edict appointing him to this office. Unfortunately the separate statements by the nobles and officials of the claims of their respective orders showed how inward-looking these men were. The *noblesse de l'épée* complained about their decline in status alongside the new official nobility. They demanded, as they had in 1614, the monopoly of ownership of fiefs ('noble' land), a third of the places in the king's council, reservation of a third of ecclesiastical benefices, and the establishment of military schools without fees. It is likely that Richelieu listened to these ideas, which corresponded to some extent to his own view of the place of nobility in society, with more sympathy than to those of the officials, who were determined to yield no ground to the state. They claimed greater power for Parlements, notably in the registration of contracts of tax farms, they protested against the activities of *intendants* and called for the abolition of that post.

Against the backing for Richelieu's naval plans had to be set the rejection of the financial manœuvres upon which these and other state projects depended. The government had presented the *notables* with its problems and the *notables* had handed them back unsolved. Divided, reactionary, defensive, the *notables* had failed, and in failing had declared themselves redundant. Richelieu and his fellow-ministers must go on less by deliberate design than by the patent impossibility of achieving progress in any other way to build up the machinery of absolute government. In the face of obstruction by grandees and Parlements the royal government must go on. This meant in practice that *intendants* were given more work to do. It also meant that taxes were increased, that more loans were raised (in 1627-9 loans brought about 18 million a year into the Treasury, about 40 per cent of total receipts) and more offices created in order to be sold. The power of the state was outwardly enhanced as the rebels were defeated and Parlements subdued. But the state grew upon insecure foundations; it was a weakness that persisted to the end, until the Revolution, when *notables* and then the Estates met once more to consider the state of the nation.

After 1626 it was evident that commercial plans had to be modified at least until fiscal conditions improved; this was a remote prospect after the decisions of the *notables* even before the declaration of open war in 1635 committed Richelieu to spending far more than could be raised by existing taxes. It is not, therefore, surprising that there was a vast difference between what Richelieu projected and what he achieved. He was never able to concentrate for long upon the economic development that he knew to be urgent. And yet the years of Richelieu were not barren in the economic sphere. Like his successor Mazarin he was increasingly taken up with the short-term necessities of finance and his *surintendants* were primarily tax-raisers searching intensively, even recklessly, to find the means of financing a war without bankruptcy or revolt. Richelieu was content to leave this business to them. He would even profess to be ignorant in matters of finance. To Bullion, joint *surintendant* with Bouthillier after 1632, a loyal ally though always protesting that he was at the end of his tether, he said: 'I confess fully my ignorance in financial matters and realise that your knowledge is so vast that the only advice I can give you is to use those people whom you will find most useful to the king's service, and I assure you that I will second you in every way'. He would speak loftily of money as merely a means to a greater end: 'For no sum of money is the safety of the state too dearly bought'. What else could he do? We should not be misled by such rhetoric. Overworked and preoccupied as he was with the life-and-death struggle with Spain he did not cease to be an imaginative and skilled projector; nor did he lose the instinct for economy and good management that he displayed in handling his own estates.

Inevitably his thinking was 'mercantilist', drawing upon the conventional reasoning of a society in which merchants were the dynamic element and were beginning to compel governments to think of their interests; analyses and solutions to their problems were couched in terms which were similar if not identical in England, Holland or France. 'Mercantilism' (a term which seventeenth century writers did not use but was coined incidentally in the physiocrat era), was essentially a form of economic nationalism. Theory and practice grew piecemeal with little intellectual coherence or system. In France, for instance, it can be traced back at least to the fifteenth century and to a concern that was widely expressed in edicts, *cahiers* and debates about the loss of money, expenditure on costly goods made elsewhere and payments to the Papacy, for it was one of the elements in Gallicanism. There was much sheer prejudice against foreigners and simple, almost superstitious reverence for gold and silver; the special interests of monopolists and the restrictive outlook of the guilds played their part. As the European states took on more commitments and found themselves affected by the rapid inflation in the costs of war in the sixteenth century, it became painfully obvious that there was a direct connection between the material well-being of subjects and the solvency and effectiveness of the state.

'The wealth of subjects is the wealth of the king.' The author of the *Discourse of the Common Weal*, which was written in 1594 and was an early specimen of a sort of literature that was to become plentiful, was uttering a commonplace. The twentieth century reader will not feel disposed to treat as scornfully as did his predecessors the apparent obsession of seventeenth century governments with a favourable balance of trade. In France, as we have seen, anxiety about the outflow of money and the languishing state of native trade and manufactures was grounded on hard facts. The distinctive character of French writing on the subject lies in the stress on self-sufficiency. Bodin, Laffemas, Montchrétien, Richelieu all noted the contrasts between France's potential wealth and her actual state and saw salvation in intensive, aggressive exploitation and marketing of her own resources and skills. In Richelieu this is joined naturally to a keen awareness of the political and strategic issues. He specifically linked power and wealth as twin and complementary objectives. Surely there is little need for the great debate as to which of these objectives loomed largest in mercantilist theory? As well distinguish between motives of religion and state in the protagonists of the Thirty Years War. Men of the time simply did not make such distinctions which belong to a later, more fragmented approach in politics, as in intellectual life. Richelieu stressed the value of ships to take by force what could not be taken by trade because he was a practical politician envisaging the actual conditions of war with Spain; in spirit he was no different from the 'pacific' Colbert, who approved the war with Holland as a short-cut to supremacy in trade and said of the expenditure of the king upon the prestige building of Versailles: 'When your glory is at stake, what do the millions matter?'

Richelieu was grappling throughout with the problem of order and this colours his attitude to economic matters. 'Les peuples', he said, 'deviennent ingouvernables avec l'aisance.' Colbert, too, devoted much time to lecturing his *intendants* on the uses of industry as the foundation of social order. The Cardinal is hardly to be blamed for the way in which his economic objectives (busy manufactures at home, expanding trade abroad) were interfered with by the obstruction of the privileged and the exigencies of war. Rather, surely it is one mark of his stature that he never lost sight of these objectives?

More than any other statesman of the *ancien régime* Richelieu appreciated the importance of colonies. The companies that he formed or encouraged were important, even decisive, in establishing France, belatedly, in the colonial field. He believed in colonies as a means of securing advantages from that self-sufficiency and strength at sea that he intended to create. The story of these companies reveals, however, a two-way process: they grew both by private initiatives and state support. The *Compagnie de Cent Associés* (or *du Morbihan*) attracted the support of businessmen like François Fouquet, father of Louis XIV's first *surintendant* and of Père Joseph, who was interested in the missionary opportunities that might arise from trade and settlement. The non-noble members acquired automatically the privilege of hereditary nobility, a potent attraction. The company was given exclusive rights in Nouvelle France, or Canada. The towns of Brittany raised a loud protest against this monopoly and so delayed proceedings that the company was never properly constituted. It reappeared, however, as the *Compagnie de la Nacelle de Saint-Pierre,* with wider terms of reference, and was able to send twelve ships and 400 families to enlarge the settlement of Canada. Finally, in 1628, Richelieu decided upon the constitution of a third company with a specific colonising purpose, that of *la Nouvelle France,* which was directed by Razilly, on whose experience and ardour Richelieu and Père Joseph relied to put blood and bones into their optimistic design. The war with England over La Rochelle had its effects upon the settlers on the St Lawrence. Quebec was lost to the English and Samuel Champlain, the pioneer of French discovery, had to return to Paris.

The French had been established on the St Lawrence since 1593 when Champlain set up his first post on the river. Versatile, energetic, ascetic, Champlain was one of the greatest of all explorers. He became Henry IV's Geographer-Royal but could not stay in France when Canada's wastes of water and forest, her virgin lands and savage, untutored Indians were there to explore and subdue. In 1608 he persuaded a group under the Sieur de Monts to settle on the escarpment of Quebec, where Jacques Cartier had built a fort, long since rotted away. In 1611 he fixed on the site of Montreal as a centre for the fur trade. The settlements were tiny, handfuls of soldiers and *coureurs du bois,* unwilling to settle and till the soil. In Champlain himself we see the apparent contradiction of aims that is so characteristic of his time. He was utterly ruthless in exploiting the wars between the Iroquois and the Hurons, whom he supported, and wanted their war to go on lest the Iroquois should lead the Hurons to trade with the Dutch. At the same time he was dedicated to the mission of converting the Indians. In 1632, after a treaty with England had restored the former French rights, two French squadrons accompanied Champlain back to Canada. Quebec, Montreal and Trois Rivières were restored or founded, explorers went further afield amongst the boundless lakes and rivers, and the missionaries, Capuchins and Jesuits, taking their cue from the attitude of Champlain who claimed that 'the salvation of one soul is worth more than the conquest of an empire', vied with one another in evangelism and self-sacrifice. They went further even than the Spanish in their zeal to convert where they conquered, for they went to live alone among the natives. The Indians, vagrant feuding tribes, who lived by hunting, offered the intrepid missionaries an opening by their bitter divisions. The Jesuits found themselves taking sides in the battles of Iroquois and Huron; they advertised their Christianity in practical ways which the natives could understand, showed them where to settle and where to farm. Some were killed and tortured; one saw strips of his own flesh eaten before his eyes. But they left an indelible mark upon French Canada. They were followed by nuns, Ursulines and Hospitalières, teachers and nurses, intrepid women like Madame de la Peltries, who was so excited when she saw a group of converted Hurons that she fell on their necks and embraced them all. The vision of Père Joseph, the Catholic ideal at its most ambitious, was thus realised by ordinary French men and women.

Razilly had designs upon Acadia but died, in 1635, before he could accomplish anything. Champlain died in the same year at Quebec. His colony survived but was slow to grow; in 1643 there were only 300 Frenchmen in Canada as against the 4,000 envisaged by Richelieu. When Colbert sent out Jean Talon to organise and develop it in 1663 there were about 2,500 inhabitants but they were living in relative security: Quebec had about 500 then, of whom 15 per cent were members of religious communities. Other French establishments were founded at this time. The Caribbean especially attracted adventurers from the western countries. The corsairs of St Malo and Dieppe had for some time been raiding and privateering amongst the islands. In 1625 two captains from Dieppe, Esnambuc and Roissey, landed on St Christophe where they found already there a small band of Huguenot refugees eking

o

out a precarious existence by selling tobacco to the Dutch. They returned to France to secure the patronage of the crown and were allowed to form the *Compagnie de Saint Christophe et des Îles*. The colonists had to fight with a rival group of English; then in 1630 a Spanish fleet, en route for Brazil, sacked the settlement. It survived however, and Richelieu was sufficiently interested in the possibilities to enlarge the company under the new name of the *Compagnie des Îles d'Amérique,* with exclusive rights over any lands that it could obtain. What the government wanted and what the subscribers wanted were not the same. Those of St Christophe, for example, wanted to sell their tobacco and cotton to the Dutch ships, which visited more regularly than the French. In France itself the robustly independent *armateurs,* the captains of the Norman and Breton ports, did all they could to undermine the privileged companies. But the capital of these companies allowed for greater development than any individual could envisage. Colonists went out to the West Indian islands, one after another, Saint-Domingue, Guadeloupe, Martinique, in sponsored groups of a hundred: peasants who could not hope to find land in France, debtors, young men looking for excitement. Huguenots were not allowed. Already the distinctive character of French colonisation was emerging, though it was left to Colbert to put his stamp upon the idea of the colonies as images of France, Catholic, seigneurial and authoritarian. How very different from the exodus of religious communities which formed the early colonies of New England, mistrusted by the English government and left largely to fend for themselves! The settlers were often miserable, working in a climate which the white man could scarcely endure on plantations which were later to be worked by slaves. Slaves, and the cultivation of sugar, were to transform the economy of the islands about the middle of the century.

Support was not only forthcoming from the crown. The region between the Amazon and the Orinoco, the Island of Cap Verte, Senegal, Gambia were all at different times settled under the auspices of companies based on Dieppe, St Malo and Rouen. In 1642 a company under the Duc de la Meilleraye took possession of Madagascar and founded there Fort-Dauphin. But it was Canada that interested Richelieu most, because the trade in furs would not entail a corresponding loss of money. Mediterranean trade he suspected at first as opening the way to a flood of expensive luxuries, silks, carpets, china, spices, which France could ill afford. It was his policy, along traditional lines, to stop spending on luxuries: for instance he forbade all but the nobility to wear silk and tried to restrict the use of carriages, legislation like that issued in Spain at the time and no more effective. But he was too intelligent to persist in sumptuary laws that were ignored and he was flexible enough to change his mind when well-advised. He received a treatise written by a merchant of Marseilles analysing the effect of Levantine trade upon that city and incorporated its arguments in the *Testament*, where he argues that only half the imports into Marseilles were paid for in silver, the rest in exports: by encouraging those industries which catered for Eastern needs, honey, wine, paper, cloth, a favourable balance could be achieved and the merchants and workers of the south enriched. Many of the imports into Marseilles were in fact re-exported to Spain, which paid in silver. So, as Richelieu wrote, right against the grain of strict mercantilist thinking, 'The silver that is carried to the east does not have its origin in France but in Spain, and it comes to us thence through trade in the same goods that we get from the Levant'. He took steps to protect Mediterranean traders against the depredations of pirates. With the Barbary corsairs he negotiated a treaty through the mediation of a Corsican, Sanson Napollon, who set up a fortified headquarters at de la Calle, from which he patrolled the seas. To Morocco he sent Razilly, who brought sufficient pressure to bear on the sheikh, Abd-el-Malek, to make a treaty (1631) along the lines of France's arrangement with Turkey: a preferential tariff, a consulate, and guarantee for the Catholic worship of French subjects.

Richelieu began to dream of a great extension of Mediterranean trade to the east. A confidential envoy, des Hayes de Courmenin, was instructed to prospect but he received no encouragement from the ambassador in Constantinople, Harlay de Césy, and gave up. Richelieu persisted, however, with the encouragement of Père Joseph, who believed that alliance with Persia, Turkey's enemy, would yield favourable openings for trade and missionaries. The Shah of Persia wanted to prevent the Turks from levying tolls on the caravans which passed through territory held by the Turks. The ports of the Indian Ocean offered an alternative outlet for their wares; they were already frequented by English and Dutch ships. About 1629 Richelieu was considering a scheme for diverting Persian traffic toward the Caspian Sea and from there using the great Russian rivers to reach Archangel on the White

Sea, or Narva on the Baltic. From these ports, however, it was necessary to use the Sound, controlled by Denmark, whose tolls had already caused French ships to abandon the Baltic. Courmenin was sent on a more successful mission: in 1629 King Christian of Denmark conceded favourable tariffs to the French and Csar Michael signed a commercial treaty. The French gained from this *grand dessein* (as Hauser has somewhat effusively called Richelieu's trading strategy) some trade with Russia and better conditions for operations in the Baltic. But even if Richelieu took very seriously the idea of diverting eastern trade from its traditional routes, it is certain that nothing came of it.

He came to the conclusion, like Colbert after him, that France would stand to gain less by discouraging expenditure on luxuries than by fostering the growth of native industries to supply both home and foreign demand. Following the initiatives of the Duc de Nevers, privileges were granted which led to the foundation of a French glass industry. He gave new encouragement to the workshops at la Savonnerie and Beauvais. The new silk factory at Tours received special support. In his *Testament* he enthuses about the splendid quality of the products of Touraine, with the affectionate pride of a Frenchman for his own *pays*: the plush, taffeta, velvet, silk and cloth of gold were all better than those of Spain, Italy or England. The silk industry spread to Lyons and was soon employing 40,000 people.

Richelieu, like Sully before him, was aware of the importance of mines: Baron de Beausoleil, who was believed to be dabbling in black magic because of his experiments in metals, was commissioned to make a survey of mines in the kingdom. In the north of France sugar refining was promoted, an industry with great prospects. Always open to new ideas, the more ambitious the better, Richelieu was at once attracted by the scheme presented to him in 1633 by Antoine Baudan, master of royal works in Languedoc, for digging a canal through the Midi to link the Atlantic and Mediterranean. This had to await Riquet and the backing of Colbert for its construction; it was finished in 1681. But the work of rendering the great rivers navigable went on and in 1642 the important canal joining the Seine and the Loire was opened. It was still often cheaper at this time to travel by sea than by land, despite the efforts of the crown for a hundred years to remedy the situation. Richelieu did succeed in reducing most of the road and river tolls. He also instituted a vital reform in setting up a royal postal service. In 1630 this service was made an office for one or two *surintendants des postes*; under them were *maîtres des couriers* who were allowed to farm out their responsibilities. This arrangement shows that the fiscal and administrative interests of the crown were not necessarily opposed: society gained an organised service, rapid distribution of letters and parcels through official stages; the government acquired a new range of offices to sell.

## 17. Defender of the Faith

There was an inherent difficulty in Richelieu's double rôle as Cardinal of the world-wide Church and as First Minister of France. He had risen as a spokesman for the party of the *dévôts*, he had been a zealous diocesan bishop and expressed pronounced views upon doctrine, administration and Christian conduct. Among the vital themes in the life of the Church at this time were personal devotion, mission, and ecclesiastical authority. The devotional revival had a strong mystical element and the devout tended to form groups which were wrapped in their own concerns to the point of behaving secretively and flouting authority. At home the missionary effort was directed against profligacy and irreligion in general, against the Huguenots in particular. Richelieu's decision, on political grounds, that the state could not bring material pressure to bear on the Huguenots convinced many Catholics that he was no longer concerned with the interests of the Church. The reform movement, with which he was intimately associated, was notable for the advance of religious orders which owed allegiance not primarily to the king but to the Pope, and derived its strength from the reassertion of the Pope's authority since the Council of Trent. At the same time one of the strongest forces in French life, especially in the establishment of Paris, the Sorbonne and Parlement, but permeating official life everywhere, was Gallicanism. Clearly Richelieu's position was ambiguous. The question asked by friends like Vincent de Paul and Père Joseph who looked to him to direct and encourage the reform movement, and understood the strains imposed on him, might take some such form as this: in the process of deciding what was best for the state, under all the pressures, in all the compromises involved in political questions, could the Cardinal-statesman remain true to the ideals and precepts of the young bishop of Luçon? They might have added: could he keep anything of his inner life of the spirit intact? Vincent de Paul was fortunate in that his worldly concerns stemmed naturally from his spiritual convictions: the organisation of charity involved no contradictions. Less fortunate in his vocation, Père Joseph was worn down, though he persisted to the end in the disciplines of meditation, by the disillusioning process of diplomacy, envisaged by him as but a means to the great end of the crusade, and he saw that vision grow fainter with the years: a bitter experience. Richelieu hoped that the Capuchin would succeed him but he died first and was saved the final trials of supreme power. What then of Richelieu? How did he deal with the problems of Church and state: with the Huguenots after 1629, with the Gallicans, with inconvenient fanatics?

'Le reste est un ouvrage qu'il fault attendre du ciel sans y apporter jamais aucune violence que celle de la bonne vie et du exemple.' In the spirit of these words Richelieu pursued a consistent policy of conciliation towards the Huguenots after the fall of La Rochelle. He may have listened sympathetically to plans for negotiated reunion of the Churches. When Grotius, the travelling savant and keen advocate of reunion, author of *De Jure Belli et Pacis,* Dutchman by birth, but for some time the king of Sweden's emissary, was in Paris, Richelieu gave him long audiences on the subject, though he found the man tedious. On Richelieu's advice the Jesuit Audebert proposed to Huguenots that there should be a conference at which pastors and priests might elucidate the points of disagreement. The ex-Jesuit Veron, *curé* of Charenton where the Huguenots of Paris worshipped, outlined a system of Catholic belief to which he hoped Protestants would be able to subscribe: he was allowed to expound his thesis openly at Saint-Germain until silenced by the authorities at Rome. It is likely that Richelieu treated schemes for reunion by negotiation as chimerical and no more practicable by negotiation than by force. He believed undoubtedly that time was on his side and figures support him: between 1627 and 1637 the number of pastors fell everywhere by at least a tenth, and congregations proportionately. Sometimes the fall was drastic, as in the small town of Leyrac: from 300 in 1627 to 60 in 1661. Richelieu's principle seemed to be that tolerance would soften hearts and prepare the way for conviction of mind and conversion by the rational process in which he put most trust. It was in line with the gentle approach of Vincent de Paul, who never forgot, in his zeal for conversion, the kindness of his Huguenot friend Jean Beynier in his early days at Châtillon-des-Dombes, and who always referred to the Huguenots as *les frères séparés.* Successive edicts of the council forbade Catholics to describe Protestants publicly as heretics. In 1637 Secretary of State la Vrillière repudiated a decision of the Bishop of Montpellier condemning mixed marriages. More surprisingly, Protestants obtained official aid for holding their synods, even a grant for their schools. Here and there individual Church leaders enjoyed friendly relations: the noted pastor of Saumur, Amyrault, dined with the Bishop of Chartres, to the disgust of some of his fellow-pastors. Rivet, a member of the central Huguenot council, was a friend of Père Mersenne. Such instances can be multiplied but it is doubtful whether they are representative of ordinary opinion. Pastors were hooted in the streets of Paris, as Catholics were in London. Powerful interests worked for the destruction of heresy. The *Compagnie du Saint Sacrement* made it one of its chief aims and challenged every appointment of a Huguenot to a high post. The Church Assembly was gradually building up to the pitch of fervour which made it such a relentless advocate of coercion in the reign of Louis XIV. In 1655 it was to call explicitly for the suppression of the 'synagogues de Satan'. If the Huguenots were safe for the time being, despite the mounting pressures, it was because Richelieu had the sense to realise that conciliation suited the needs of the state. His constructive efforts to foster peaceful co-existence point also to a magnanimity for which he has not received full credit.

Richelieu could not avoid being in the centre of the long-standing Gallican controversy, which erupted at the meetings of the States-General and the *notables*. Louis XIV was later able to exploit Gallican sentiment and it became an important element in the united and fervent royalist spirit of his reign. His policy involved him, however, in a costly quarrel with the Papacy; more-over when, at the end of his reign, he wanted Papal support in matters of doctrine for his attack upon the Jansenists, he had to reverse his strategy, with damaging results. The problem was in essence simple. Catholicism was the soul of the Bourbon monarchy. The strength of Catholicism lay in acceptance of the authority of the Pope in points of doctrine. But it was not easy to isolate authority in doctrine from authority in other concerns of the Church, and a long tradition in France questioned the validity of this latter authority. Gallicans believed, in short, that the king should be master in his own house.

The development of this view, natural as it sounds, must be examined; one might as well try to understand English history without some account of the Reformation as French history without the Gallican movement, which reaches back to the fourteenth century and the Avignon 'captivity' of the Popes, when the monarchy was in an exceptionally strong bargaining position. The Pragmatic Sanction of Bourges (1438) had affirmed the Conciliar doctrines to which French clergy and lawyers were to have recourse whenever the Pope's authority was in question. The Concordat of Bologna, in 1516, the year after Francis I's victory at Marignano and the year before Luther initiated the reform movement which Francis might well have been tempted to follow—or to lead—if he had not already secured some of the authority he needed over the Church, gave the French king the right to nominate to benefices: a compromise between open schism, English-style, and that full acceptance of Papal authority which even Spain would not endure. Gallicanism and civil war together cut France off from many of the Catholic reform movements of the second half of the century; while the dogmas of the Council of Trent were formally received, the disciplinary decrees were mostly ignored. The high claims of the Papacy were accepted only by the small Ultramontane group associated with the ambitions of the Guises and the interference of Spain. Gallican feeling was often a sort of patriotism, one expression of the secular, *politique*, zenophobic spirit which carried Henry IV to the throne. Henry IV embodied the sense of nationhood, and he favoured compromise; yet he admitted the Jesuits back into France and his reign saw the beginnings of the revival of the international religious orders owing unequivocal allegiance to Rome.

To the more secular-minded Gallicans in Parlement the whole movement of Catholic reform was suspect. One element among the lawyers was simply anti-clerical; there was professional suspicion of the priest. Ever since the quarrel between Philip the Fair and Pope Boniface VIII lawyers had argued in Parlement that the Pope was a temporal ruler with sovereignty only in his own land. Kingdoms had been established by God long before the name of Pope existed: the Pope was therefore a usurper when he interfered with a dynastic question. When Henry IV was excommunicated, the magistrates declared the Bull to be 'worthless, damnable, full of sacrilege and imposture'. It was generally held, moreover, though not always rightly, that the Pope favoured the Habsburgs. Parlement men, brought up on Canon law, were able to discuss relations of king and Pope as knowledgeably as their

common lawyer contemporaries in England asserting political
rights against the monarchy—but with the opposite effect, for it
became axiomatic in Parlement that there could be no ecclesiastical
exception to the authority of the king. 'The king of France is
Emperor in his own realm.'

One extension of this idea was that of Pierre Pithou, who based
a treatise, in 1594, on the idea that 'the king, being anointed with
holy oil, was personally responsible to God for the Church in his
lands'. Another was that of Edmond Richer, head of the Faculty
of Theology in Paris. Writing in 1611, soon after the assassination
of Henry IV had fanned indignation against the Jesuits, who were
generally assumed to have instigated the crime, he asserted the
supreme importance of the bishops: 'A bishop in his diocese is the
real ruler of his Church' and 'Bishops are an essential part of the
Church and the Pope is an accessory'.[1] In 1614 the Gallican
question produced the sharpest arguments of the States-General.
In 1615 Parlement declared that it was illegal to question the
Gallican principles; in the ensuing years it was vigilant in censoring
all books, like that of Mariana, *De Rege et Regis Institutione*, which
expressed the Ultramontane view. In 1626 the official representatives to the *notables* insisted upon treating the Papal nuncio as a
foreign representative, which angered the king and put the
government in an embarrassing position, since the last thing that
Richelieu could do at that juncture was to offend the Pope; his
position in Italy was already precarious enough. In April 1626
Richelieu had revealed his own position when he ordered that the
book of the Jesuit Santarelli, which asserted that the Pope had the
right to depose when kings were heretical or offended against the
law of the state, or even when they were incompetent, be burnt by

[1] The influence of Richer was to prove long-lasting. His name and
writing inspired the lower clergy in the eighteenth century who voiced
their resentment of the privilege and wealth of the upper clergy and
their wish to participate more in Church government. Richer might not
have been disturbed by this development. He was by way of being a
demagogue, called 'Stentor' on account of his loud voice, a passionate
debater, and a man of quarrelsome disposition. He was never given a
chance to produce a coherent programme but he represented powerful
elements in Paris opinion, and in the Church at large. Obsessively anti-
Jesuit, he seems to have wanted to restore the power of the mediaeval
university of Paris, and to renew the French Church from a dynamic
centre. There is a detailed study of this Gracchus-figure by E. Préclin in
*Revue d'Histoire Moderne*, 28 and 29, July and September 1930.

the common executioner, and further requested the Jesuit provincial and the heads of three Jesuit houses to repudiate the doctrine. They did so, but with a modification which provoked Parlement to demand the suppression of all Jesuit colleges.

Richelieu was able to mollify them. He wanted above all to keep the temperature down, to impress the Pope without going too far to meet the Ultramontanes. Richerism continued to win followers, however, with its author still active in Paris though he had lost his post at the Sorbonne. In 1629 a new issue agitated the parties: should the oath to be taken by bachelors of theology include respect for the Holy See? Spada, the nuncio, asked Richelieu to intervene. When he returned from Italy at the end of the year he tackled Richer in private debate. Evidently he took him seriously, equally he was confident in his own power of theological reasoning. Richer signed at last a declaration that the Holy See was 'mother and mistress of all Churches and infallible seat of truth' and Richelieu recorded, with justifiable pride in his *Mémoires*, that he had won the heretic over by force of argument. Richer claimed that he had been overawed by the Cardinal, and tricked. With Gallicans claiming to be the patriots and Ultramontanes naturally uneasy about the prospect of alliance with heretics against Catholic Spain, the doctrinal issue could easily develop into a political crisis. Urban VIII was pleased with Richelieu and signified it by making his brother Alphonse, the Bishop of Lyons, a Cardinal. But Richelieu could not escape the anger of the *dévôts*, who linked the boldness of the Gallicans (their latest move was to suggest the creation of apostolic delegates in France to judge all appeals to Rome) with Richelieu's foreign policy.

In 1635 the question of Gaston's marriage touched the Gallican nerve once more; fortunately Richelieu was more secure but it was awkward. For once he was at odds with Père Joseph. In July 1635 the Church Assembly had accepted the report of the special commission appointed by Richelieu to consider Gaston's marriage to Marguérite of Lorraine; in their view a royal marriage was invalid unless it received the royal consent, this being a custom of France 'affirmed by legitimate prescription and authorised by the Church'. Gaston was then summoned to Richelieu's own room at Rueil to sign a document recognising that the marriage was null; he did as he was told, but Marguérite appealed to Rome. The Pope was called on to decide whether a marriage depended upon the mutual consent of the parties alone, or whether the state might require the additional consent of an outside party. The danger from the Pope's point of view was that to accept the latter was to let the state usurp the Church's claim to universal jurisdiction by making conditions about a sacrament that had been ordained by Christ. Richelieu had sent Alphonse, Cardinal of Lyon and, since 1632, *Grand Aumônier* of France, to Rome in 1634, and he endeared himself to Urban by his unworldliness and intelligence. In 1636 he was reinforced by the Bishop of Montpellier, who had been chairman of the marriage commission; the latter became ill and left Alphonse to handle the case, but he was too timid to do so. The Pope, in July, reserved the question for his decision, which meant that it was shelved indefinitely. Père Joseph, meanwhile, being concerned about the way in which Marguérite was wronged, and opposed to what seemed to him unfeeling legalism with a noxious Gallican flavour, strove to influence the conscience of the king. Eventually Louis was persuaded to offer Gaston the chance of remarriage, to put the matter beyond doubt for as long as he lived, but Richelieu managed to forestall the event, aided by Gaston's outrageous behaviour. In 1643 Gaston and Marguérite went through another marriage; their implacable enemy was dead, Gaston ageing, she in tears at the thought that she might have been living all that time in mortal sin.

In 1641 Pierre de Marca's book *De Concordia Sacerdotii et Imperii* appeared under Richelieu's patronage and dedicated to him. We may conclude that its moderate thesis conformed with Richelieu's ideas about the proper relationship between Rome and the Church in France: de Marca argued for an equilibrium between the primacy of Rome and the requirements of the civil power. Some believed that the logical development of Richelieu's secular foreign policy would be a break with Rome, the convocation of a national council and the proclamation of Richelieu as patriarch of the Gallican Church. That such a programme was appealing to Richelieu is certain; it would be one way of consolidating his power, of evoking a nationalist response from the solid Gallican party, among the bourgeoisie. Richelieu was prepared to use the threat of schism as a means of bringing pressure on Rome: in 1639 the threat was taken very seriously by Urban VIII's special nuncio Scotti, who reported that schism was imminent. In the last analysis however, Richelieu was too aware of the value and convenience of Rome as the guardian of truth and court of final appeal. As a good Catholic and a good Frenchman he pursued the middle way.

Richelieu was intimately concerned, through his dealings with Duvergier de Hauranne, Abbé de St Cyran, in the early stages of the Jansenist movement. So called after the Flemish theologian Cornelius Jansen, it might equally well be called St Cyranism, for many of its early characteristics stemmed from the character and beliefs of that remarkable man. The relationship between the Cardinal and the Basque priest whom he once called 'more dangerous than six armies' raises some vital questions, political as well as theological; it is also flavoured with the mystery and intrigue which always hung about Jansenism, not only because of the hostility towards anything heterodox of both Richelieu and Louis XIV, who later devoted so much effort to crushing the movement, but also because of the conviction of Jansenists that they were the elect, and the determination of some of them to behave like a secret society. Under persecution these traits became naturally more pronounced but we see them at the outset, in the use of cypher words in the correspondence of Jansen and St Cyran about the purification of the Church.

Cornelius Jansen, who was promoted to the bishopric of Ypres by the Spanish in return for his services to them, was a public figure in a minor way: he was known to detest the French. He was also a formidable scholar, devoted to the study of St Augustine. In the writings of this saint, the greatest of the Early Fathers for both Catholic and Protestant, he believed that he found the true principles which Christendom had lost in the Middle Ages, when it was dominated by the scholastics, and had not recovered in the age of humanism, with its formal devotions and rational or merely ethical approaches to faith. The *Augustinus*, Jansen's life's work, published in 1640 two years after his death, presented the saint's views in the fullest manner. He is supposed to have read the anti-Pelagian passages thirty times to ensure that he missed nothing, but in his scrutiny of the letter he undoubtedly missed much of the spirit of the saint's work. Augustine was reflecting ardently upon the miracle of his own conversion and so he insisted upon the depravity of man and his consequent dependence upon divine grace; he also concluded that grace was given to those for whom it was predestined and correspondingly withheld from others, who suffered in this way the penalty of man's original fall. Jansen's enormous tome, 'born in the library of an intellectual', as Brémond said, lifted Augustine's view from the frame of the man's life and teaching and presented it, scrupulously but selectively edited, as the pure ideal from which the Church had fallen. Theology for Jansen was an exercise in the mobilisation of texts; for all his scholarship he was a propagandist, though he died, as he had lived, in the assurance of orthodoxy.

He began the book with an attack upon Jesuit views and he must have known that he was treading dangerously. Calvin had pressed Augustine's logic to its appalling conclusion that the majority whom grace did not touch were irrevocably damned while, among Catholics, Jesuits and Dominicans had long been quarrelling about grace and will. Molinists, followers of the Jesuit Molina (1535-1601), professor of theology at Evora, held broadly that grace was only efficacious so far as the will co-operates: God leaving man free to resist grace which, without man's cooperation, is powerless. Dominicans held a modified Augustinianism: sufficient grace is a divine premonition given to all, preparing the soul for efficient grace which is needful for man's acts to be justified before God. Thus stated, the doctrines seem neat, the differences clear. But what anguish, what gritty marathons of debate, what subtleties of interpretation lay behind the simple formulas! Between 1594 and 1605 the matter was debated at Rome in the *Congregatio De Auxiliis*, without conclusion, though the Jesuits may have been lucky to escape condemnation. So the Catholic was left to choose between the Dominican view that stressed the prerogative of an omnipotent God, and Jesuit insistence upon man's will. The fatalistic Spanish Dominicans, guardian order of the Inquisition, felt bound to uphold, for purity's sake, the view that the elect of God were few. The missionary, outward-looking Society of Jesus required by contrast a working guide for sinners, to leave scope for their work of conversion. In this way the theological battle reflected, as it always will, basic attitudes and practical needs.

Jansen angered Richelieu with his hostile pamphlet, *Mars Gallicus*, published in 1635. He was already a marked man for he had known St Cyran since 1611: for five years the two men had worked together intensively on Church history and theology. Since then they had kept in touch, corresponded voluminously and laboured to fulfil their self-imposed design of reforming the Church, as Jansen went ever deeper into Augustine and St Cyran widened his range of contacts in France. They were very different,

the burrowing scholar of Ypres and the mystic, *exalté*, the friend
of Bérulle, but their work was complementary. Their correspondence left little doubt in Richelieu's mind that they meant
business. But what business? What was *l'affaire Pilmot*, which
takes its name from one of the code words they used? Was it a
plot to overthrow the Church as the Jesuits suspected? Was there
no connection between Jansen's antipathy to France and the
opposition of the *dévôts* to the anti-Spanish trend of Richelieu's
policy? Could Richelieu, surrounded as he was by plots, look with
equanimity at the prospect of the activist St Cyran succeeding the
relatively gentle Bérulle as the prophet of the *dévôts*? Bérulle,
looking for the triumph of Catholicism in Europe, and Richelieu,
working for the ascendancy of France, had moved apart by 1628
to points at which their perspectives were different, their policies
opposed. For the last year or so of his life Bérulle was
out of favour at court but he was revered by many Catholics
and in a few hours of a successful coup the position of the two
men could have been reversed. It is arguable that Richelieu
acted against St Cyran more stringently than was necessary, but
he did not act out of ignorance, nor without long trial of alternative methods. The year before he imprisoned St Cyran, he
offered him a bishopric!

When Richelieu was bishop of Luçon, Duvergier (from 1620
Abbé de St Cyran) was the vicar-general of the neighbouring
bishop of Poitiers, de la Rochepousay. In 1609 Duvergier had
written a study of the duties of the Christian to the king, which
had some topicality after the assassination of Henry IV in the
following year. During Condé's rebellion in 1614, de la Rochepousay took up arms and shut the gates of Poitiers against him.
Duvergier appeared in print again to defend his warlike bishop.
Richelieu approved such forthright attitudes, while Duvergier and
Rochepousay helped to secure Richelieu's election to the States-
General. From admiration of a strong and vivid personality
Richelieu turned gradually to distrust as the abbé went about
building his private empire of souls. 'His entrails are on fire and he
mistakes the vapours for inspiration': something of the Cardinal's
dislike for ecstasies and irrationalities in thought and conduct is
conveyed by these words. A man of extremes, St Cyran invited
extreme judgements, then as now. From him, through his devoted
pupils, Jansenism acquired some of the traits which make it so
compelling and, in different ways, so admirable and detestable.

From the start the keynote was exaggeration, in language, theology and attitudes.

St Cyran's theology rested upon the need to stand aside and let God's grace operate through a passive spirit, but his own personality was wilful; it seems he could be affected, self-important, morbid—yet we have to set against these impressions the respect of some of the most notable Catholics of his time. Bérulle met St Cyran in 1620. The founder of the Oratory, author of *Les Grandeurs de Jésus*, was Augustinian in his emphasis upon the dependence of the creature before the creator and redeemer. St Cyran was deeply impressed by his personality, absorbed more perhaps of his theology than of the Christo-centric spirit that informed it, and defended him passionately against the assaults of his rivals, notably the Jesuits. He also assisted Vincent de Paul in organising the charitable organisation of St Lazare. Monsieur Vincent was sometimes exasperated with St Cyran but believed him to be a good man. Zamet, Bishop of Langres and spiritual director of the abbey of Port Royal, introduced St Cyran to the abbess, Mère Angélique (Jacqueline Arnauld), and she took St Cyran as director in place of Zamet; thenceforward she and her sister nuns of the reformed abbey followed St Cyran as prophet and, after his imprisonment, martyr too. Among lay supporters there were the Prince of Condé, Procureur-Général Molé and Avocat-Général Bignon. Then in 1637 Antoine le Maître, Mère Angélique's nephew and a brilliant young advocate, declared in an open letter to the Chancellor his intention of living henceforward in retreat and penitence, without becoming a monk or even being ordained; he went off to be the first of the 'solitaries' of a new male community, Port Royal des Champs. There was a stir of protest from those who deplored a waste of talent and feared escapism, especially from the Jesuits who had been embroiled with the Arnauld clan since Antoine Arnauld the elder's celebrated denunciation of them as accomplices in assassination. 'Boutique de Satan' he had called them. We see the strands coming together: puritanism, the anti-Jesuit caucus, a professional *élite* of lawyers. It needed only a big issue and a man of genius to create a movement of real importance. The issue was provided by the publication of the *Fréquente Communion* by Antoine Arnauld the younger in 1643, the genius by Blaise Pascal. But the battle over Arnauld and his book, the publication of *Lettres Provinciales* and Pascal's attack on the Jesuits, lay in the future. When Richelieu sent St Cyran to prison in 1638 he may have thought that he had dealt with the trouble in time. As he observed to a friend: 'If Luther and Calvin had been clapped into gaol the moment they started dogmatising, the nations would have been saved a lot of trouble'.

Besides the range of his contacts, the extravagance of St Cyran's theology had convinced Richelieu that he was dangerous. He went further even than Calvin in asserting that the mass of men were damned. The only mortals who could be sure of salvation were baptised children who died in infancy. Those who dared to presume they were saved must discipline the flesh and eschew the world and its vanities, which included the imaginative arts as well as the more obvious perils of dancing and gambling. Conversion, the process by which it was intimated to the few that they were saved, was a violent process, a sudden Pauline impact of grace upon the soul. St Cyran announced that Luther had erred not in fundamentals but in form, and he told the startled Vincent de Paul that God had revealed to him that there was no longer a Church but only a river of slime where once there had been clear flowing water. He called the Council of Trent an assembly of mere scholastics. In a book which he published under the pseudonym of 'Aurelius' he advocated an extreme Gallican form of Church government. When the Sorbonne took notice of this, Richelieu issued an *arrêt* referring the book to a special commission for examination.

As a theologian Richelieu had made a special study of the question of contrition. As he saw it now, the essential question concerned the state of mind in which the penitent goes to confession. In what circumstances was absolution effective? If the Jansenists had their way, he thought, only the elect, far advanced in sanctity, would dare to be penitents. After Arnauld's publication of the *Fréquente Communion*, the same could be said of the Mass. St Cyran's biographer, Lancelot, who had been a regular communicant, began his career at Port Royal by going without communion from Candlemas to Easter. Arnauld described the practice of voluntary abstention as 'a living image of the penitence of former times'. The way beckoned to a desert of scruples: there would be oases for the elect, but what of the ordinary Christian? The matter was well put by François de Sales, who asked a nun of Port Royal whether they would do well 'not to take such big fish and to take more of them.' Richelieu was surely right in his assessment of the drift of St Cyranist theology. Inclined as he was

P

to mistrust the validity of emotional experience in the sacraments as in life, he preferred to emphasise the mental process: the intention of the penitent to avoid sin in the future. The difference was emphasised by the publication by a priest of the Oratory of an edition of St Augustine's *Treatise on Virginity* with notes which were obviously inspired by Jansenism. The author, Séguenot, bared his flank to attack by adopting the Lutheran idea that all grace justifies or condemns its object, that good works are not productive of grace, and that all the actions, even of Christ, are predestined. Forced poverty, he said, is the result of divine will and is therefore more a source of grace than voluntary poverty, which is not: monastic vows were therefore worthless. Père Joseph went through the book and prepared a list of errors for Richelieu, who then summoned the superior of the Oratorians, Père de Condren. The latter took a cool view of St Cyran and revealed that 'this great lover of novelty' was the man behind the book. Séguenot was promptly sent to the Bastille, St Cyran to Vincennes. The same day, 14th May 1638, Jansen died, his great work, which was to cause such a furore, still unpublished. St Cyran was treated considerately, allowed books and communication with his friends. Though he went through agonies of self-doubt he became inevitably a martyr for the cause. He came out in 1643, only to die a few months later. His body was cut up for relics for the faithful.

In an age that was, in Bérulle's phrase, 'passionnée pour la méthode', in a society that yearned for stability and order after the radical religious and political changes of the Reformation and sought these ideals in its literature and arts as well as in government, Richelieu deliberately set out to promote orthodoxy and to suppress minorities where they threatened the interests of the state. He took it for granted that public issues of theology were issues of state. In his writings he always refers to dangers to the Church as dangers to France. Like any artist or dramatist of his time, like the mathematician Descartes whose masterpiece, *Discours de la Méthode*, perhaps the most influential single book of its time, was published in 1637, like the architect Jacques Lemercier, who was building the Palais-Cardinal and was soon to start work on the severe rectangular designs of Richelieu's new town and private court in Poitou, Richelieu believed in logic and regulation, in Church as in state. He upheld the principles of the Council of Trent, those precise definitions of truth that were to fix the

Church in a rigid mould for centuries to come. Only on the obedient acceptance of the basic certainties could the Church flourish and society rest secure. The faith of the Church could then be exhibited with all the splendour of ritual. He found his ideal, not in the arcane gatherings of Port Royal, the soul-searchings of a small, upper-class clique, but in the splendid interiors of the new churches in the baroque style, lavish with allegorical aids to popular devotion, painted heavens, trumpeting cherubs, rich altars and lofty pulpits, where science and art combined to provide the setting for sermon and mass. There is no inconsistency here. The exuberance of this style grew out of beliefs that were firmly held because they were plainly defined. It appealed to ordinary people who could not, in Richelieu's pessimistic and condescending view, live peaceably or well without spiritual sustenance.

It would have been surprising if Richelieu, who was so suspicious of unorthodoxy, had dealt mercifully with the case of Canon Urbain Grandier, *curé* of the church of St Pierre in Loudun, condemned for sorcery and burnt alive in the town market place in August 1634. It might, however, have been better for his reputation if he had accepted the allegations less uncritically. Grandier was robust, intelligent and a forceful local personality, evidently restless in his vocation. He led the local opposition to the government's order that the town walls should be destroyed. He also acquired notoriety by a book in which he seriously argued against the principle of celibacy, and which naturally raised questions about his own conduct. He had already been forced to appeal to Parlement against proceedings taken against him by his bishop and parishioners. Then it was reported that there were cases of demoniac possession at the convent of the Ursulines, whose young abbess, Mme de Belcier, and another nun, Mme de Razilly, were said to be pregnant. Grandier had no official dealings with this convent, whose spiritual director, Canon Mignon, was one of his loudest critics. The nuns were exorcised and interrogated; they named Grandier as the author of their possession. In an atmosphere of group hysteria they assented, perhaps too readily, to the suggestions of their exorcisers, or recalled the scraps of gossip which had penetrated the convent from the town. No one concerned seems to have questioned the reality of this possession, for sorcery was as real to them as the devil.

Richelieu had already sent a *conseiller d'état*, Laubardemont, to supervise the destruction of the town's walls and he reported that he found the town and district agitated by the affair of the nuns; everywhere there were ribaldry and recriminations. The new chancellor, Séguier, was an authoritarian, ministers were on their guard against local disturbances which could fester until they became dangerous, and Richelieu took a personal interest. He knew the town well as it was near his family estates and was notorious for violence and duelling, and Mme de Razilly was a protégée of his, the daughter of an old friend. Indignation, the disgust of a fastidious mind at the suggestions of embarrassing disorder where above all order should be maintained, the desire to teach the town and thereby the country a lesson, may all have played their part. At a recent trial in the *Chambre de l'Arsenal*, another priest, Bouchard, had been condemned to death as a sorcerer. When Laubardemont was ordered to arrest Grandier and set up a special court to try him, he must have felt that severity was expected. In the event Grandier was condemned in an archaic trial by nothing more substantial than the allegations of the nuns, whose paroxysms weighed more with the judges than his own reasonable defence. He died well, maintaining his innocence to the end. Of such a case a Voltaire would have made a *cause célèbre* for all the ingredients were there, the injustice, the superstition, the remote authority that stirred him so greatly in the Calas case. In our century it has provided a brilliant writer with a rich field of psychological study.[1]

[1] Aldous Huxley, *The Devils of Loudun*. London, 1952.

## 18. Lonely Eminence

The Cardinal became a rich man. He was a pluralist on a scale which suggests that he took every chance of an important ecclesiastical vacancy to add to his own collection and that he cynically exploited his power and the weakness of the system. Given that pluralism, despite the efforts of the reformers, was an accepted way of providing a sufficient revenue for a man with great responsibilities, he is open to the charge of avarice. His benefices have been estimated to be worth $1\frac{1}{2}$ million livres a year, the major part of his fortune, though he also derived large revenues from the governorship of Brittany and from his private estates, much augmented since he came to power. He spent lavishly on building and entertainments at a time when millions of Frenchmen were living in dire poverty (but this contrast may not have struck his contemporaries; grandees were expected to live grandly). His household of about 150 was a miniature court; again this is not surprising, for it was necessary for him to impress in the manner of the time. What Burckhardt calls the 'mummery' of outward display was important as an argument of power. He was also a man of sensibility who made the most of opportunities to gratify his tastes. Of course he aroused loathing and mockery among those who would have imitated him if they could.

In this matter we cannot judge him as a private citizen but as a servant of the state. He and his household were an establishment parallel to that of the king himself: his court was also a chancery, a close-knit, working body of agents and advisers, secretaries, publicists and clients. Security was provided by guards, at first about thirty but, by 1639, a hundred horse and a company of musketeers. At this time, when Richelieu was extending the authority and activity of the state so enormously, the machinery for doing so was still primitive. Just as he used his accumulation of Church office to exercise a degree of centralised power over the Church, to reform the monasteries and the conduct of dioceses, so he developed in his household the specialised services which he required to assist him in the government of the country. In terms, therefore, of the job he was doing, his establishment cannot be called excessive; and its domestic expenses were at least half a million livres a year.

His manner of life was intense and exacting. He set a formidable example of dedicated and unremitting work. He was often on the move, apart from the periods spent with the army and separated from the king, maintaining with difficulty and expense a second centre of government. It was his habit to take most of his meals by himself and this may have helped him to preserve some detachment; one cannot say privacy, for he was almost always accompanied by secretaries and guards. He would retire before midnight, sleep a bit, then write and dictate to secretaries in the small hours; another short sleep and he would be ready for his twelve-hour working day. He knew that he must use every moment well. What sustained him in this efficient, sacrificial programme? His faith in God? His vision of the destiny of France? A complete absorption in the details of a power such as few men had enjoyed before? Or a simple determination not to be beaten? We may see all these forces at work and still be left with an impression of genius which does not lend itself to precise analysis. When men identify themselves closely with an ideal there is likely to be an element of self-delusion and great men are not exempt from this. Richelieu, like Colbert and Napoleon, experienced the intoxication of giving himself to an ideal of glory. Of these three very different men, Richelieu was the most circumscribed in his field of action due to bad health and political difficulties. To cut a way through, to win a degree of freedom of manœuvre, he had to use every resource of brain and nerve. His ability to command and to take initiatives in a situation which would have forced other men on to the defensive commands our admiration.

Few men have attracted more enmity than Richelieu. Most of the hostile propaganda can be discounted as the work of disappointed or injured men, embroidered sometimes with scabrous gossip. As his enemies saw him he was power-drunk, mean, cruel, even ridiculous. This Cardinal, a consummate hypocrite, employed hacks to write his theological discourses, entertained Marion de Lorme,[1] kept his widowed niece Marie Madeleine as

[1] G. Montgrédien, in *Marion de Lorme et ses amours,* Paris, 1940, suggests, with little justification that Richelieu had a weakness for this notorious courtesan.

his mistress and tried to seduce Anne of Austria! The portraits of Richelieu that appear in the memoirs of Cardinal de Retz or of that John Aubrey of the French court, Tallement des Réaux, are historical curiosities, not to be taken seriously. And yet Richelieu did make more enemies than was necessary, and he aroused disgust in some people on first acquaintance. His critics scored points when they ridiculed his vanity, as when he elaborated his family tree after becoming *duc et pair*. He was liable to be defensively cold towards women and unnecessarily rude and hurtful in a way which grew more pronounced with age. The elegant cavalier of his youth was not entirely lost, but courtliness turned sour. It may have hurt him more to be mocked than to be hated, and derision was a powerful weapon in the hands of enemies like Mme de Chevreuse. With his sickly pallor and hollow cheeks, periodic fevers and, latterly, painful haemorrhoids, his invalidism was a stock joke in Anne of Austria's circle at court. Richelieu, the fastidious celibate, was also roused to physical aversion by a certain sort of robust, gay, outgoing person—Buckingham and Bassompierre both offended him mortally—but this may have been because he associated the type with reckless irresponsibility. Like many overworked men, he often resorted to sarcasm. It was only those who knew him best and had seen him with his defences down, who shared his work and worries and could appreciate the extent of his problems, Père Joseph, Bouthillier and, not least, the king, who felt warmly towards him.

As so often with great public figures we are left with contrasts. He was more vulnerable and interesting than the icy, unnaturally calm figure of legend, the incarnation of intellect and will that is presented by the superb, baroque portraits of Philippe de Champaigne. The statesman whose consistency and logical application of selected policies were so impressive to his enemies was also the tense, waspish, anxious invalid who was liable to sudden rage or tears and found it hard, even when appearing most impassive, to keep his prejudices under control. The theologian, so methodical in his exposition, was also superstitious to the point of naïveté. Posterity has fastened naturally on the outward style of the man, his dramatic gestures and compelling authority. And he could reduce strong men and women to near paralysis in private confrontations. Was it only fear of what he could do, the shadow of the Bastille? Was it a majestic presence, a persuasiveness that could charm and bemuse, or a voice that assumed and got consent?

He was sometimes hectoring, as the delegates of La Rochelle found in 1628. There was undoubtedly something of the bully in him when he was dealing with fools, by his standards a large class. His brother Alphonse, promoted and used by the Cardinal, was treated so brusquely on occasion that he must have wished himself back in his Carthusian retreat. There was no room in Richelieu's guarded, suspicious world for muddlers or meddlers: better an innocent man or two in the Bastille than a failure and change of government, with the disintegration that would follow. Alongside the portrait of remote splendour, then, let us put a human being, Gallic and volatile, harassed, hypersensitive, impulsively emotional, sometimes cruel, always in his lowest moments lifting his eyes to a vision of the destiny of France; and see him at his desk, forcing tired eyes to focus upon the endless documents, dictating to his secretaries or pondering policy with Père Joseph; or, more pleasantly, listening intently to musicians or actors; or just by himself, meditating, writing, revealing and fulfilling himself on paper—where there was no opposition and where he could justify himself to future generations.

We learn something of Richelieu's mind from the character of the man who was for many years his closest friend and who, like Richelieu, had to live by the double standard of God and the world. 'I swear the devil must be in this friar's body', said the Duc de Bouillon on one occasion: 'he penetrates my most secret thoughts, knows things that I have communicated only to a few people of tried discretion.' François Leclerc du Tremblay (1577-1638) came from a line of notable lawyers and administrators on his father's side; his mother Marie de la Fayette was of the landed nobility. From one of the four baronies in the family, François was known, when at court, as the Baron de Maffliers. Though Marie's parents were Huguenots she was brought up as a Catholic in order that she might enter a convent and save them a dowry; she married instead and produced three sons of whom the eldest, François, turned out to be precociously clever. At the age of ten he was accomplished in Latin and Greek, he had already shown an acute sensibility in his awareness of religion, and at the boarding school in Paris to which he asked his parents to send him (lest he should be spoilt at home!) he met Pierre Bérulle, a kindred spirit and like him passionately serious beyond his years. Later, at the academy of Pluvinel, he acquired the polite accomplishments which he was soon to renounce, though he never lost his perfect manners. Under the influence of Bérulle, Du Val and Mme Acarie the vocation which he seems to have known instinctively from boyhood took more precise form. At Mme Acarie's he met Benet of Canfield, the English Capuchin, 'master of the masters' in Brémond's phrase, teacher, by example and writings, of a whole generation of mystics. Against the opposition of his mother he became a Capuchin and took the name 'Father Joseph'. Like other well-born friars (for he was not unique in his class in choosing this ascetic path) he was attracted by the extreme severity of the rule, the evangelical poverty and the constant challenge of dealing with the poorest and lowest in what François called 'a soldier's life'. He was also intent, with exceptional force of mind and will, on arriving at the higher state of the mystic: the annihilation of the self in the awareness of being with God. His fellow Capuchin, Ange de Joyeuse, described him in 1601 as 'the perfect Capuchin and the most consummate religious of his province, indeed of the whole order'. One vital element in his pursuit of perfection was scholarship: he read avidly, wrote readily, but his sight began to fail and this may have played an important part in turning him towards a more active rôle. Placed in charge of a Capuchin house of novices at Meudon, he did not confine himself to them but taught and preached in the countryside around Paris. As his fame as a preacher spread he was given more difficult assignments. In 1609 perseverance was rewarded by a notable triumph when he secured the establishment of a Capuchin house in Saumur against the opposition of Du Plessis-Mornay and the Huguenot leaders of the town.

With the co-adjutrix of Fontevrault, Antoinette d'Orléans, he began the reform of the greatest abbey in France until the point when Mme d'Orléans' new community of contemplatives (those nuns who accepted her reforms) were promoted to the status of a new order, the Congregation of Our Lady of Calvary. Father Joseph was given the task of advising this order whose principal devotion was that nearest to his own heart, that of Mary at the foot of the Cross. To this task alone he gave what would have been a life's work for many men; it has been reckoned that his letters and meditations composed for the Calvarians would fill altogether thirty octavo volumes or 15,000 pages! Most of his time was already spent on foot, tramping around the countryside inspecting Capuchin houses. He entered into the political world in 1615 when he acted as self-appointed mediator between Condé and Marie de Médicis. From then on he moved steadily closer to the centre of affairs, acknowledged as master of negotiation and acceptable to princes and magnates because of the unique combination he presented of gentleman and prophet. The governments of Europe were soon to know the relentless friar who walked to Rome or Ratisbon, fixing his mind upon the Cross or on the work of his Capuchins abroad, on his great vision of a European crusade, or on the immediate diplomatic moves by which the Habsburgs might be defeated; the unkempt, red-bearded figure with prominent blue eyes, who carried under his dusty cloak the sealed instructions of the king of France. The paradox of the mystic who dedicated so much of his life to the compromising work of diplomacy baffles us as it baffled contemporaries. Clues lie in the nature of his relationship with Richelieu. The Cardinal had two nicknames for him: Ezéchiely, the visionary and zealot, and Tenebroso-Cavernoso, the reserved, calmly resourceful, enigmatic diplomat.

He first met Richelieu when he was dealing with the Abbey of Fontevrault. Luçon was nearby and Father Joseph found its bishop a sympathetic ally and ready listener. If Richelieu was struck by the friar's fiery zeal, Father Joseph recognised in him a quality that was different but perhaps complementary to his own, a largeness of vision, a cool mind: 'I saw that young eagle before he had yet left the eyrie as he gazed without winking into the sun'. Both men were ambitious, though their tactical aims and priorities were different. Richelieu might think that Father Joseph's idea of a crusade against the Turks was impracticable while Spain remained in a position to dominate Europe, but it was an ideal with which he could sympathise. Father Joseph came to see in him the man to lead the party of those who wanted to reform the Church and strengthen the state. He resolved to use his influence to advance Richelieu's cause. A visit to Rome extended that influence enormously. He returned in 1617 with a pontifical letter addressed to the court of Spain empowering him to negotiate for the crusade; he expressed his elation in verse, a long epic in Latin about Turks and crusaders, and religious lyrics in French.

While he was in Rome, Richelieu had risen to power—and fallen. Father Joseph walked to Madrid, two companions dying of heat exhaustion on the way, and found that Spanish enthusiasm for the crusade was tempered by a shrewd idea that if, as Father Joseph naïvely suggested, France were to lead it, France would correspondingly benefit from it. Out of this rebuff grew a distrust

of Spain which was strengthened by Habsburg victories in the
Bohemian war and which came in the end to replace the crusade as
an immediate objective. He helped the Duc de Nevers to organise
an international army, the Christian Militia; it gained recruits but
suffered a fatal blow when Philip IV refused to allow its establishment in any of his possessions. After Nevers' ships had been
seized by the Huguenots, only the *Turciad*, a verse epic of 4,637
lines completed in 1625, was left to bear witness to Father Joseph's
dream; it pleased Pope Urban VIII who called it the 'Christian
*Aeneid*', but has had few admirers since.

Father Joseph was probably never happier than in these years
when as well as working for the crusade he was leading and
inspiring a campaign of evangelisation in Poitou and neighbouring provinces. But he was being drawn inexorably to Paris
and the court, and he did not resist the process. He became
unofficial confessor to Louis XIII and he won and held the
allegiance of Gaston of Orléans. He was not always discriminating
in the service he would render to Richelieu. In 1622 he acted as
intermediary in the contract of marriage between Richelieu's niece
Mlle de Pontcourlay and Luynes' nephew de Combalet, a match
which enriched Richelieu's family and strengthened the position
he had already secured by the Peace of Angoulême. When the
question of an attack upon Béarn was discussed, it was Father
Joseph, according to the Cardinal de Retz, speaking 'like the
prophets of the Old Testament' who swayed the council to decide
to proceed, though his chief work in this campaign, and later
when Richelieu was besieging La Rochelle, was the conversion of
the Huguenots. Like Richelieu, he did not believe that coercion
was enough by itself: 'forced religion is no longer religion', he
said.

Richelieu recognised what he owed to Father Joseph, 'Next to
God, the principal instrument of my present fortune,' as he said in
a letter to the Capuchin urging him to come to Paris. Father
Joseph came, having secured the necessary dispensation from the
general of his order, and became what he was to remain until his
death in 1638, Richelieu's aide, personal envoy and special adviser,
the *eminence grise* who was no less remarkable, though less sinister,
than the legend that began to grow about him in his lifetime and
which is conveyed by the anonymous wit who scribbled on his
tombstone a few days after his death: 'Is it not a strange thing,
that a demon should be so near to an angel?'

In the years after Ratisbon, he came to divide his time between his cell at the convent of the Rue Saint-Honoré and the apartments provided for him in Richelieu's country house at Rueil or at the Palais-Cardinal. In palace or convent he kept the rule of his order without relaxation. To state business and religious life he brought rare powers of intellectual concentration and physical endurance; he was living two full lives in one. He had the toughness and pragmatism that seem sometimes to go with spiritual insight. D'Avaux, his fellow diplomat, said that he seemed to have prescribed for himself a special rule of his own: 'having regularly practised meditation he could judge in a more orderly fashion of things and affairs'. Something of the man's inner compulsions can be inferred from the mortifications he inflicted on himself. As if his bed of planks, the ragged hair shirt, and the raw wounds of regular penitential scourgings were not enough, he added, ostensibly to stimulate fading sight, regular cauterisings of the back of his head. He could school himself to endure pain and drive his weary body, but the price he paid for immersing himself in the political world was not only physical: he sacrificed his peace of mind. He could not endure noise and had guards posted at his gates to drive away barking dogs. The mystic lost what he had held to be most precious, the constant awareness of God, the experience of union, the highest state of the mystic. There is a disillusionment about his last years, no less poignant for being the consequence of his deliberate choice. 'One must expel the life of self-will; in every panting breath, one must hunt down one's nature in an implacable course towards perfection' he had written; but after increasingly frantic efforts to find spiritual fulfilment he was oppressed by a sense of failure and wrote sometimes in a vein that suggests he had come to doubt his own salvation. For this neither the red hat of the Cardinal which the Pope was about to grant at the time of his death, nor the capture of Breisach, for all its strategic significance, would have been sufficient compensation. He tasted the bitterness that comes to those who hope to satisfy their highest aspirations through political action. Between the part of him that yearned for glory and the part that tramped the stony road that led to the mystic's heaven, Father Joseph could not be satisfied. As he well knew, 'the more of the creature, the less of God'. So our last impression of Father Joseph differs from that of Charles de Condren, Bérulle's successor as General of the Oratory, who declined an invitation to preach at Father

Joseph's funeral because he could not commend a man who had
lent himself to the unscrupulous designs of the Cardinal and was
therefore hated by all Frenchmen. It is rather of a perfectionist,
cruelly self-deceiving, essentially worldly, perhaps, for all his
heroic asceticism.

When the Capuchin died Richelieu was deprived of his chief
support. Father Joseph had perfectly complemented his own
character. Richelieu needed his ardent conviction and prophetic
insights. He knew the dangers and risks that surrounded him and
he was not an optimist, but when Father Joseph was there
enthusiasm and the vision of victory were always at hand. The
purposefulness of his devotion impressed the Cardinal as it did the
king; they were men who expected faith to bring results. Who but
Father Joseph could translate the revelations of his Calvarian nuns
into bracing and practical advice upon the duties of kingship?
Richelieu found time to compose, between 1636 and 1639, his
*Treatise of Christian Perfection* in which he advocated the mystical
goal of the practice of the presence of God. Whether it is seen as a
personal apologia, a sort of settling of accounts with God, or as a
heartfelt statement of what he felt to be most important, it is an
extraordinary work when we consider what else he was doing in
these years. We can see Father Joseph's influence in this as in other
manifestations of the deepening piety of Richelieu's later years.
Father Joseph gave him strength and serenity at a time when he
might otherwise have succumbed to the prolonged ordeal.

## 19. The Cultivated Statesman

No study of Richelieu is complete without consideration of his rôle as patron, intellectual and artist. Nor would he have wished to be judged on his political achievements alone. He was able to talk and write on equal terms with theologians, philosophers, poets and playwrights. He helped to make literature respectable at court where, as Chapelain wrote: 'poet, singer, ballet-dancer, beggar, buffoon and parasite' had been 'synonymous and inter-changeable terms'. Those whom he helped were not usually unappreciative though few expressed it so bluntly as Benserade in his epitaph: 'Here lies Cardinal Richelieu, more's the pity! And what upsets me—my pension goes with him.' Richelieu's patron-age was discriminating and influential because he did not think of the artist as a peripheral figure to be used to embellish a scene or praise a patron, but as a vital force in society. In the France of Descartes, Corneille and Philippe de Champaigne, where among fashionable people it was an offence to be stupid, where Arch-bishop de Gondi was a figure of fun because of his ignorance of theology and philosophy, the fact that the first minister was acknowledged to have a brilliant mind, that he wrote theological treatises, political maxims, verses, plays, listened every day to his private orchestra and went whenever he could to the theatre, was crucially important. Literature and the arts flourished in the glow of Richelieu's favour; there was little of the heavy direction or concern for outward appearances alone that characterised the court patronage of Louis XIV. Then again there did not occur that alienation of intellectuals from the régime which is so conspicuous a feature of France in the eighteenth century. We should beware of ascribing too much to the influence of one man, but it is a remarkable fact that in the great age that followed Richelieu's lifetime, writers and artists to a man accepted and supported absolute monarchy: Pascal, Racine, Boileau, Bossuet. Criticism was stilled, anarchy rejected; there was a consensus, and order ruled supreme.

Richelieu could not neglect the possibilities of propaganda. He did not have the field to himself. Indeed he was subjected to a stream of criticism, ranging from scurrilous personal abuse to reasoned argument. But he was not content to remain on the defensive against writers like de Morgues and du Chastelet. More than any statesman before him he used writers to present his aims and principles to the literate public. There was a great increase in this period of pamphlets and periodicals. The first printed newspaper, the *Strassburger Zeitung,* appeared in 1609. Throughout the Thirty Years War the rival apologists kept religious issues alive, each dwelling upon the atrocities and blasphemies of the other side. Richelieu knew that his particular audience was sophisticated and trained to argue and to weigh moral issues in precise terms. Where but in France could a theological dispute, that of the Jesuits and Jansenists, become a matter of intense public interest and debate? He was well served by several writers and there is little doubt that they were carefully briefed. He retained Fancan from about 1616 and later Cassan, as official publicists. François Fancan, canon of St Germain-l'Auxerrois, was an able polemical writer, a *bon Français,* that is to say a follower in the *politique* tradition of putting country before creed, and a violent critic of Spain. His powerful allegory, *France Mourante* (1623) dwelt upon the misfortunes which had befallen France, attacked the Brûlarts and Condé and urged the king to employ Richelieu instead. Was he too brilliant, or too independent for Richelieu? He was active on his behalf until 1627 when he was suddenly disgraced and sent to the Bastille, for no clear reason. He died there.[1] In 1632, when there was reason to fear Gustavus' intentions concerning the Rhineland, Cassan wrote a book arguing that the antiquity of rights (French claims to the Rhineland going back to King

---

[1] The reader may pursue these questions further in the article by G. Fagniez, 'Fancan et Richelieu' in *Revue Historique,* 1911. Fancan was essentially a free-lance, a man of convictions passionately held, neither subservient like Cassan, nor devoted like Father Joseph. He was more secular in outlook than Richelieu could ever be. He was violently anti-Jesuit and critical of the development of monasticism. His bold over-simplifications of policy served Richelieu well when he aspired to power, but irritated him when he was in power. Furthermore it is likely that he ranged himself among the opponents of the Gaston-Montpensier marriage, and that he was too much attached to the always suspect Duc de Soissons. Matthieu de Morgues alleged that Father Joseph was instrumental in his downfall.

Dagobert) does not reduce but actually improves their validity: it was dedicated to the Cardinal. A regular means of influencing domestic opinion was provided by the government newspapers, *Mercure* and the *Gazette*. The latter was started as a private venture by a doctor, Theophraste Renaudot, but taken under Richelieu's protection. When war came it was useful to be able to dress up small victories and cover up reverses. 'The *Gazette* shall play its part', Richelieu wrote, 'or Renaudot will lose the pension he has enjoyed up to the present.'

There were essays in political theory to take the war of ideas on to a loftier plane. In Balzac's *Prince* (1631) Machiavelli was adapted to the needs of the time with a new statement of the morality of the state. In his *Souveraineté du Roy* (1632) Lebret expounded a view of Divine Right which anticipated the extreme development of the idea by admirers of Louis XIV. Sovereignty, said Lebret, 'is supreme power bestowed on an individual, which gives him the right to command absolutely and which has for its end the repose and advantage of the public'. He further argued that all institutions and customs could be changed by the king 'for all persons, being equally subjects of the same king, are equally subject to the same law'. Where in this is the doctrine of fundamental laws of the state, whose ruler, in Loyseau's words, 'must exercise his sovereignty according to its own proper nature and the forms and conditions under which it is established'? The doctrine was flexible. Richelieu, for example, found it convenient to appeal to it in matters of diplomacy, but as it was expounded by Parlement, which Loyseau regarded as the prime defender of the fundamental laws, it stood in the way of policies aimed at increasing royal power in the country.

Richelieu therefore preferred to stress another traditional idea, that the king was absolute only when he acted within the limits of Christian morality. The public good, he wrote in *Testament Politique,* should be the sole end of the prince and his advisers. 'It is impossible to conceive how much good a prince, and those whom he employs to do his business, can do if they religiously follow this principle'; he contrasts this with 'the evil which a state suffers when they prefer the interests of individuals to those of the public'. Since 'Christian morality' is open to wide and subjective interpretation, the public good is easily liberated from moral restraints: it is a short step from the criterion of public good to that of *raison d'état*, a phrase often credited to Richelieu. He may not have coined it but he acted always on the assumption that acts that would be immoral in a private person might be justifiable if they were for the advantage of the state. The ruler must on occasion make, interpret and unmake laws, make wars (just wars), make and, under certain conditions, break treaties, raise taxes, and strike, if need be on mere suspicion, against the enemies of the state.

Before we consider further the Cardinal's own contribution to the contemporary dialogue of ideas it is necessary to outline the context of his thinking. As a statesman his position was unique; to some extent he was above the mêlée because he was able to command and to follow his own taste and ideas. He was also, however, a product of the age, sensitively aware of the cultural tendencies of the time. He was something of a Cartesian, something of an *honnête homme*. If in all his attitudes there was an obsession with the dangers of *dérèglement*, in this he was expressing as well as furthering the master-principle of cultural life in his time. He was also opposing an individualist concept which had a strong following; though among a minority, it was precisely this minority which challenged his rule and philosophy at all points.

The French upper and middle classes were the best educated in Europe. The advance of humanist ideas in the sixteenth century, the stimulus provided by the Reformation and the growth of a serious-minded Calvinist élite were elements in this situation. The distinctive feature, however, was the success of the Jesuits in adapting humanist ideals and methods, responding to the demand for a superior education for the well-to-do, and creating a system which married the principles of those who ran the schools to the needs and fashions of society in a way which suggests comparisons with English public schools of the nineteenth century. When the Jesuits were readmitted to France in 1603 they were severely restricted: only in three towns were they allowed to open new schools. These restrictions were flouted despite protests from the Sorbonne and they soon came near to having a monopoly of secondary education; even their rivals copied their methods. Their boarding schools provided an intensive formal training and a way of life.

A group of six Jesuits, each from a different country, had worked for fourteen years to produce the *Ratio Studiorum*. The essence of their curriculum and methods was that the mediaeval schoolmen were abandoned in favour of the classics. The emphasis

Q

was more upon style and attitudes than on ideas; at least ideas were
taught, through examples, rather than allowed to form in enquiry
and free study. The teacher embodied the authority of the parent
and the sanctions of the Church and his pupils were expected to
accept rather than to criticise. If the boy had to be punished,
flogging was administered by a servant while the master looked
away in sorrow. The Jesuits measured the success of their schools
partly by the extent to which their pupils respected and supported
the order in adult life and this depended upon establishing a
relationship of trust and respect at school. Pupils did not, of
course, necessarily become *dévôts* or find themselves drawn to the
exacting rule, the committed life of the Fathers. They may not all
have become competent Latinists nor shone in the social graces,
deportment, elocution and etiquette that were regarded as essential
parts of the finished gentleman, *honnête homme et chrétien*; but they
would become accustomed to corporate discipline, steeped in the
ideals and manners of Roman culture, conditioned to accept rule
and regularity by the elaborate rules of their own community and
the constant elevation of classical models: Cincinnatus and his
heroic simplicity, Themistocles and his magnanimity, Socrates and
his temperance. They were trained to recognise good taste and
harmony in their study of antiquity, and they learned that to
innovate was to undermine. The enclosed world of school and life
outside were less at variance than might have been expected, for
when they left school they found Jesuits influential everywhere, but
especially at court, renouncing the world, yet living in it and
using its methods—the paradox which was the source of their
strength. They came out steeped in Latin, ready to become
lawyers and diplomats, eager material for the expansion of the
bureaucracy.

The better educated of the upper classes continued to look in
their reading for a guide to their changing rôle in society; many
of them found it in the late classical authors, Seneca and Plutarch.
In Plutarch's tales of individual heroism might be found the Stoic
philosophy as it was practised by men of action. The will used
reason to control the passions: man was armed against the assaults
of fortune; in good times and bad he could live nobly. To live
nobly was to be true to one's destiny. Virtue was conceived in
individualistic terms and was necessarily self-centred; *devoir* was
the duty of being worthy to oneself. Despite the Stoic notion of
self-control a man might find his destiny in the single-minded

pursuit of his passions. *La gloire* (and how profoundly this concept has marked the French nation) was an ideal to be cherished for itself, pursued like a lover, with audacity and without limit. The plays of Corneille expressed a morality and mood in a way that appealed immensely to the upper classes. In plays like *Cinna* (the favourite of his contemporaries), *Horace* and *Polyeucte*, the plot is relatively simple and the play revolves round the conflict of passion and duty, between love and patriotic obligation, for example. His heroes are not so much real persons as posturing, declaiming embodiments of abstract qualities, intellect, pride and will, so placed in relation to events and to fate that their qualities are put to the test. The drama comes from argument and the cumulative effect of long tirades which should be heard rather than read for full effect. For Corneille the lowest thing was personal humiliation, the highest was self-mastery. The man who achieved this could pursue some ideal higher than self, honour, loyalty, even revenge. One can see why so many of his audience were intoxicated by Corneille; young nobles who conceived themselves to be repressed by Richelieu, lawyers who dreamed of becoming Gracchi, tribunes of the people: they were the *frondeurs* of the next generation.

The seventeenth century was 'the century of mathematics'. Logarithms were being brought into use, the slide-rule was invented. Notation, with most of the signs familiar to us, was being simplified and extended. Descartes contributed to mathematics the idea of the property of the curve and its use, in relation to fixed lines at right angles, and in equations which fixed that relationship. Pascal laid the foundations of integral calculus in an essay on conics which he wrote while still at school. The publication in 1647 of his work on the vacuum contributed to the solution of the problem which stood in the way of great advances in physics. So mathematics was unlocking ancient doors. Men were learning to think mathematically. To Descartes, as to Pascal, mathematics was impressive not only for its own sake but for the keys that its orderly, exact and related truths seemed to provide to the mysteries of mind, nature and universe. The basis of Descartes' philosophy was mathematics. As opposed to Bacon, who believed that new knowledge might be got by amassing facts and proceeding thence to general laws, he held that philosophy must proceed from what is clear and capable of definition to the explanation of what is complex and uncertain. Indeed he believed that learning might

impede reason by implanting conscious prejudice: the study of
Latin and history were of no assistance to him in the search for
truth.

'Sometimes one man', wrote Fontenelle of Descartes, 'gives the
tone to a whole century.' The limitation of the objectives of
science to what could be calculated, and the view of the universe as
a mechanism which affected theology and indeed all thought, so
profoundly bear the stamp of Descartes. *L'esprit de géométrie* was
the religion of the best minds of the time and pervaded every
realm of thought and art. 'The Eternal Word has turned Cartesian',
said Jurieu at the end of the century. As Fontenelle was to write:
'The geometric spirit is not so attached to geometry that it cannot
be disentangled and carried over in to other areas of knowledge'.
A work on politics, on criticism, perhaps even on eloquence will
be better, all other things being equal, if it is written by the hand
of a geometer. It played a part in the victory of rule in the arts and
in literature, in the insistence upon proportion and restraint.

It has been said of the painting of Vermeer that it shows not
only the light of Holland but also what Descartes called 'the
natural light of mind'. Is this not also true of Philippe de Champaigne, whose severely ordered design and rejection of all ornament not strictly relevant to the subject is Cartesian as much as
Jansenist? It is certainly true of Poussin. This great painter was
born in a peasant family in Normandy but lived in Rome for
forty years and was only once tempted to Paris for a stay of two
years. Many of his patrons were, however, French and his work is
the embodiment of French classicism, though, like Claude le
Lorrain, his scenery was usually Italian. Poussin's method illumines
the artistic values of his time. He believed that the processes
involved in artistic creation were essentially rational. Imagination
had to be moulded by rules of reason into forms of absolute
clarity, suited exactly to the subject. His approach was intellectual
and deliberate: he always began a painting by reading all he could
about a subject; to ensure verisimilitude he used to make a puppet
show of wax models, and from these he made larger models. He
never painted from life and his work has therefore a cold, marble
character, appealing like a work of architecture as much to mind
as to heart. Later the *Académie de Peinture et de Sculpture* was to
make this method the required standard for a painter who wished
to be accepted, and under the guidance of 'reason, rules and the
best masters' the *Académie* laid down laws of composition.

perspective and proportion. Lecturing to the *Académie*, le Brun
was able to take a painting of Poussin, *The Gathering of Manna,* and
trace the ancient models for every figure in the composition.

The structure of the state could likewise be thought of in
rational, geometrical terms. As le Bret wrote, 'Sovereignty is no
more divisible than is the point in geometry': in other words there
must be no competition with royal authority. An echo of this can
be heard in the terms of the royal declaration of 1652: 'All
authority belongs to us. We hold it of God alone, and no person
of whatever quality he may be can pretend to any part of it.'
Along with the belief in the power of reason to disclose the whole
truth went the mathematician's habit of dismissing exceptions.
Belief in reason was the essence of Richelieu's thought. As he
wrote: 'The light of natural reason enables everyone to know that
since man is endowed with reason, he must do nothing except by
reason, for otherwise he would act contrary to his nature and, as
a result, contrary to Him who is its Author'. The theological
conclusion is as typical as the neat logic that leads to it.

But Richelieu the rationalist, who frequented the *salons* and was
painted by Champaigne, was also the practising politician, a
pessimist about human nature, who knew very well that men did
not behave predictably and who had constantly to adjust his
policies and methods to meet changing circumstances and human
wilfulness. The state must be powerful, he thought, not only
because it embodied a rational principle, but because men were
irrational and must therefore be restrained to save them from the
consequences of their conduct. It is this combination of the intellectual, the empiricist, and the creative artist which makes his
writing so interesting.

We have seen that Richelieu took to his pen when he wanted to
instruct and persuade and clarify issues, sometimes for his own
benefit as well as for others. The memoirs, which did not appear
until eighteen years after his death, and first under the title *Histoire
de la Mère et du Fils,* were not his work alone. It is likely that he
meant the Bishop of St Malo, who had worked for some years in
Richelieu's household, to compose something out of the papers
that he put at his disposal; it is also likely that he dictated certain
passages. The memoirs are an account of Richelieu's rise to power
and ministry in the early years. He was never complacent about
the way in which he had secured power, nor about his choice of
policies. Sensitive about the moral issues as well as about the

methods he had pursued, he wanted to justify to posterity the part he had played in a decisive decade. He wrote lucidly and power-fully, not only with a polish that betrays a deliberate and studied artistry, but also with a penetration and force that tells us that what he wrote was distilled from experience. His *Testament* and *Maximes* are struggle recollected in tranquillity.

The *Testament Politique* may well have been intended as a manual of instruction for Louis XIII after Richelieu's death, and is in form only an enlarged version of the memoranda which he regularly composed for his master; like those weighty, personal documents it contains a ranging survey of political and diplomatic problems, together with personal advice attuned to the awkward character of the king.[1] The *Testament* also contains rules and

---

[1] The question of the authenticity of the *Testament Politique* and its value as historical evidence is much disputed. The extreme view that it is a complete fraud, a later compilation falsely ascribed to the Cardinal, is no longer taken seriously. There remain two distinctive and plausible views. That of the late Louis André, supported broadly by Mousnier, is that the *Testament* represents Richelieu's wish to leave a record of the reign and to pass on to the king the benefit of his own experience. André sees it as belonging to the middle period, being mainly done about 1634-8, influenced by Père Joseph, but substantially Richelieu's work (though largely by dictation to secretaries) and characteristic of his methods (like his lengthy memoranda to the king) and of his style and beliefs. The other view is held notably by E. Esmonin, who sees the *Testament* as a compilation by secretaries and authentic only in so much as it is a mosaic of fragments of Richelieu's own writing pieced together by a later hand, possibly the Abbé de Bourzeis. He would say, therefore, that for Richelieu's ideas the reader should go to his authentic cor-respondence rather than to the *Testament*. Tapié brings the two views together in a convincing way by an imaginative reconstruction of the way in which Richelieu worked, giving to secretaries a general idea, a canvas as it were, documents to work on and a number of dictated passages on matters that he regarded as especially important. (Did Tapié, one wonders, have the statesman-historian Churchill in mind?) So Tapié, finding numerous passages emanating from Richelieu's chancellery and bearing the authentic stamp of his experience and intelligence, concludes that the *Testament* was written 'on the initiative and under the control of Richelieu, containing in all parts Richelieu's thought'.

The reader who is curious to pursue the matter may find the debate a fascinating one. The considered reflections of a statesman are valuable evidence, but only if it is reasonably certain that they are authentic. The protagonists use evidence and construct their arguments with a blend of logic and passion that provides a fine example of historical

reflections of a more general character upon matters of statecraft. For instance, he devoted a long passage to the faults of the French army. 'There is no nation in the world so unfit for war as ours.' He goes on to argue that the French, valiant, courteous and humane as they were, were unreliable, impatient, unaccustomed to endure fatigue and hardship, caring little for their country. This was the weapon with which he had tried to make his diplomacy effective! Richelieu plainly felt that he had never had the military support that he deserved, and the record of the French armies in this period bear him out. 'The most powerful state in the world cannot boast of enjoying an assured security if it cannot defend itself against an unexpected invasion.' Elsewhere in the *Testament* Richelieu affirms the necessity of negotiation: always be ready to negotiate. He was not thinking only of foreign diplomacy but of all affairs; from his first appearance on the political scene in the States-General of 1614 to the unravelling of the last conspiracy against him, he had had to negotiate in order to survive. First and foremost he was a diplomat. We see in the *Testament* how the notion of prestige dominates his thinking, a natural preoccupation of the diplomat: 'The slightest loss of this kind (reputation) means that the king has nothing else to lose'.

At times diplomacy was not enough: examples were necessary. The passage that follows is crucial, indeed it might be regarded as the summary and justification of his work. Those who find it repellent should consider the context—incessant conspiracy and fear of assassination that was all too well founded not only in the existence of plots against him but in the recent history of public figures: Louis XIII's two predecessors had died in this way. 'Laws are wholly useless unless followed by enforcement which is so

polemics. Sure proofs evade them, but this does not dampen their ardour.

H. Hauser, 'Testament Politique', *Bulletin de la Société d'Histoire Moderne,* April, 1935.

L. André, 'Testament Politique', *Bull. Soc. Hist. Mod.,* Paris, 1947. (The best edition of the *Testament*, though scholars disagree about his handling of the text.)

E. Esmonin, 'Testament Politique', *Bull. Soc. Hist. Mod.,* January, 1937; and same journal, October, 1951.

R. Mousnier, 'Testament Politique', *Rev. Hist.,* 1949 (review of André's edition).

Ed. Mousnier, Esmonin & V. L. Tapié, 'Observations sur le Testament Politique, *Bull. Soc. Hist. Mod.,* December 1951-January 1952.

absolutely necessary that although in the ordinary course of affairs justice requires authentic proof, the same is not true of those which concern the state, because in such cases persuasive interference must sometimes be held to be sufficient, for parties and cabals which are formed against public security ordinarily act with such cunning and secrecy that there is never any clear proof except in the event, when the matter is beyond remedy'. The *Testament* would not, however, be such an impressive document if the author were solely concerned with matters of order and security. Naturally these loomed large. Long passages deal, however, with economic and fiscal problems and show how ready he was to modify, in the light of experience, the ideas of his youth.

In one important point the Cardinal was as much aware of the importance of trade and the burden of taxes as he had been in his younger days, but he was now oppressed by a sense of failure. He recognises the gap between the ideal and the reality. It is necessary not to overcharge the people lest they be ruined, and equity as well as interest requires 'a proportion between what the prince demands from the subjects and what they can pay without notable inconvenience'. But the *taille* alone had doubled since he came to power and was more than forty million by 1636. He reiterated his faith in France's manufactures and alluded constantly to the prospect of peace, the essential condition for what today would be called a 'take-off' in the economy. 'It is a common statement, but true, that as states often increase their extent in war, they usually enrich themselves in peace by commerce.' He had been absorbed with the preliminary stage, with strengthening a precarious state; had he been granted the health and strength, he would have devoted equal effort to the realisation of the second stage. This, at any rate, is what he wanted posterity to think. Through the *Testament* runs a continuing and touching paradox. Alongside the disillusionment, the acceptance of fallibility in human beings, institutions and schemes, we find an underlying confidence in his treatment of the major themes. He projected a future in which France would be the greatest and richest of countries and he based this surprisingly on his assessment of his fellow-countrymen. 'The French are capable of anything provided that those who command them are capable of showing them what they must do.' Richelieu the patriot was never wholly submerged by Richelieu the cynic.

The *Maximes d'État* were only jottings by comparison with the extended argument of the *Testament*. If they represent his considered views on certain topics they can also be misleading if quoted in isolation. The writing of maxims was a popular diversion of the time; the art of conveying the essence of wisdom in a sentence was cultivated in the *salons*. He probably enjoyed the exercise, much as he enjoyed writing verses. The formula was to be neat and striking. Richelieu knew very well that statesmanship was more than an academic exercise. As he wrote, 'Nothing can be more dangerous in a state than those who will govern kingdoms by the maxims they find in books'. We can derive some of the maxims from his own experience. 'Secrecy is the first essential in matters of state'. 'To make a law and not to see it put into action is to authorise what you have yourself forbidden.' Sometimes we have a valuable *précis* of a whole area of thought: 'One would have to be a very bad theologian not to know that the king receives his crown and his temporal power from God alone'. 'In popular opinion, matters falsely presented are very willingly accepted as true.' Some of his remarks must, however, be taken with a pinch of salt. 'People are like mules which, being used to labour, are spoiled more by rest than by labour' (the writer, let it not be forgotten, seldom ceased from working himself and lived an ascetic life amidst the splendour of his household). Others he would have done well to act on himself. He offended many by his sarcastic tongue, yet wrote: 'Wounds inflicted by the sword are more easily healed than those inflicted by the tongue'.

One characteristic act of Richelieu was the foundation of the *Académie Française* in 1635. This body stood for purity and discipline in language against the *dérèglement* which Richelieu deplored in the arts as in politics. The *Académie* was also the natural product of the culture of the time and of the *salon* in particular. The *salon* is a distinctive expression of French culture. In this period it is inseparable from the name of the Marquise de Rambouillet whose *hôtel* in the rue Saint-Thomas du Louvre, only a few steps away from the palace, has an essential place in the history of the time as the focus for many years of the social and intellectual life of the capital. Lesser *salons* might be the scene of idle scandal and intrigue or the pretentious nonsense later satirised by Molière in *Les Précieuses Ridicules*. But in her boudoir of blue velvet and silver this formidable hostess enjoyed an ascendancy so unchallenged that historians write of her following as 'a movement'. Here there was a free-for-all of the talents, a mixing of aristocrat and bourgeois, subject only to the rules of *honnêteté*. This word defies translation but it represents something significant: the *honnête homme* is the intellectual concept of the gentleman, the evolution from the warrior hero type, with the aid of the fashionable new academies and the material improvements that brought comfort and elegance into rich men's lives, into a model of civility. The phrase was popularised by Nicholas Faret, who used it as the title of his treatise on correct deportment or *bienséance*. His subtitle was *L'Art de Plaire à la Cour,* but the notion meant more than a code of manners since it embraced an interest in ideas and literature. The *honnête homme* 'ne se pique de rien', cultivated *générosité*, the open-mindedness which he was expected to learn from the rule of reason, and the 'mean' that the classical authors extolled.

At Mme de Rambouillet's meetings themes were set for discussion upon the most difficult questions of language, ethics and, of course, love. When Madeleine de Scudéry took upon herself the mantle of Mme de Rambouillet, her own interests as a romantic novelist dominated the discussions. The character of love was analysed tirelessly and with as many refinements as among the selfless heroes and heroines of her novels. Refinement of feeling was the soul of *préciosité*. Tedious, precious, artificial it all might seem. The cultivation of wit for its own sake suggests sterility. At their best, however, the *salons* provided a milieu for free discussion amongst very different people and talents. When the two sexes met and talked in an atmosphere of equality the way was open to that feminisation of French culture which was so strong an influence in the *grand siècle*. The idealisation of love and worship of heroism could be pretty disastrous when the lovers and heroes were playing the game of politics. The history of the Fronde is evidence of this, with its theatrical atmosphere of make-believe, resounding gestures and sordid manœuvres, gallantries and reckless promiscuity, political motives almost lost in a tangle of personal interests and love affairs—a 'war of chamber pots' that left its mark also in hundreds of devastated villages. *Frondeurs* might be habitués of the *salons*. In the character of the Cardinal de Retz we see a fine example. But in the long run the *salon* tamed the anarchists and the Corneillian hero became the *honnête homme*; extremes went out of fashion. The decline of duelling witnesses to the process.

Just as the *salons* of the eighteenth century helped to prepare for the Revolution, so the *salons* of Richelieu's day conditioned people to accept absolute monarchy. Here Richelieu was swimming with the tide. There was a growing body of Frenchmen who were becoming convinced that disorder was dangerous. Even without him there would have been a movement towards order and restraint. The arbiters of the *salons* were concerned above all for precision in the use of words and the excision of exaggeration and vulgarity. It was appropriate that Richelieu should be the man who founded the *Académie*. There is an analogy between the way in which the systematic and dictatorial refinement of the language led to the supremacy of French as the European language of diplomacy and culture for the next hundred years, and the pioneer work of the Cardinal in government which led also to Louis XIV, Versailles and the years of mastery. The *Académie* was intended to hold a watching brief over the language, to preserve its purity by its decrees and publications. This work was to be crowned by the publication of a dictionary, not in the event until 1694. Its authority grew, meanwhile, until it came to be regarded as the public guardian of taste; in this rôle it promoted orthodoxy and supported those who were already trying to influence taste in this way. Malherbe had been a pioneer: poet and translator, patronised by Marie de Médicis, very much a court writer, he taught that poetry was a craft and that the poet must preserve balance and eschew vulgarity. Vincent Voiture, habitué of Mme de Rambouillet's *salon* and acknowledged master of the art of conversation, was a gentler critic than Malherbe; his irony and finesse have led some critics to see him as a lesser Voltaire. While drawing-room poets were setting new standards of delicacy and tact in language, grammarians were examining the proper uses of words, with the aim of eliminating obscurity and fitting the language for the clear expression of ideas and the converse of society. Besides the self-imposed task of removing common and provincial idioms, they set themselves to assimilate the new abstract and technical terms, usually Latin-derived. Latin was giving way to French as the language of scholarship. Descartes' use of French for the *Discours de la Méthode* (1637) was a landmark in this process. As a medium for expressing ideas, French enjoys a natural advantage over English, for instance, in its subjunctive forms, which enable the writer to pass from opinion to fact, from hypothetical to categorical, without fear of misunderstanding, by changing a letter or two in a word. In the process of bringing the language under the control of *les règles*, Jean Chapelain was a central figure. He was the leader of the triumvirate (the others were Conrart and Balzac) who ruled the literary world in Richelieu's day. It was from their circle that the idea of the *Académie* came, apparently by way of Boisrobert, an absentee prior and elegant court poet in Richelieu's entourage, to the attention of Richelieu. Chapelain, as Richelieu's literary adviser, drew up the regulations of the *Académie*. He maintained that an artist could only achieve beauty by conforming to the rules which he claimed were based on reason but were derived entirely from classical writers. An academic approach to the arts can be dangerous and he made himself look silly by criticising *Le Cid* on the grounds that it broke the three dramatic unities, defying probability, unity of place and moral decorum. His own epic, *La Pucelle*, is a tedious work.

An important assumption of the *salons* was that good writing belonged exclusively to polite society. In the hands of Claude de Vaugelas, whose *Rémarques sur la Langue Française* summarised a lifetime's consideration of the niceties of language, this élite was interpreted very narrowly. He disallowed the claims to influence of both Parlement and the Sorbonne! The consequence of such a doctrine was that literature became, even more than painting and sculpture, an expression of aristocratic values. The Prince of Condé (father of the 'great Condé') and Gaston of Orléans used, allegedly, to have a censor in their houses so that if any of their families spoke a word that savoured of the Palais de Justice or the Sorbonne he should incur a fine. Long before the *Académie* put the seal of authority upon the choice of words with the publication of the Dictionary, such words as *cracher* or *vomir* were eliminated as plebeian or crude. Corneille went so far as to revise his plays in order to remove archaic words.

As an active patron and a mild dictator in fields where he was able to exert influence, Richelieu played no small part in this literary movement. As a patron he aided struggling men of letters with more discernment and generosity than either Fouquet, the plutocratic *surintendant* of the Mazarin period, Mazarin himself, or even Louis XIV, whose disembursements to the arts were negligible in relation to the total budget, and who left it largely to Colbert. Colbert systematised patronage, ran it on business-like lines and expected the artists on the pay-roll to render their due in advertisement of the régime, even when they were not working directly for the king. Louis and Colbert were sincere in their appreciation of the arts, but in times of retrenchment the artists were the first to suffer. By contrast Richelieu was himself an artist who delighted in poetry and plays. It was a bond between him and the king. On the eve of war, in March 1635, king and Cardinal were engrossed in plans for the production of the *Ballet of the Blackbird*, of which the *Gazette* loyally recorded that Louis 'devised the dance figures and the music and designed the costumes'. In January 1641 Richelieu mounted a theatrical party and ball in the Palais-Cardinal, attended by the king and queen: the central feature was a play, *Mirame*, a satire of political flavour on the peoples of Europe, in which he had collaborated. In the same season he celebrated the opening of the new theatre he had built by arranging a ballet on the success of French arms.

His love of formal beauty, taste for magnificence and constant concern for reputation and the view of posterity lead us to expect that Richelieu would be an ambitious builder. In an age of exciting developments in architectural style he aspired to what his money could buy and built in the grand manner. Shortly after coming into office he bought a whole block of buildings along the rue St Honoré, demolished them and commissioned Jacques Lemercier to build him a palace on the site. Lemercier, who brought from his training at Rome the academic, classical style just before its full baroque flowering, created a masterpiece, the Palais-Cardinal which is now the Palais-Royal; it was at least as fine as any of the royal palaces. He was next employed on embellishing the Sorbonne, of which Richelieu was Rector, by constructing a church whose great cupola, surmounted by a cross, is one of the landmarks of Paris today. Richelieu was buried there, as he intended, in the atmosphere of scholarship and debate that he had found so congenial. But Lemercier's most spectacular commission was reserved for Richelieu's birthplace in Poitou. Here on the site of the old family *château*, enclosing the apartments where he was born, his master of works, Nicholas Durand, supervised the construction of a new *château*. In 1631 his estate was elevated into a *duché-pairé*, summit of the hierarchy of title. On the estate, outside the walls of the *château*, the new town of 'Richelieu' was built, on a severe rectangular design. This was indeed a *folie de grandeur*. The town was designed to house Richelieu's officials, servants and clients, and it was hoped that neighbouring gentry would build *hôtels* there, as some did, under the regulations of Richelieu's architect. As well as a fine church in the 'Jesuit' style, there was a house of the *Pères de la Mission*, Vincent de Paul's organisation, in which Richelieu took great interest. Provision for them was made in a special clause in his will. The town lies off the main routes, in quiet countryside. It had, and has, no economic justification.

Locke visited it in 1678 and was impressed. 'This morning we left Richelieu, the most compleat peice of building in France, where in the out side is an exact symetry, in the inside convenience and beauty, the richest guilding and best statues that are to be seen anywhere, the avenues on all sides exceeding handsome and magnificence on all sides. . . . The towne is built with the same exactness that the house, and though by its natural situation it has not the convenience to be a town of great trade, yet the great priviledges the Cardinal has got setled upon it, being a free towne, exempte from Taile and salt, cheape living in it will always keep it full of people and the houses deare in it.'

It is today much as it was in the seventeenth century, quiet and shabby but miraculously intact within its walls, a chequerboard of houses, the larger ones in the main streets gabled behind courtyards. The *château* has gone, destroyed in the Revolution, but the park remains, with its splendid avenues of chestnut trees. The market is as it was built, with its magnificent beamed roof. Only on market days does the town come to life. Otherwise the town sleeps, an exquisite memorial to the Cardinal's pride.

## 20. Limited Objectives

In December 1636, while the Habsburg armies were completing their retreat from France, Ferdinand, king of Hungary, was elected king of the Romans; two months later his father died and he became Emperor under what still seemed to be favourable auspices. The leading German states supported him, neither Sweden nor France presented insuperable military difficulties, Spain was still formidable, Bavaria was a potent ally and his own troops had a fair record of success since the elimination of Wallenstein. The Austrian hereditary lands formed, if not a single unit, at least a more coherent group than they had in 1618, and the reign began with hopeful plans for reconstruction. If in retrospect Corbie looks like a turning-point in the war, it was not evident at the time. Among the French there was as much anxiety as relief. The frontier provinces were beginning to experience the horrors with which Germans had long been familiar. In the so-called 'war of the two Burgundies', the nobility and peasantry of the Spanish provinces joined with Gallas' Spaniards and Croats to make systematic war and pillage against their French neighbours. In the work of the Lorraine artist Callot there survives a vivid impression of the sufferings of the helpless people in a territory that changed hands several times during this period. His famous series, *Les Misères de Guerre,* was actually executed in 1633, the year of Richelieu's invasion of Lorraine, but the message transcends time and place. Pictures like the famous one in which a priest stands on a ladder, giving absolution to a man who is about to join a row of victims already hanging like scarecrows from a tree in the middle of a ring of soldiers, are civilisation's commentary on the unpleasantness of war. The next few years saw the crushing of local revolts, experience gained at some cost in the campaigns on the frontiers and in north Italy, the sporadic disturbances of faction and the constant worry of a deteriorating financial state as deficit was piled on deficit. France's problems were different from those of

Spain; for one thing her material resources were far greater. The Spanish were about to experience a sequence of calamities from which the country could not recover; the Fronde was later to show that the French government was also strained to breaking point by the demands of war upon a precarious political structure.

The escalation of government expenditure on war after 1635 coincided with a severe phase in the recession of demand and trade which affected all Europe to some extent at this time. The main argument of those who were opposed to the extension of hostilities from the Mantuan crisis to the final commitment to war against Spain was that the economy could not sustain the necessary expansion of the armed forces. Richelieu willed the end and believed that the nation must provide the means. He was aware of the sacrifice involved though he was probably more concerned about the damage to his expansionist plans for trade and manufactures than about the livelihood of the peasant. His choice of war was dictated, we have seen, by many considerations, but it was the choice of the lesser of two evils, one that he believed was required, if not dictated, by the preponderance of Habsburg arms and the threat to France's security. 'Guns or butter?' Defence budgets are notoriously hard to evaluate, and they can usually be defended only by reference to hypothetical situations. We are in no better situation to decide whether Richelieu was right than were his contemporaries, though we can perceive more clearly from this distance the nature of the problem.

In a survey prepared for the Cardinal in 1639 by Galand as a prelude to a comprehensive reform when peace should permit, the revenue from all taxes, and from the crown lands was estimated to be 79 million livres. After deducting 47 million livres attributable to the expense of collecting, the actual Treasury receipt was therefore 32 million livres. The load that was imposed upon the tax-paying population was growing fast but the state was not benefiting proportionately. With more officials there were less people to pay the *taille*; as the debt rose, interest on the debt became a greater charge upon the revenue. After 1630 there began a period of devaluation. Foreigners found that French silver was becoming cheaper in relation to gold and bought it; the shortage of silver that resulted had a depressing effect on trade. The government was eventually forced to have recourse to an official devaluation (Edicts of March and June 1636). The mass of people were trapped in a static if not actually deteriorating situation;

taxes went up while incomes stood still until the burden became intolerable and the victims sought relief by rebelling, not against the king but against the officers who, they claimed, were abusing their powers.

The drain of silver was most noticeable in the provinces, in areas of deep country and small towns, where money transactions were usually in coins of small denomination. These coins were often in a poor state, *monnaie noir,* and 'bad coin drives out good'. Merchants exploited this situation whenever possible. Good money was hoarded. When the tax-payer was faced by the demands of the collector he might borrow from some local notable, who received goods or services in exchange. At the same time in the larger towns, especially in Paris, luxurious fashions caused a steady outflow of available specie. Jewels, fine silks, spices and exotic merchandise were brought from the east by travelling merchants to the great fairs. No wonder that Laffemas attacked the merchants of Lyons so violently. So good money was drawn from the countryside to certain privileged centres, and thence abroad.

The distress of *journaliers* and *ouvriers,* the poor sediment of country and town, was exacerbated by the fact that others were evidently benefiting from the economic needs of the government. There was always scope among merchants and middlemen, among master craftsmen and the richer peasants, for the slow, patient accumulation of capital, the nest-egg of today which might be the base for the fortune of tomorrow. At the top of the ladder there were families like the Legendres of Rouen, importers of luxury goods, money changers and brokers, farmers and lessees of other men's estates committed to making the most of the feudal dues, tax-farmers, 'a sort of pirates', in the words of a crown official before the *notables* in 1626, 'who take the best part of your revenues before they arrive at their proper destination'. The tax-farmers were hated more than any class of men since their exactions seemed to be largely for their own benefit. The extent of the piracy is hard to measure. The job of the *traitant* was a risky one. In 1641, two leading *traitants,* Sabathier and Barbier, became bankrupt and the government declined to help them. The *traitant's* demands grew proportionately with the needs of the state until by the end of the century he might expect a return of about 25 per cent. In Richelieu's day 20 per cent was not uncommon; enough to incur the hatred of the peasant and the

R

jealous official alike. In 1648 Parlement excluded from their courts all *traitants*, their agents, even their sons and sons-in-law. But to raise high taxes without recourse to private enterprise was beyond the capacity of any state, though Sweden and Holland, relatively small and exceptionally well-governed, were showing the way to greater efficiency. So long as the *traitants* were operating in a seller's market, when the government's needs gave them the edge in bargaining, abuse of the system would persist. An administrative revolution was half of what was needed to remedy the situation; the other half was a sustained attempt by the government to live within its means. This in turn required peace. The only period of significant reform after the death of Henry IV was the decade of the sixties when Colbert was able to double the yield of the *taille* while actually lowering its rate: this was a decade of peace, broken by only a year of war.

One aspect of the state's predicament was the mass creation of offices. They were created in order to be sold because they provided quick, easily raised cash to bridge part of the gap between income and expenditure. They were bought avidly though from time to time the market was temporarily saturated and prices fell as they will on any exchange where supply exceeds demand: an office was a straightforward investment, the best available after land, with commerce and industry taking for most bourgeois a bad third place. Land came first because it was reliable, permanent and brought prestige. Inside every bourgeois was a seigneur, waiting his chance to emerge, to rationalise and exploit the feudal dues in a business-like way. But allowing for regional and temporary variations, the values of offices increased more rapidly than comparable investment in land. Through land and office together, substantial bourgeois grew richer in a society which, in terms of total product, was almost standing still, partly because they were not contributing proportionately, either in the form of investment in industry or in taxes. It is against this background that we have to look at the failure of Richelieu's blueprints for commerce and colonies, at the increase in the *taille* and the imposition of new taxes, at sales of office and mounting deficits.

What could be done by a government that was committed to large expenditures? The idea of substituting indirect taxes for direct appears in the *Testament*. In practice, of course, indirect taxes were imposed alongside the *taille* and were resented. The tax on wine played a big part in the Dijon riots in 1630, the Bordeaux riots in 1635 and the *croquant* revolt of 1636. The *édit des cabaretiers,* as it was called, had to be withdrawn. The *sol par livre* (a form of surcharge) fared little better; it raised prices and tempers.

The Church offered a tempting target with its vast estates and fine buildings. In 1640 all public institutions were required to supply details of their property and income: the resulting inventory was to provide for a fair assessment of, and tax upon, the Church's wealth, and when this became plain there was much righteous indignation. Bullion claimed that the king, as sovereign, had the right to 'make all the orders of the kingdom contribute to the cost of war'. He died at the end of the year and with his colleague Bouthillier playing a less masterful rôle, Richelieu took a hand in financial management which up till now he had left entirely to his *surintendants.* The way in which he broadened the debate about taxing the Church provides an insight into his political method and philosophy. The obstacle was formidable. The institution of *mortmain* rests on the idea that land given to the Church was inalienable. Furthermore the claim to sovereignty over the Church roused opponents of Gallicanism. So economic arguments brought ready converts to Ultramontane views. Richelieu attacked on two fronts. Parlement was served with a stern warning against any show of resistance by the Edict of February 1641 forbidding any discussion of affairs of state, administration or finance—a landmark in the progress of absolutism. Meanwhile Richelieu encouraged the brothers Dupuy to write a book on the historical origins of the liberties of the French Church. He would have preferred a moderate, pragmatic approach, relying upon precedents such as the extraordinary payments made by the Church during the Hundred Years War. Their book was so complete a statement of the Gallican position that he had to show his disapproval by accepting the dedication to himself of a reply written by Pierre de Marca, who argued for the supremacy of the Pope over a general council of the Church. Even this book Rome found erroneous in points of detail and it was put on the Index. Richelieu thus found himself involved in a quarrel with the Papacy which weakened his position when it came to persuading the French Church to accept taxation. Conversely his attempts to tax the clergy made his attitude toward Gallicanism, in the eyes of Rome, seem more radical than it actually was. Despite careful management of the elections to the Church Assembly, which met at Mantes in spring 1641 to consider the government's demand, there was hot opposition and Richelieu only secured just over half of the seven million he required of them.

'Expenditure in cash is up to forty million, the *traitants* are abandoning us, and the masses will not pay either the new or the old taxes. We are now at the bottom of the pot.' Thus Bullion to Richelieu in 1639, writing under the shadow of the Normandy risings. What, in these circumstances, could Richelieu do? The international loan market was running dry and his agent in Amsterdam, Lopez, was having to pay higher rates of interest for his money. The only way to tap native reserves of capital was to multiply offices. Fortunately the appetite of the bourgeoisie remained keen as ever. So Pelion was piled on Ossa. In the *Chambres des Comptes* alone, there were eight new masters, seven checkers, ten auditors; in the *Cour des Aides,* a complete new chamber. There were twenty-four new additions to the office of royal secretary. In the provinces new offices abounded; annexed territories were of course fair game and Metz received a Parlement. More offices were made hereditary on payment of an extra sum. In this way substantial sums were raised but the authority, competence and repute of officials declined and the older generation of office-holders grew restive. The future was being mortgaged for the sake of present survival.

Shortage of money contributed to a serious French reverse in March 1637. The Grisons, thinking that Rohan's unpaid troops were on the point of mutiny, came to terms again with the Spanish, so that Rohan was forced to evacuate the defiles: the Habsburg life-line was open again, and Rohan sought refuge in Geneva from the Cardinal's rage. In the autumn of the same year two useful allies died: the Dukes of Mantua and Savoy, both without direct heirs. In Savoy the regency went to the Duchess Chrétienne, Louis XIII's sister, but her authority had to be sustained against her brothers-in-law. One of these, Thomas, commanded a Spanish army in the Netherlands; the other, the Cardinal of Savoy, was attached to the Spanish faction in the College of Cardinals. The new ruler of Mantua was an infant and the regent was Charles of Nevers' daughter-in-law Maria, inclined to favour the Spanish. In March 1638 she signed a treaty with the Spanish governor of the Milanese, agreeing to hand over

Montferrat, with Casale, to Spain. Montiglio, the governor of Casale, was in an awkward position since there was a French garrison in the citadel; he tried to comply with the regent's order but was arrested by the Cardinal de la Valette, whom Richelieu had sent from Flanders to take command in Italy when Créqui was killed during a reconnaissance. At the court martial he was offered his life in return for a complete confession; he was then sent to France and eventually executed all the same.

The effort planned for 1638 was prodigious. France had never made war on this scale before. Counting Bernard's there were six armies: in Flanders, Marshal Châtillon; in Picardy and Champagne, Marshal de la Force; in Alsace, Bernard supported by Guébriant; in Franche-Comté, Longueville; in Guyenne, Condé; and in Italy, Créqui and la Valette. But the achievement was incommensurate. Too many officers, like Richelieu's brother-in-law, the Duc de Brézé, found some specious excuse for leaving the army in autumn: he wanted to return to his estate in Anjou to enjoy the melon harvest and get into shape for the hunting. Sheer inexperience led to expensive mistakes. When Châtillon was investing St Omer he omitted to close a canal which the Spanish used to feed and reinforce the garrison. When Thomas of Savoy and Piccolomini threatened his own supply lines, Châtillon had to abandon the siege.

In May 1638 la Valette made a show of force outside Turin. Chrétienne was reluctant at first to commit herself to a treaty but when a Spanish army invaded Montferrat she placed the Savoyard army under French direction. Suddenly the boy-duke died and Chrétienne's regency automatically lapsed. The matter of the regency of the five-year-old Charles Emmanuel II had to be referred to the Emperor. Richelieu tried to win over the Cardinal of Savoy, who now stood next in line of succession, with promises of marriage to Condé's daughter (despite his title he was not an ordained priest) and great French estates, but without success. The Emperor predictably quashed the regency of Chrétienne and sent Thomas from Flanders to execute the decree; la Valette was unable to save Turin and agreed to a two months' truce in August 1639. Chrétienne, still fearing to be too closely involved with France, refused to hand over her son to Louis XIII's protection. 'This wretched woman', as Richelieu called her, had a particular antipathy toward Richelieu; he believed that her Jesuit adviser, Père Monod, was leading her astray and had him arrested and imprisoned in Montmélian. The French position crumbled, la Valette died; when the truce expired, his successor, the Comte de Harcourt, was forced at first to retreat from Turin, leaving the garrison to hold the citadel, and the Cardinal of Savoy also captured Nice. In the following year, however, Harcourt struck back; his cavalry general, the young Turenne, who had already won acclaim in the fighting in Flanders, beat off the Spanish general Leganez, and Thomas was forced to surrender the city on terms drawn up by Mazarin, the former Papal diplomat, whom Richelieu had now persuaded to serve him instead.[1] This was not the end of the war. The brothers

---

[1] There is no satisfactory life of Mazarin and many misconceptions cling to his name. He was not for example merely a Sicilian, nor was his family obscure. His father was a Sicilian who had become chamberlain to the powerful Colonna family of Rome; his mother was a Roman. Giulio grew up in Rome and became a brilliant pupil at a Jesuit school. He was handsome, amiable, courteous and ambitious, with a love of gambling; fortunately he also had good judgement and a strong sense of self-preservation. In negotiation it was his rule to multiply personal contacts and make friends everywhere. The Papal diplomatic service provided him with many openings and wide experience in international politics. Richelieu's first reactions were guarded to say the least: 'Le Mazarini has come here to spy rather than to treat. . . . I believe that he is entirely inclined towards our enemies. . . . He is so Spanish and Savoyard that what he says ought not to be taken as Gospel.' In 1634 he wanted to be Papal nuncio in Paris; but was made instead vice-legate in Avignon, with the special mission of exploring possibilities of peace. He lost no chance of engaging Richelieu on the subject and talked so elegantly about it that Richelieu declared that he cherished peace as if it were the lady of his desires. But the Franco-Spanish war saw Mazarin's recall and the apparent failure of his mission. In reality he had laid the base of his future career. He had impressed Richelieu by his sensitive awareness of diplomatic problems, and he had made useful friends by his suavity and tact. Gaston (still heir then) he had deliberately befriended; his gallant manners had made their mark with Queen Anne. In 1636 he organised a useful supply of ammunition for the front from Avignon. When he returned to Rome it was as the unofficial ambassador of France. From 1637 to 1639 he was in Rome: fallow years, but when Father Joseph died Richelieu thought seriously of Mazarin as his successor-designate. He thought that he had 'spirit, skill and energy'. Mazarin's ambitions had lain with peace, but now he was bellicose, urging Richelieu on to the conquest of Milan and a mortal blow to Spain. He believed that Olivarez only wanted peace to free his hands for aggression elsewhere. He used every means to ingratiate himself with Richelieu: he had solicited a Cardinal's hat for Father Joseph, he purchased statues for Richelieu's garden at Rueil, and he offered his

were hard to bring to terms and a final treaty, by which the towns held by France and Spain were restored to Savoy, was not completed until 1642. By then the deterioration in Spain's whole position and in particular the Catalan revolt, had made Savoy relatively unimportant in Richelieu's strategy.

The Pyrenean front was the scene of determined Spanish thrusts in 1636-7. They entered France at both ends of the Pyrenees but failed at first in Guienne and Roussillon. In August 1637 they began the siege of Leucate, a frontier fortress between Narbonne and Perpignan. The Sieur de Barry defended the place stoutly and was eventually relieved by Schomberg, who forced the Spanish army to retreat in some disarray after a skilful night attack on their lines. When the French went over to the offensive, however, they were little more successful than their opponents. In the summer of 1638 Condé and the Duc de la Valette laid siege to Fuentarabia, with naval support from Admiral Sourdis. When at the beginning of September the assault took place it ended in defeat and panic. A contributory factor was the recalcitrance of la Valette (he was unable to work with Sourdis, like his father the Duc d'Epernon before him); he refused to press home the assault. Richelieu was confidently awaiting news of the town's fall and when he heard of the *débâcle* he was furious: 'The grief of Fuentarabia is killing me', he wrote. Condé's report dwelt severely upon la Valette's conduct, but the duke had meanwhile fled beyond the Cardinal's reach, to England. Sourdis made some determined efforts to harry Spanish shipping in their harbours; the effect was negligible but it did not matter. The victory of his nephew Pontcourlay, operating with the galleys off Genoa, delighted the Cardinal, who was directing naval operations personally. But these operations were unimportant compared with the event of October 1639, when the whole fleet of Don Antonio de Oquendo was destroyed by van Tromp off the Downs.

---

services (via Chavigny) in whatever capacity Richelieu should care to employ him. No one saw more clearly the decisive shift in the balance of power from Spain to France. In January 1640 he returned to France. In 1641 he undertook a confidential mission to Chrétienne. In December 1641 he became Cardinal. So this paradoxical person, who became a Cardinal without being a priest, became Richelieu's first lieutenant without even having become French, for he was not naturalised. This subject is explored in the article by G. Dethan, 'Mazarin avant le Ministère', *Revue Historique*, 227, 1962.

Another ambitious French design was the siege of Salses, a fortress standing out of level country on the frontier of Roussillon. Condé captured the town after a successful mining operation; the Spanish then came back under the Marques de Spinola, the great soldier's son, and spent the rest of the year trying to recapture the place, with seventeen regiments. In January Salses fell again, but the effort of Spinola had been disproportionate in the context of the whole war effort; the operation had also involved Olivarez in the direct confrontation with the Catalans that was now to be his undoing.

Catalonia had long been regarded as virtually ungovernable. Tenacious of their local privileges, aggrieved at the way in which they were excluded from the commercial benefits of Spanish empire, the Catalans refused to make any contribution to the expense of running and defending the empire. They were all the more detested by the Castilians when they refused to accept their quota in Olivarez' 'Union of Arms', the scheme by which every province of the empire was to make a proportionate contribution in soldiers to the defence of the empire. Necessity as much as inclination drove Olivarez to extreme measures: in 1637, for instance, expenditure was 13 million escudos, receipts no more than $7\frac{1}{4}$ million. In the military and financial crisis of Spain his determination to force the Catalans to pay their share is understandable, but he was gambling and may have underestimated the danger involved. It was plain to him, however, that Catalonia was a security risk, with the French on the frontier and their agents busy in the province. When in 1638 the French were besieging Fuentarabia, contingents went to its support from Aragon and Valencia, but not from Catalonia. The Catalans seemed to prefer to exploit the difficulties of the crown. In 1639, therefore, Catalonia was deliberately chosen as the front to concentrate on, so as to involve the Catalans in the common war. At last Catalan troops were sent into action. Unfortunately for Olivarez the operations were mishandled: Salses was needlessly lost and recovered only at heavy cost in Catalan lives. The Catalans were shocked into action, but not in the way Olivarez wanted.

In the winter of 1639-40 Spanish troops were quartered in Catalonia and when there was difficulty over infringement of local rights, Olivarez ordered that these be disregarded. In May there were outbreaks of peasant violence which soon merged in a general revolt. Olivarez' viceroy was murdered, royal officials were hunted down, Barcelona was taken over by the insurgents. It was no consolation to Olivarez that the revolt was from the beginning aimed as much against the Catalan upper class as against the Castilian government. He could not crush the revolt without securing peace with France. France stood now to gain immensely from the continuance of the war, and of the revolt. In September 1640 the *Diputacio* of Catalonia, led by Canon Pau Claris and Francesco de Tamarit, requested French aid, and in October they entered into an agreement with France whereby French ships were invited to use Catalan ports and 3,000 French troops were to be sent to Catalonia (and paid for by the Catalans). Richelieu did not need to be generous in this situation, for the Catalan revolt promised to be self-perpetuating. As Olivarez remarked, Spain had now another Holland to deal with.

Richelieu did not support the Catalans without qualms. It might be easier to enter than to escape from military commitment in Spain. The example of revolt was, moreover, contagious; he did not want the inhabitants of Languedoc to follow suit. He would have preferred the Catalans to set up an independent state; under French pressure Claris did indeed, in January 1641, declare a republic, but it lasted only a week. Catalonia dissolved into anarchy and class struggle and Richelieu was left, therefore, with no alternative but to intervene and direct the resistance from France. Under a French viceroy and officials the Catalans found themselves billeting, supplying and paying for French troops. In 1643 the French were successful and captured Monzon and Lerida. Thereafter the Spanish began to strike back. A stalemate eventually ensued as the French reduced their effort, until after 1648 they were only concerned with keeping a few counters for peace talks. The people became disillusioned with their 'protectors' and this change in sentiment played some part in the recapture of Barcelona by the Spanish in 1652, which was virtually the end of the revolt.

There is uncertainty about the extent to which Richelieu fomented the Catalan revolt, and the same is true of the revolt of Portugal; he was, however, not surprised by the rising of that country against a Spanish domination that had lasted sixty years, for he had already assured certain Portuguese through an agent, the Sieur de St Pé, that France would give disinterested naval and military support. Constant tax demands, resentment at the damage that the Dutch were inflicting on her eastern empire and at the apparent inability of the Spanish government to defend it, the feeble failure in 1640 of a strong naval force to beat the Dutch at Pernambuco and so to relieve Brazil, and, on top of all, Olivarez' fresh demands for military service to help suppress the Catalans, brought the aristocracy to the point of revolt. In December 1640 the palace of Lisbon was stormed by a crowd shouting for 'Don Juan IV, King of Portugal' and Philip IV's governor, Marguerite of Savoy, was made at swordpoint to order the governor of Lisbon castle to surrender it to the rebels. Philip IV could not hope to recover Portugal and long before the final defeats of Ameixial and Villa Viciosa in 1663 and 1665 which were the prelude to formal independence, the Portuguese, assisted in turn by Holland, France (until 1659) and England, were acting as a sovereign nation. The revolts of Catalonia and Portugal shattered Spain's war effort. With two new fronts to be financed and only meagre contributions coming from the New World, Olivarez had to have resort to reckless *vellon* (copper-silver alloy) issues and then to an arbitrary deflation of 25 per cent. In January 1643 Olivarez was given leave to retire, leisure at last to contemplate the failure of his plans and the irreparable ruin of Spain.

Even as late as 1640 it was less Spain's overall military weakness than her inability to concentrate with sufficient force at one point that was causing failure. After Richelieu's entry into the war the over-extension of Spanish forces that had begun with the Mantuan affair in 1630 became really serious. It would have mattered less if the imperialists could have held their own in Germany. The revival of Holland after 1637, marked by the capture of Breda in October 1637 by Frederick Henry, was followed by great new efforts by Sweden, once more playing an aggressive rôle; after hard bargaining between Salvius, Oxenstierna's vice-chancellor, and Richelieu's plenipotentiary, d'Avaux, a treaty was signed between France and Sweden by which the latter was to receive 400,000 thalers a year in return for her undertaking to maintain the war against the Emperor. The Dutch, too, were amply subsidised by the Cardinal. No less important was Bernard of Saxe-Weimar, for so long as he maintained himself in Alsace and the Black Forest the imperialists would be unlikely to invade France. In 1638 Bernard went over to the offensive, attacked imperial encampments in January, secured towns and villages on the way to Breisach and then began the siege of that town above the Rhine which gave the imperialists entry to Alsace and thence to either Franche-Comté or Lorraine; if taken, it would block communication between the Rhine and Flanders. So far he had received little French support; indeed the French army in Franche-Comté could not move in the winter; there would have been massive desertions and the commissariat would have broken down, even if the eighty-year-old commander la Force could have summoned the energy and resource to march. As it was, the army moved slowly in the spring to divert some of the imperialists from the vital siege. In August Turenne joined Bernard after defeating the Bavarian Goetz at Wittenweier, and the siege was regularly formed. In October Charles of Lorraine attempted to relieve the town but was repelled by Bernard at Sennheim. The inhabitants clung on through nightmarish weeks of hunger; it is at this siege that one of the few well-authenticated cases of cannibalism that figures so much in the propaganda of both sides occurred: famished soldiers of the garrison ate the flesh of some dead prisoners. At last Breisach surrendered, on 17th December. In Paris Father Joseph lay dying and the news of the triumph reached Paris too late to cheer him on his way. The pleasant legend that Richelieu leaned over his bedside and whispered 'Father Joseph, Breisach is ours' may not be true but does justly emphasise the importance of this place in the strategy to which the great Capuchin and his master had devoted themselves.

In Flanders the Cardinal Infant, now discredited by his failure to relieve Breda, could expect little help from Spain and send none to Germany: in 1639 the French were to demonstrate their ascendancy by the capture of Hesdin, under the direction of la Meilleraye, grand-master of artillery. The Emperor had lost his best general, Werth, and Gallas had squandered his early reputation; now known as 'the spoiler of armies', he was becoming casual, lazy and a notorious drunkard. Apart from him, neither Goetz, who had replaced Werth in command of the Bavarians, nor Hatzfeld were commanders of the first rank. The appointment of the Emperor's brother Leopold as commander-in-chief did not improve matters; he was an intelligent man but no general. Bernard could be relied upon to hold his own with them.

But what were Bernard's intentions? After his success at Breisach, he asserted his rights against the French crown. In the original treaty of 1635, Richelieu had granted him permission to keep Alsace. Now that he held it he demanded that possession should be converted into outright sovereignty, the issue that Richelieu had been careful to evade. Patriotic motives have been ascribed to Bernard in his attitude towards Richelieu but it should be remembered that he made no attempt to use his influence and success to create the united German party that could alone give some protection to German interests. His obstinate refusal to yield to French pressure suggests a simpler answer: he wanted to exchange the precarious credit of the successful soldier of fortune for the solid revenues of the territorial prince. If he entertained ambitions beyond Alsace we can only guess at them for in July 1639 he died of a sudden fever. In his will he left Alsace to his elder brother William, who could hardly have taken it even if he had wanted to, and, failing his brother, to the king of France. He left his army to his second-in-command, Erlach, who promptly offered it to the highest bidder. The young Elector Palatine, Charles Louis set out boldly to join the troops. He had a party amongst them and was a serious contender, but he was foolish enough to travel across French territory. Richelieu seized him and held him prisoner in Vincennes until his own deal was made. In October a treaty was signed between the Bernardines and Richelieu by which they were to continue under French pay and to follow the French commander, although allowed to keep their own entity and their own general, who could keep Breisach and some other towns under the French crown. There was now no German commander left to exert an independent influence on the course of the war. Richelieu had been as lucky in the death of Bernard, aged only thirty-five, as he had been in that of Gustavus.

The capture of Breisach brings us to an issue which cannot be avoided. What was Richelieu's policy with regard to the Rhine? Did he think in terms of a frontier as has been alleged, notably by writers of an older school nourished on the idea of 'natural frontiers', partisans perhaps in controversies stimulated by the Franco-German wars? Mommsen[1] was the first German historian to suggest that Richelieu's policy was essentially defensive and Zeller[2] thought the same. But Burkhardt[3] considered that Richelieu exaggerated the menace of Spain in order to rally support for an aggressive policy. So although it is certain that the

[1] G. Mommsen, *Richelieu,* Berlin, 1922.
[2] G. Zeller. In various works, as '*L'Organisation défensive des frontières du Nord et de l'Est au XVIIe Siècle*'.
[3] C. J. Burkhardt, *Richelieu,* vol. iii.

Rhine as a 'natural frontier' is anachronistic, belonging to a later
century and to sentiments of romanticism and nationalism,
Richelieu's motives remain an open question.

The most useful clues are to be found not in his own writing
for posterity, but in his instructions to ambassadors and advice
to the king. The best source, as it happens, belongs to the year
after his death, namely the instructions to the ambassadors at
Munster in 1643, for these are a summary of his views of a
lifetime, faithfully reproduced by his successor. The French were
to negotiate for Breisach and the 'forest towns', Colmar, Schle-
stadt, Bedfort, Saverne, Haguenau and other places already
occupied between Lorraine and the Rhine. While other towns
were negotiable, Breisach must be kept. In short, Richelieu wanted
access to the Rhine and a passage across it; he did not want the
Rhine. It was the same with Pinerolo, where he wanted a fortress,
not a line. He never talked the language of wholesale annexation,
like Vergennes in the eighteenth century: 'Without doubt the
Rhinelands are very tempting; they lend themselves in a marvellous
way to the rounding-off of France'. A passage in Richelieu's instructions indicates his thinking: 'The princes of Germany will recognise that the princes of Austria have no other end but to make
Germany subject to them; by contrast it is by the actions of France
that they have secured their liberty and they ought all to join with
France in working to preserve for France this place Breisach'.
It was consistent with Richelieu's policy throughout to keep
open the possibility of crossing the Rhine on behalf of feeble or
oppressed princes.

Carefully limited objectives pursued with a steady eye to what
was essential: this view of his aims is borne out by his methods.
He preferred to use diplomacy, backed by force only when it was
unavoidable. When in 1631-2 the Swedish advance to the Rhine
presented a threat to France's interests in the area and even to
her own security, military action was clearly unthinkable. Richelieu
adopted instead a policy which Marshal de Marillac had suggested
two years before when the imperialists had occupied Vic. He
offered 'protection' to all princes who asked for it. From this he
he hoped to gain advanced positions with good communications
in friendly country, the extension of French political influence and
a timely advertisement of his concern for Catholic interests—all
without the open confrontation which he must try to avoid. Only
the Elector of Trier, who was also Bishop of Spier, was able to

accept 'protection', and he signed a convention in April 1632 by
which the French were allowed to garrison Ehrenbreitstein and
Philipsburg. Trier was not molested by the Swedes and the French
gained a valuable bridgehead. Richelieu wanted to appear modest
in his demands in Germany, but the occupation was puffed at
as a notable advance. Bignon, *avocat-royal*, at a *lit de justice* spoke
of success in Germany which had 'carried the frontiers of
France to the Rhine'. The Elector was afraid that Trier would
go the way of the *Trois Evêches* (Metz, Toul and Verdun), refused
to accept the word 'protection', preferring 'aid', and protested
against the conduct of the occupying troops. But he was weak and
isolated, and Richelieu was able to consolidate. The Elector had
to offer him the high dignity of provost of the cathedral chapter
and he only accepted on condition that the succession to the
archbishopric itself was put at his disposal! Was it the prelude to
annexation? There was no need for it, for Richelieu's interest
was always strategic and he had achieved his goal in a cheap and
convenient way. 'Protection' was none the less a positive concept.
In his famous memorandum of January 1629 he declared the
protection of weak and vulnerable princes to be the mission of
the king, as it would make him 'the most powerful monarch in
the world and the most esteemed prince'. Bussy-Lameth, elated,
perhaps, by the importance of his job as first governor of Trier,
expressed a confident view in a letter to Bouthillier which may
have been typical of the way in which many of his countrymen
were beginning to think: French arms were so successful in
Germany 'that we will establish the French language and, if God
pleases, even settle the Empire upon the house of our kings'.
With the authority of the Emperor already waning in the lands
between Rhine and Meuse, there was a tempting vacuum. It
remains unlikely that Richelieu, anchored in the experience of the
past and concerned with bases and spheres of influence more than
with accretions of territory to a country which was already too
large to manage, was thinking of a general advance. He was alive
to the value of French influence in Germany as a means of checking
the Emperor and as a result of his policy this was enhanced by the
Peace of Westphalia, that 'finest jewel in the French crown'.
Louis XIV later squandered the store of influence and good will
that he inherited from the Cardinals by an aggressive policy
aimed at enlarging the country and rounding off earlier acqui-
sitions. Richelieu would have been more subtle.

## 21. 'The Highest Degree of Glory'

In June 1640 Richelieu received in private, in the country, the Spanish emissary Jacques de Brecht, who brought Olivarez' proposals of peace. In a moment of confidence after the temporary Spanish success in Savoy, Olivarez had decided to tempt the Cardinal into negotiations which might have the effect of splitting France from her allies: a key proposal was that Holland should be made to return the part of Brazil she had conquered. Richelieu was, however, determined not to risk the alliance of Holland and he was happy to let the grievance about Brazil rouse Portuguese feeling against Spain. He had been anxious to keep open the possibility of negotiation. The visit of the priest Bachelier to Olivarez in January 1637 was officially to secure for Anne of Austria a relic of St Isidore of Seville, supposedly efficacious in the case of barren women; Bachelier had also conveyed peace proposals to Olivarez, who had rejected them.

Now it seemed that it was Richelieu who thought that he had more to gain by fighting on. He is open to the charge of hypocrisy in his talk of peace, but is this fair? If his reputation abroad is anything to go by, it is. Even his allies had little good to say about him. The Swedish emissary, Grotius, who had been treated by the Cardinal with some contempt, expressed his mistrust. The Prince of Orange had reason to be grateful to France but he had no love of Richelieu. Olivarez believed that 'he was the author of all the persecution and damage that Christendom suffered' and that 'everything he said was plain fraud'. His relations with Rome had deteriorated steadily since the relatively friendly period of the Mantuan War. Despite the emollient diplomacy of his brother Alphonse and the pleading of Mazarin, Urban became convinced that Richelieu was an enemy of peace. The appointment of d'Estrées, a violent man, in place of Alphonse in 1637 made matters worse: he began by fighting his way into the Quirinal. The Papal legate in Paris, Ranuccio Scotti, came to Paris in 1640 to discuss terms of peace but behaved foolishly in a situation calling for tact. For Richelieu was busy with his plans for taxing the Church and had summoned Gallican arguments to his aid. The enthusiasts went further than the Cardinal wished, as we have seen. Urban VIII was more concerned than he needed to be about the danger of schism but he correctly perceived that Richelieu in 1640 had travelled a long way from his zealous, orthodox, Tridentine youth, when he had defended the Papal cause at the States-General of 1614. Misrepresented at Rome, hated in Madrid and Vienna, suspected in Germany, libelled by the antagonised members of the royal family, Chrétienne of Savoy, Henriette of England, Marie de Médicis (and of course that model of Catholic propriety, Charles of Lorraine), Richelieu was generally held to be a tyrant and the principal obstacle to peace in Europe. The truth is that he was too good a Catholic to be content indefinitely with the alliance of heretics, too intelligent not to see that war was damaging the French economy—and yet it was natural that he should wish to make the most of advantages for which he had worked so long. He would wait until he could negotiate from proven strength.

In the same month that Richelieu rejected the peace offers with assurances of personal regard for the man he so detested, Olivarez' whole position was wrecked by the revolt of Catalonia. In the summer of 1640, moreover, French armies mounted a successful offensive in Flanders, resulting in the capture of Arras and the occupation of Picardy. The king was present with a great concourse of courtiers to see the fall of Arras after a laborious siege: a foretaste of the easier triumphs of Louis XIV. A sign of the times was the defection of Charles of Lorraine, who had long been a thorn in Richelieu's flesh. He came to Paris and made a treaty in March 1641 which gave him possession of his estates in return for acceptance of vassal status, the cession to France of Clermont, Stenay, Jametz and Dun, the provisional occupation of Nancy and a promise that he would not conclude any alliance with France's enemies. He made a solemn pledge of his good faith in a special ceremony, but he had already entrusted to a lawyer a private disavowal of these promises on the ground that they were made under constraint. For Richelieu, however, the duke's temporary commitment was invaluable, advertising the power of France and the clemency that would be offered to those who were prepared to submit.

The Cardinal Infant recognised before his death in November

1641 that there was a limit to what could be achieved by his armies, despite heroic efforts in that year which prevented the Dutch from gaining more than one town, Gennep, from their spirited attacks. He wrote that there was only one chance left, to support the partisans of Spain within France so as to enable them to bring pressure on the French government. There was still no shortage of collaborators. In the spring of 1641 the Comte de Soissons, a prince of the blood and Thomas of Savoy's brother-in-law, the Duc de Guise, and Turenne's elder brother, the Duc de Bouillon, came together in a conspiracy, financed by Spanish gold and encouraged by the widespread discontent about the government's latest tax levies. Soissons was popular in Champagne, of which he had formerly been governor. From Bouillon's frontier fortress of Sédan the magnates marched into France with imperialist troops under Lamboi. Marshal Châtillon barred their way but was defeated at Marfée in July. At the end of the battle Soissons was killed, possibly by an agent of Richelieu fighting in the rebel ranks; by another account he blew his brains out when he carelessly lifted his visor with his loaded pistol. When Louis XIII led his troops towards Sédan, Bouillon decided that the game was up and made his peace with Louis. Meanwhile Charles of Lorraine had reverted to his old rôle of imperialist general with as much bad judgement as bad faith: his duchy was once more occupied by the French.

The episode of Soissons serves as a reminder that Richelieu was never free from anxiety about enemies within the frontier. The last year of his life saw an absurd but also alarming climax of factiousness. The Cinq Mars affair which engrossed Richelieu in his last months of life might have been conceived by some dramatist with an eye for the far-fetched and romantic as a means of bringing down the curtain without anti-climax. Cinq Mars embodied so much of what Richelieu had fought against that his defiance and downfall come appropriately at the end of the play. The artist in Richelieu might have found grim amusement in a human problem of his own making. It is more likely that he rued the day when he first introduced Cinq Mars to Louis XIII.

Cinq Mars had been at first only a pawn in the game of palace politics, which Richelieu played with unremitting concentration to the end. The point of the game, as he saw it, was to keep the king from being controlled by one or other group of the

s

Cardinal's enemies: key figures were Queen Anne and the royal confessor.

The queen's position was an unhappy one. In her private conduct she seems to have been blameless and dignified. She allowed herself, however, to become compromised in the intrigues of the pro-Spanish party. Slighted by the king's passion for Mlle de la Fayette, inclined by faith and family feeling to sympathy with Spain, egged on by Mme de Chevreuse, her indiscretion is understandable; it was also, to Richelieu, dangerous treason. His spies reported in 1637 that Anne was making frequent visits to the Convent of Val-de-Grâce, rue Saint-Jacques; a letter intercepted from the Spanish envoy in Brussels to the queen looked like a reply to one from the queen. Throughout the summer the net was drawn around her, then in August, an Angevin gentleman, la Porte, one of her messengers, was arrested and cross-examined, but he staunchly maintained the queen's innocence. The Archbishop of Paris and the Chancellor then interrogated the Abbess of Val-de-Grâce, a native of Franche-Comté, Louise de Milly: she too was stubbornly uncooperative and was deposed. Séguier at last went to the queen herself. Anne denied that she had been corresponding with the Spanish and sent an emissary to Richelieu protesting her innocence. He said that he was unconvinced and demanded proof. The queen then saw Richelieu in person, whom she found respectful but adamant; somehow he convinced her that it was in her best interests to reveal all. So she explained the elaborate chain of communication from the queen to la Porte, then Auger, the English ambassador's secretary; to Gerbin, his colleague in Brussels, and from Gerbin to Mirabel, the Spanish ambassador. The main object of this intrigue was to prevent the alliance of France and England which the Spanish greatly feared. The queen was advised, for her part, by her exiled friend, Mme de Chevreuse. Richelieu, whose whole conduct of the affair shows him at his most patient, impressive and, to the queen, evidently awe-inspiring, refused to take the queen's hand when she wept and begged for mercy, but he interceded for her with the king. He consummated his victory by conditions which were not excessively harsh: she was forbidden to correspond with Mme de Chevreuse and was only allowed to have in her household persons acceptable to the king. The king and queen signed this curious treaty. La Porte was pressed by Richelieu no further; he admired the man's loyalty. Mme de Chevreuse rode from Couzières to her Spanish friends across the frontier, disguised as a man; from Flanders she went to London, never to return in Richelieu's lifetime.

Richelieu's personal influence on the king was great, and fortified by a war which made them in a sense partners in an enterprise they both understood. But Louis' emotional life gave cause for concern. He became no less impulsive and unpredictable as he grew older and more pious. At the same time he remained acutely aware of his responsibilities as ruler, and advisers found a sensitive spot when they talked of the sufferings of the people or reminded him that France was in alliance with heretics, an aspect of Richelieu's policy which he could never fully accept. It was possible to construct a composite picture which might so shock the king that he would turn against his minister: peasant revolts, penal taxes, Catholics fighting Catholics while heresy raised its head all over Germany, faithful subjects turned against him by the Cardinal's intransigence, his own family alienated. If Louis once accepted this picture, then Richelieu and all he had achieved would be undone. For this reason he used his influence to disgrace Père Caussin, Louis' Jesuit confessor, whom he knew to be working upon the king's scruples in November 1638. Advent was then treated like Lent, as a time for penitence and mortification. Richelieu secured in Caussin's place, at Christmas 1638, the appointment of another Jesuit, Père Sirmond, older and more accommodating.

A week or so before, Louis had signed a solemn engagement placing his realm under the protection of the Virgin Mary and promised to mark the Feast of the Assumption by special devotions which, in the form of the Procession of the Vow of Louis XIII, continued to be celebrated in some places long after his death. Various explanations have been offered for this gesture of royal piety: a bid, inspired perhaps by Richelieu, to recover the initiative of faith for France, to show Europe that the Habsburgs were not the only zealous Catholics, or an offering to God by way of supplication for the particular favour required by Louis and his country, the birth of a male heir. These considerations may have played their part but it is likely that the idea sprang in the first place from Louis' sincere desire for peace, tinged with thankfulness for the deliverance of the year of Corbie. That a son and heir was born to Anne of Austria in September 1638 after twenty-two years of married life was undoubtedly seen as a sign that God smiled on the Bourbons. Gossip embellished the event with the tale of a December night spent together unexpectedly after a storm had driven the king to take shelter in the Louvre, from which the birth of Louis, *le Dieu-Donné*, this *enfant du miracle,* nine months later was the result. There is no reason to suppose that the king had entirely neglected his marital duties in all the years before. If not a miracle however, the queen's pregnancy was a surprising piece of good fortune after two miscarriages many years before. The succession was assured and Orléans ceased to be the heir apparent. A few days after the birth of the future Louis XIV, an infant daughter was born to Philip IV and Marianna of Austria. This child, Maria Theresa, was to be Louis XIV's bride: no sooner had the news of the birth reached Paris than there was speculation about the possibility of a marriage engagement which should seal a peace—a new alignment of the powers. As Chavigny put it: 'Might not the coincidence of these two births bring about one day a great union and a great blessing to Christendom?' Richelieu and Olivarez thought in the same terms. Two years later another son was born to the queen. Richelieu no longer had to work under the depressing knowledge that when Louis died, his persistent enemy would become king.

The king's marriage had produced a son. It was too late otherwise to repair the marriage; any feeling that had once existed had grown cold in years of misunderstanding and reproach. Yet Louis needed, even if he could not maintain, a steady attachment. He was loyal in his way to those whom he had once loved. For years he clung to Mademoiselle de Hautefort, though she seems to have been bored and puzzled by his devotion and repaid his heavy attentions with mockery. In the spring of 1635 he was diverted from her by a sudden passion for Louise de la Fayette, who came from a noble but impoverished family in the Auvergne, and had entered the queen's service five years before at the age of twelve. She was shy and simple in her tastes, a sensitive puritan, who loved country life. Though she felt affection for the king and talked happily to him about horses, she shrank from him when he became explicit about his passion. Richelieu only became alarmed by the affair when he realised that the king was obsessed; when she expressed her wish to take the veil he was relieved. Louis respected the girl's decision as a true vocation, though it was also her only way out of an intolerable dilemma. He made no attempt to conceal the grief of separation and used to visit her, to talk for hours to the pale figure behind the grille. He referred to her loss as his 'greatest sacrifice'. 'So, Sire, you have been to see the poor prisoner', said a courtier, after one of these visits. 'No', said the king, 'It is I who am in prison.' He returned without enthusiasm to Mademoiselle de Hautefort. Always she had perhaps been more of a friend than a mistress; now they bickered aimlessly. He forbade her to marry but denied her the status of his official mistress. Louis evidently yearned for some more exciting relationship. Before he was forty he had become an ageing invalid. Suffering from insomnia, gout, a chronic chesty cough, he wanted distraction.

Henri d'Effiat, Marquis de Cinq Mars, was eighteen when Louis made him Grand Master of the Wardrobe. He was the second son of the Marquis d'Effiat, diplomat and soldier, who had served Richelieu well but died young. Richelieu wanted to help the family and this handsome and graceful youth struck him as being likely to appeal to the king; he might fill the gap left by the departure of Saint-Simon as a protégé, son and companion to the lonely king. A steadier, less selfish boy would have been spoiled by the attention that Cinq Mars now received. He was greedy and heartless, clever enough to exploit the situation, but not to see the responsibilities it entailed. He was spoiled by the flattery of the courtiers, the interest of women and the slavish affection of the king. The most experienced and cynical observers, those who knew the king best, even Richelieu, must have been shaken by the king's surrender. Everything that he had kept in check he now released. His chaste, devout, intense temperament was at Cinq Mars' mercy for he loved him obsessively and would not let him go. The relationship was stormy and destructive. Emotional quarrels were followed by humiliating reconciliations. Cinq Mars seemed to delight in flouting the wishes of the king and the conventions of the court. Louis wished to educate him in war, religion and social conduct; Cinq Mars escaped to the brothels of the Marais and the company of the notorious Marion De Lorme. Louis reported to the Cardinal his quarrels with Cinq Mars in all their pathos and absurdity. Richelieu did not need to do more than watch, for Cinq Mars was clearly bent on self-destruction. First he demanded a royal bride; then he joined in a plot against the Cardinal. His pretext was Richelieu's refusal to let him marry the daughter of the Duc de Nevers, Marie de Gonzague; not surprising in the context of Richelieu's Italian policy.

Through Gaston, Cinq Mars' conspiracy was linked first to the revolt of Soissons. How dangerous was this combination? The part played in the Soissons plot by Jean de Gondi, better known as the Cardinal de Retz that he later became, and leading *frondeur*, is worth notice for what it reveals of the motives and outlook of a young man who, for all his modish singularity and exceptional ambition, fairly represents the political and social attitudes of some of his class. Retz's uncle was Archbishop of Paris, notoriously incompetent and disreputable, and Retz aspired to succeed him. One aunt was the scandalous Mme de Fargis who played a leading part in the Day of Dupes intrigue, subsequently acted as intermediary between Anne and the Spanish, and vied with Mme de Chevreuse in her amours. Gondi's family tradition embraced extremes of piety (as exemplified by his father, Vincent de Paul's patron, ex-general of galleys, Philippe de Gondi, now Père de Gondi, Oratorian) and of rakishness, as in Albert de Gondi (his grandfather, the successful soldier, Cathérine de Médicis' adviser, and the real founder of the family fortunes). Gondi himself recognised the validity of the first, but inclined to the second extreme. He admitted that he pursued a career in the Church to gratify his ambition; if his own mendacious but revealing memoirs are to be believed, he also pursued, not without success, some of the most attractive women of the day. One was Anne de Rohan, the Princesse de Guémenée, sister-in-law of Mme de Chevreuse. Dueller, gallant, in his own opinion the epitome of *le généreux*, he seems to have moulded himself deliberately in the image of the hero of Corneille, for whom self-fulfilment was all.

He wrote in 1639 a study of the Conspiracy of Fieschi which he circulated in manuscript. Fieschi was the leader of a coup in 1547 aimed against the ruling Doria family of Genoa. The Italian Mascardi's account of the coup, translated by Bouchard, was unflattering to the conspirators and Bouchard actually claimed that Richelieu had commissioned his translation. Gondi interpreted the affair in a way that showed that his sympathies were with the conspirators: 'Vain, high-handed and insolent' was his description of Jannetin Doria: his readers recognised Richelieu. The Cardinal had already been crossed by Gondi in his capacity as Rector of the Sorbonne when Gondi had obtained the prize from the professors for his examination for the master's licence against Richelieu's own cousin, Henri de la Mothe-Houdancourt, and made the contest an occasion for a studied defiance of the

Cardinal. It was as well for Gondi that Richelieu did not also know of his connections with the assassination plots of 1636-7. Mme de Fargis' son, la Rochepot, and his associates, Montrésor and Saint-Ibal, followers of Soissons, planned to kill the Cardinal on two occasions. Once was when he was to baptise Gaston's daughter, *la grande Mademoiselle*, in the Tuileries; Richelieu was ill and could not come.

Another plot came nearer to fruition, at Amiens, at a council of war planning the relief of Corbie, when Montrésor and Saint-Ibal were poised to kill Richelieu, only waiting for Gaston's signal. He did not give it, and the conspirators made off, fearing treachery like all Gaston's intimates. Richelieu, acting on suspicions, exiled Père de Gondi but took no action against his son, Jean, who later claimed that the assassination would have been 'a crime which appeared to me consecrated by great examples and justified and made honourable by great peril'. He soon became involved again with the Soissons group, though he thought that the leader was too undecided to be a *chef du parti* and lacking in that 'heroic judgement, whose main function is to distinguish the extraordinary from the impossible'. Despite his misgivings he set about forming a group in Paris from the political prisoners of the Bastille, a mixed group of survivors and victims of earlier affairs, including Bassompierre, de Vitry (Concini's assassin), du Fargis and his wife's lover Cramail, la Porte and Vautier (Anne's courier and Marie's doctor respectively). Cramail, an intelligent man and Richelieu's bitter enemy, worked on this group, while Gondi sought followers amongst officers in the Paris militia, disgruntled officials and, anticipating the methods of the demagogues of the Revolution, the artisans and labourers who were the natural radicals of the Paris streets. Exploiting the pious reputation of his parents, he worked under cover of Vincent de Paul's Mission at Saint-Lazare, and dispersed 'alms' provided by Soissons. But Soissons was killed, his rising ended in farce and Gondi's plans for seizing the Bastille, the Arsenal and the Palais de Justice were never put to the test. An interesting chapter of history remained unwritten. Gondi played no part in the Cinq Mars affair.

Cinq Mars' main collaborators were the Marquis de Fontrailles, a born intriguer and a man for whom Richelieu had not tried to conceal his dislike, and François-Auguste de Thou, a young lawyer, ambitious to rise with Cinq Mars. It was easy for them to play on Cinq Mars' dislike of the Cardinal. He was told that

Richelieu had edited the despatches in the *Mercure* which described the capture of Arras, where Cinq Mars commanded the 'Immortals', a squabbling band of aristocratic volunteers, so that Cinq Mars' unlucky part (his horse was shot under him and he was unjustly accused of cowardice) would not be known. Then there was the proposed marriage of Cinq Mars and Marie de Gonzague; the latter, nearly thirty, regarded Richelieu as the cause of her frustrations and hated him. She was a cousin of Charles of Lorraine who had rejoined the Spaniards in July 1641. After the death of Soissons at Marfée in that month Bouillon might have been expected to remain loyal for a time; he had been given command of the army in Savoy opposed to Thomas but somehow he and the ever-credulous Gaston were persuaded that the king himself was ready to dismiss the Cardinal. Faction was running high at court with 'royalists' opposed to 'Cardinalists', and the conduct of Cinq Mars strained relations between the two sick men. Louis' views were enigmatic as ever but the plot grew on wishful thinking.

In February 1642 the government was on the move again, as Louis decided that he would conduct the siege of Perpignan in person, Richelieu had to be with him and he went escorted by his own guards, travelling a day or so's journey behind the court. Meanwhile Fontrailles was negotiating a treaty with the Spanish by whose reckless terms Gaston guaranteed internal support for an invading Spanish army. The lack of realism is as startling as the treachery, for the Spanish were in no state to invade; from the imperialists there was little danger after Torstenson's invasion of the hereditary lands in the spring of 1642. When the court reached Lyons, Richelieu's brother sang a Te Deum for the French victory of Kempfen in a cathedral hung with captured Austrian banners. If there was a plan to murder Richelieu on his way south it had miscarried. Then Fontrailles returned from Spain to find that de Thou had failed to bring in other nobles, notably Mercoeur and Beaufort; when he heard that Cinq Mars' downfall was imminent he left for England, there to write his version of events. It was just as well, for Richelieu obtained somehow a copy of the treaty, possibly from the queen herself, who, fearing that she might be separated from her children, had alerted his suspicions by well-planted hints.

Once given material proof Richelieu acted fast. He sent Chavigny to the king at Narbonne. Cinq Mars and Bouillon were arrested at once. After some weeks of wandering about the Auvergne hills

Gaston wrote the expected confession. He was coaxed back to France in August and completed Richelieu's case by naming Cinq Mars and Bouillon as accomplices. Meanwhile in July, neglected, unregretted, Gaston's mother had died in Cologne. 'I am happy to have seen', Richelieu wrote, 'that she had great repentance of her sins and that she pardoned generously those whom she held to be her enemies.' He was probably sincere in his feelings about the woman who had been his first important patron: in the last sentence in his will he stressed that he had never 'failed in all the obedience or the respect which I owed to the queen mother, in spite of all the calumnies with which some have tried to blacken my reputation in this respect'.

Richelieu was amazingly busy in these last months of his life. From his bed he gave audiences, dictated and read despatches, interrogated de Thou whom he had detained at Tarascon and then took with him in his barge, and grimly prepared for the final act of authority which he knew was required. In mid-August he travelled up the Rhône to Valence. Preceded by a frigate and a boat-load of musketeers, followed by other boats of clerics, soldiers and officials of his household, accompanied by bands of pikemen marching along the banks, he lay in his barge of crimson and gold, his bed draped in purple taffeta, a wasted figure covered in ulcerous sores, his right arm already paralysed. In early September he reached Lyons where, as usual, part of the wall of a house had to be broken down so that his litter could be lifted into his bedroom. Here Cinq Mars and de Thou were tried after being trapped into betraying one another. Louis himself offered evidence; disillusioned at last with Cinq Mars he wrote that he was 'an impostor and calumniator'. Richelieu had moved again when Séguier, who presided over the court in person, brought him the verdict: guilty of high treason for being parties to the agreement with Spain. There was to be no reprieve; indeed, Richelieu went so far as to rusticate Cinq Mars' mother to Touraine and to order the destruction of the Château Cinq Mars. To Chavigny he wrote in terms which tell of his personal satisfaction as much as the relief of the statesman: 'Perpignan is in the hands of the king and M. le Grand and M. de Thou are in the next world . . . these are two results of God's goodness towards the king and his state'. Cinq Mars died with bravado, after having refused to share a scaffold with de Thou on the grounds that he was a commoner. While an unpractised executioner was botching his job and rousing the fury of the crowd, Louis XIII was playing chess. Looking at his watch, he said, 'I wonder how the Grand Master looks now', and went on with his game.

Richelieu's conduct of the Cinq Mars affair may seem callous and vindictive: could he not have sealed his own triumph of survival at the last by an act of clemency towards two foolish young men? He knew that he had not long to live and had already made a will in seventeen pages of precise detail. It is possible that he had lived with pain and anxiety so long that generous human feelings were overlaid by the desire to punish. One has to recall that it had become habitual with him to think of human questions only in terms of the state. He had worked for its security and prestige to such effect that the tide of war was visibly turning; at home all attempts to deflect him from his course, to halt the extension of the powers of state, had failed. But the recent conduct of the king upon whom all depended, the range and virulence of opposition exposed by the Cinq Mars affair, emphasised that constant vigilance was necessary. His own experience had shown that selective punishment—and Richelieu's victims did not die in droves—had a salutary effect. Was he to change his formula now? He was ready to bequeath his power to his chosen successor. It was intolerable to think that the succession, the continuity of policy, could be jeopardised by reckless individuals at a time when a favourable peace could be envisaged, and when, therefore, long-postponed plans for developing the resources of the country could be resumed. The war must be pursued vigorously to the end if the negotiators were to secure the maximum advantages; at the same time France had to present an appearance of stability, her king above any suspicion that he preferred the interests of friends to the well-being of the state, her nobles loyal to the king.

From Nemours the Cardinal travelled in a carriage to Fontaine-bleau. The king visited him at the Hotel d'Albret; supported by Chavigny and Sublet de Noyers, Richelieu lifted himself with difficulty from his chair. The king embraced him, then they had a long, private talk, the first for months. At such a time, we may guess, the king glimpsed something of the value of the partnership which had proved so successful against all odds and predictions. In October Richelieu went on to Paris. From the Palais-Cardinal he composed a memorandum for the king recalling the details of the Cinq Mars affair. He had not lost his skill in persuasion; like a tutor to an awkward student he rubbed in the lessons, then stated his terms. He would resign unless the king agreed to his propositions. The king must not let favourites interfere with political matters, he must close his ear to scandal about his ministers, check the truth of charges before acting against them and punish those who were guilty of slander; he must keep the secrets of council meetings. With the brutal frankness which characterised this remarkable relationship, he went on to remind the king of the way he had been treated after the death of Concini, 'banished from the king and the queen-mother, and from the kingdom, on unfounded suspicions'. On 5th November, when the king had not responded, Richelieu offered his resignation. Chavigny urged his master's case, but the king kept his thoughts to himself; he was enjoying his last hunting season. Chavigny was sufficiently worried to warn Richelieu that he might be attacked and to advise him to have his guards constantly in attendance. On the 13th Richelieu wrote to the king again, asking on what conditions he would agree to peace. Plainly he was concerned for his successor, his policy and his relations with the king. On the 20th the king broke his silence and Richelieu could have asked for no more: the minister should not retire, but act with more freedom and power than ever. He declared that he had given little heed to Cinq Mars' allegations against the Cardinal and promised that he would keep secret anything that the Cardinal wished. In a review of the diplomatic situation he showed that he understood the position well: he would not compromise over the main places at issue—Lorraine, Arras, Perpignan, Breisach or Pinerolo—and he would support Charles Emmanuel of Savoy. A week later Cinq Mars' remaining associates were dismissed from the court.

On 28th November Richelieu became feverish and complained of a pain in the side: he had pleurisy. Bleedings only weakened him; soon he was choking and spitting blood. Almost to the end there were decisions to be made. The Duc de Bouillon should be pardoned in return for the cession of his fortress of Sédan, military appointments were proposed for the coming campaigns; Bouillon's younger brother Turenne was recommended for one command, while for Flanders Richelieu wanted Condé's eldest son, the Duc d'Enghien, soon to earn fame on the battlefield of Rocroy. When, on 2nd December, he was reported to be weakening, the king came to see him. Accounts of their last hours together, as of his last statements, accord authentically and touchingly with what else we know of them. Louis, who could assume a daunting majesty, could also be homely and spontaneous. He sat with his hand in the Cardinal's, talked tenderly to him, and fed him with spoonfuls of egg yolk. He dallied afterwards to look at Richelieu's pictures, then went over to the Louvre to await the result of the illness. Richelieu, as Griffet records, said some words of farewell which he had no doubt composed beforehand. 'I have the consolation of leaving your kingdom in the highest degree of glory and reputation which it has ever had, and all your enemies beaten and humiliated.' He then commended his nephews and relations to the king: 'I shall give them my blessing only provided they do not depart from the fidelity and obedience which they owe to you'. He advised the king to appoint Mazarin as his successor and to keep the other ministers in office. All this the king was to do. The Bishop of Chartres heard his confession. For the extreme unction he asked for the *curé* of St Eustâche, the parish priest whose predecessor had baptised him. He was heard to say: 'My Master, my Judge who will shortly judge me: I pray Him with all my heart to condemn me if I have ever had any intention other than the good of religion and the state'. There was a report after his death that when asked to pardon his enemies he had said that he had 'none except those of the state'. His niece, the Duchesse d'Aiguillon, declared that a nun had seen in a vision that the Cardinal would not die of this illness. Richelieu summarised his whole way of thinking, so different from Father Joseph's, when he answered her: 'Niece, there are no truths but those in the gospel: one should believe in them alone'. She was with him until he asked her to leave so that she should not witness his last sufferings. The king visited him again; also, surprisingly, Gaston of Orléans. On the morning of 4th December the Bishop of Chartres began to read the prayers for the dying; at about midday they held a candle to his nostrils; it did not flicker. His last recorded words were that he wished he had a thousand lives to give them all for the faith of the Church.

The body of Richelieu lay in state for several days while Parisians filed before it, with feelings as much of curiosity and awe perhaps as of sorrow. Only the sunken ivory of face and hands were visible among the scarlet of the Cardinal's robes; his hat and ducal coronet lay at his feet, and with them a monstrance with a silver crucifix which gleamed in the light of the candles like the hope of salvation in a darkening world. On either side of him, monks chanted the penitential psalms. On 13th December after dark, they carried him across the river to the Church of the Sorbonne, which he had commissioned Lemercier to build; there his bones lie today under a huge monument of bronze.

Chavigny and Noyers had taken the news of Richelieu's death to the king in the Louvre. On the same day the king informed Cardinal Mazarin that he wished him to carry on and to devote the same care to affairs of state as his predecessor; Mazarin tried, perhaps sincerely, to refuse, but yielded to the king's persuasion. Though some notable prisoners were released from the Bastille, the administration continued with little outward change: Séguier, Chavigny, Noyers remained in office. To prevent any move by Gaston, the king arranged for an emergency session of Parlement to declare with due formality that the Duc de Orléans was incapable of administration. If his disappointment was keen, it was short-lived, for within two months the king fell ill once more. Louis missed his old doctor, Hérouard, but even he could have done little for him now; the tuberculosis was far advanced. He regretted not being able to live long enough to avoid a regency. The Dauphin, aged five, was officially baptised and the king asked him afterwards, 'What is your name now?' 'Louis XIV', said the confident boy. 'Not yet', the king replied sharply. On 14th May the court assembled round his bed to see him receive the Last Unction. The queen and her sons, kneeling at the bedside, saw him take off his crucifix and give it to his confessor: 'For Sister Louise-Angélique de la Fayette'. Shortly afterwards, in all the publicity, crush, squalor of a royal death scene, the principal died, his finger on his lips in a last enigmatic gesture. St Simon, his former equerry, watched the coffin lowered into the vault and said that he wished to throw himself in after it for 'that incomparable king, brilliant, pious, modest and loyal, was a hero, a son worthy of Saint Louis'. The account may have been touched up by St Simon's son, who was not fond of Louis XIV, and looked back on Louis XIII's reign as a golden age.

Others were looking forward to a different sort of golden age when Louis died. Louis had arranged for a regency council containing Mazarin, Séguier, Chavigny and other experienced ministers. Anne of Austria, showing more sense than either friends or enemies would have credited her with, secured from

Parlement recognition of herself as regent with full powers and then staggered Richelieu's former opponents by confirming Mazarin in his position as first minister. Continuity could not, however, be preserved so easily. Richelieu's following of ministers, Sublet, Chavigny, Bouthillier, Séguier, lost cohesion after his death, jockeyed jealously for supremacy or survival and were all in turn disgraced except Séguier, who was able, from the eminence of the Chancellor's office, to keep his head above faction. In 1643 the *Cabale des Importants* brought together some of Richelieu's old enemies, Mme de Chevreuse, the Ducs de Mercoeur and Vendôme and the latter's son, Beaufort, in a plot to remove Mazarin and reverse his policy. They failed and Mazarin survived, with the support and affection of the queen mother and regent, but difficulties beset him. Peace negotiations were painfully slow and after the great victory of Rocroy in May 1643 the French did not manage to mount a decisive campaign.

Like Richelieu, Mazarin lived financially from hand to mouth. It says much for his skill that he was able to fend off trouble until 1648. The outbreak of the Fronde in that year had many causes. It was a year of famine. Mazarin's *surintendant* Particelli d'Emeri had devised unpopular taxes and adjusted and postponed the payment of interest on the *rentes*. Parlement's 'constitutional' resistance was largely a protest on behalf of privilege, economic, social and official. The nobility joined in with a clamour of demands, governorships, titles, pensions: all an echo of 1614 and the minority of Marie de Médicis. In their different ways Gaston, Bouillon, Beaufort, Conti, Longueville, de Retz, Condé, even for a time Turenne, all exploited the situation. Although the alliance of nobility and *parlementaires* soon dissolved as the civil war became more destructive and solid citizens were reminded of the value of order, for a time Anne and her son were in a difficult and dangerous position.

That the monarchy survived and emerged immeasurably stronger owed much to Mazarin's adroit diplomacy and gift for survival. It is also a reflection on the work of his predecessor. That the forms of centralised government were attacked so violently after his death shows how much had been achieved. The *intendants* were resented because they were effective. Magnates and office-holders fought hard for their feudal, separatist causes, but they were a small minority even among the privileged classes. A solid body of upper-class Frenchmen were now convinced that their future and the country's lay with the maintenance and extension of the powers of the state: to say that Richelieu's work had been purely destructive is to ignore its survival and subsequent extension. Louis XIV began his rule in an atmosphere of acceptance and adulation. The great feudatories flocked to court, Parlement did what it was told without demur. The Fronde was the natural consequence of Richelieu's administration, a backlash that would not have surprised him at all; nor would its defeat, nor the splendid flowering of absolutism when, in the person of Louis XIV, there evolved the king who could be his own first minister.

# Bibliography

In this bibliography I indicate books and articles that I have found especially useful or those which the reader may wish to know about for his own further studies.

The main bibliography for the period is provided by E. Bourgeois and L. André, *Les Sources de l'Histoire de France, dix-septième siècle*, 8 vols. (1913-35). The handbook of E. Préclin et V. L. Tapié, *Le XVIIe siècle*, vol. vii of *Clio: Introduction aux études historiques* (1949), is invaluable. It gives a summary of the facts, a full bibliography and a statement of 'L'état actuel des questions'.

Richelieu's letters and despatches may be studied in the eight-volume edition, ed. D. L. M. Avenel, *Lettres, instructions diplomatiques et papiers d'Etat du Cardinal de Richelieu* (1853-77).

The standard edition of the *Mémoires* is that which was undertaken under the auspices of the Société de l'histoire de France in 10 vols. (1908-31).

Other compilations include:

> *Extraits des œuvres du Cardinal de Richelieu, pub. avec une introduction et notes de Roger Gancheron et une notice de Jacques Bainville* (1929).
>
> *Maximes d'Etat et fragments politiques, pub. par Georges Hanotaux dans les documents inédits sur l'histoire de France, série 2. Melanges historiques, vol. iii, Paris 1880*, edited by J. and R. Wittlmann (1944).
>
> *Testament Politique d'Armand du Plessis, Cardinal duc le Richelieu* The standard edition (but for criticisms of it and the authenticity of the original see pages 246-7n.) is the *Edition critique publiée avec une introduction et des notes par Louis André et une préface de Léon Noël* (1947).

The following are compilations of prime importance:
   G. Fagniez, *Le Père Joseph et Richelieu,* 2 vols. (1894). A

narrative of Père Joseph's diplomatic papers: source for the diplomatic and ecclesiastical activities of Richelieu up till 1638.

A. Leman, *Urbain VIII et la rivalité de la France et de la maison d'Autriche de 1631 à 1635* (1919).

A. Leman, *Richelieu et Olivares. Leurs negociations secrètes de 1636 à 1642 pour le rétablissement de la paix* (1938).

Both the above are based on diplomatic documents in the archives of Paris, Rome, Simancas and Vienna.

ed. R. Mousnier, *Lettres et mémoires adressés au chancelier Séguier, 1633-49* (1964).

See also page 158 n.

GENERAL HISTORIES OF EUROPE

P. Chaunu, *La Civilisation de l'Europe Classique* (1966).

H. Hauser, *La Préponderance Espagnole* (1559-1660), vol. x in the series '*Peuples et Civilisations*' (1935).

R. Mousnier, *Le XVIe et XVIIe Siècles* in the *Histoire Générale des Civilisations* (1949).

*The New Cambridge Modern History,* Vol. iv (1970) covers this period.

D. Ogg, *Europe in the Seventeenth Century* (9th edition, 1971); an idiosyncratic, stimulating book: the author is unsympathetic to Richelieu. His use of the word 'dictator' has twentieth-century overtones.

G. N. Clark's study of European institutions and ideas, *The Seventeenth Century* (2nd edition, 1945), is outstanding.

Among recent text books:

D. Maland, *Europe in the Seventeenth Century* (1966).

D. H. Pennington, *Europe in the Seventeenth Century* (1970).

C. J. Friederich, *The Age of Baroque* (1960); stimulating—but should the term 'baroque' be applied so widely outside the arts?

Some introductions to French history in this period:

J. Lough, *An Introduction to Seventeenth-Century France* (1954).

R. Mandrou, *La France aux XIIe et XVIIIe siècles: Essai de psychologie historique* (1970).

J. H. Mariejol, 'Henri IV et Louis XIII' in Lavisse, ed., *Histoire de France,* vol. vi, part 2 (1908).

V. L. Tapié, *La France de Louis XIII et de Richelieu* (1952).

G. R. R. Treasure, *Seventeenth Century France* (1966).

T

The essential guide to institutions:

M. Marion, *Dictionnaire des institutions de la France aux XVIIe et XVIIIe siècles* (1923. Also paperback 1968).

LIVES OF RICHELIEU

G. Hanotaux, *Richelieu,* 6 vols. (1893-1947), later volumes compiled by Duc de la Force.

Vicomte d'Avenel, *Richelieu et la monarchie absolue,* 4 vols. (2nd edition, 1895).

L. Battifol, *Richelieu et le Roi Louis XIII* (1934).

C. J. Burckhardt, *Richelieu,* 3 vols. (1940-66) (the first two have been translated into English).

A. Bailly, *Richelieu* (1934).

J. Bainville, *Richelieu, 1585-1642* (1935).

H. Belloc, *Richelieu, 1585-1642* (1930).

H. Carré, *La jeunesse et la marche au pouvoir de Richelieu* (1944).

F. Funck-Brentano, *Richelieu* (1938).

R. Lodge, *Richelieu* (1896).

J. B. Perkins, *Richelieu and the Growth of French Power* (1900).

D. P. O'Connell, *Richelieu* (1968); the latest life: particularly strong on diplomatic and strategic aspects.

Comte de Saint-Aulaire, *Richelieu* (2nd edition, 1960).

C. V. Wedgwood, *Richelieu and the French Monarchy* (1954).

OTHER BIOGRAPHIES

L. Batiffol, *Marie de Médicis* (1905).

L. Batiffol, *La Duchesse de Chevreuse* (1913).

H. Chapman, 'Louis XIII' in *Privileged Persons* (1966).

L. Dedouvres, *Politique et apôtre—le Père Joseph de Paris* (1932).

G. Dethan, *Gaston d'Orléans* (1959).

C. Herbillon, *Anne d'Autriche* (1939).

M. Houssaye, *Le Cardinal de Bérulle et le Cardinal de Richelieu* (1875).

G. Montgrédien, *Le Bourreau du Cardinal de Richelieu Isaac de Laffemas* (1929).

M. Roberts, *Gustavus Adolphus;* a history of Sweden 1611-32, 2 vols. (1953-58).

J. H. H. Salmon, *Cardinal de Retz* (1969).

B. Zeller, *Le Connétable de Luynes* (1879).

SOCIETY AND ECONOMY

M. Baulant and J. Meuvret, *Prix des céréales extraits de la Mercuriale de Paris (1520-1698)*, 2 vols. (1960-2).

M. Bloch, *French Rural History* (trans. by Sondheimer, 1966).

P. Boissonade, *Le Socialisme d'Etat, 1559-1661* (1927).

L. A. Boiteux, *Richelieu, grand maître de la navigation et du commerce de France* (1955).

Cambridge Economic History, vol. iv, *The Economy of Expanding Europe in the Sixteenth and Seventeenth Centuries*.

C. Cole, *French Mercantilist Doctrines before Colbert* (1931).

P. Goubert, *Beauvais et le Beauvaisis de 1600 à 1730: contribution à l'histoire sociale de la France du XVIIe siècle* (1960).

H. Hauser, *La Pensée et l'action économique du Cardinal Richelieu* (1944).

E. Hecksher, *Mercantilism* (trans. by M. Schapiro—2 vols., 1935).

W. H. Lewis, *The Splendid Century* (1953): essays on French life.

E. le Roy Ladurie, *Les Paysans de Languedoc* (1966).

F. Mauro, *L'Expansion Européene 1600-1870* (1964).

E. Magne, *La Vie Quotidienne au temps de Louis XIII* (1948).

R. Mousnier, *La Vénalité des Offices sous Henri IV et Louis XIII* (1949).

J. Nef, *Industry and Government in France and England* (1940).

B. Porchnev, *Les soulèvements populaires en France de 1623 à 1648* (1963).

G. Roupnel, *La Ville et la Campagne au XVIIe siècle* (1922).

H. Sée, *Histoire économique de la France*, 2 vols. (1939-42).

H. Sée, *L'évolution commerciale et industrielle de la France sous l'ancien régime* (1948).

G. Schmoller, *The Mercantile System and its Historical Significance* (1910).

F. C. Spooner, *L'économie mondiale et les frappes monétaires en France, 1493-1680* (1956).

A. Vene, *Montchrétien et le nationalisme économique* (1923).


POLITICAL, ADMINISTRATIVE, DIPLOMATIC AND MILITARY

A. Bailly, *Mazarin* (1935).

L. Batiffol, *La Journée des Dupes* (1925).

L. A. Boiteux, *Richelieu, grand maître de la navigation et du commerce de France* (1955).

E. Bourgeois, *Manual historique de politique étrangère*, 1, *1610-1789* (1892).

R. la Bruyère, *La Marine de Richelieu* (1968).

G. Castellan, *Histoire de l'Armée* (1958). A short account in the *Que sais-je?* series.

J. P. Charmeil, *Les Trésoriers de France à l'époque de la Fronde* (1964).

G. N. Clark, *War and Society in the 17th Century—six lectures* (1958).

L. Dollot, *Les Cardinaux-Ministres sous la Monarchie Française* (1952).

J. H. Elliott, *The Revolt of the Catalans. A Study in the Decline of Spain* (1963).

P. Erlanger, *Cinq Mars. La passion et la fatalité* (1964).

E. Everat, *Michel de Marillac, sa vie, ses œuvres* (1894).

L. Fraineau, *La dernière guerre de La Rochelle, 1627-1628* (1916).

Hon. E. Godley, *The Great Condé: A Life of Louis II de Bourbon, Prince of Condé* (1915).

G. Lacour-Gayet, *La marine française sous les regnes de Louis XIII et Louis XIV* (1911).

J. R. Major, *Representative Institutions in Renaissance France* (1960).

G. Mattingley, *Renaissance Diplomacy* (1955).

R. Mousnier, *La Vénalité des offices sous Henri IV et Louis XIII* (1945).

H. Nicolson, *Diplomacy* (1930). A general study.

G. Pagès, *La Guerre de Trente Ans* (1939; English version translated by D. Maland, 1971).

G. Pagès, *La Naissance du Grand Siècle, 1598-1661* (1948).

O. Ranum, *Richelieu and the Councillors of Louis XIII* (1963).

O. Ranum, *Paris in the Age of Absolutism* (1968).

J. Petit, *L'Assemblée des Notables de 1626-7* (1936).

ed. J. Poujol, *Claude de Seyssel, 'La Monarchie de France'* (1961).

I. S. Revaly, *Le Cardinal de Richelieu et la restauration de Portugal* (1950).

S. H. Steinberg, *The Thirty Years War* (1967).

J. H. Shennan, *The Parlement of Paris* (1968).

N. Sutherland, *The French Secretaries of State in the Age of Catherine de Medicis* (1912).

V. L. Tapié, *La politique étrangère de la France et le début de la guerre de trente ans, 1616-21* (1934).

P. de Vaissière, *L'affaire du maréchal de Marillac* (1924).

C. Vassal-Reig, *La guerre en Rousillon sous Louis XIII, 1635-39* (1934).

C. Vassal-Reig, *Richelieu et la Catalogne* (1935).

C. Vassal-Reig, *La Prise de Perpignan, 1641-2* (1934).

F. Vaux de Foletiers, *La Siège de La Rochelle* (1931).

P. Villemain, *Journal des assiégés de La Rochelle, 1627-8* (1958).

J. M. Wallace-Hadrill and J. McManners, *France, Government and Society* (1957). (Relevant essay: M. Prestwich, 'Making of Absolute Monarchy'.)

C. V. Wedgwood, *The Thirty Years War* (1938).

B. Zeller, *Etudes critiques sur le regne de Louis XIII de 1621 à 1624; la cour, le gouvernement, la diplomatie* (1880).

G. Zeller, *L'Organisation défensive des frontières du nord et de l'est au XVIIe siècle* (1928).

POLITICAL IDEAS, SCIENCE, PHILOSOPHY

J. W. Allen, *History of Political Thought in the Sixteenth Century* (1938).

M. Bloch, *Les rois thaumaturges* (1924).

J. Bronowski and B. Maglish, *The Western Intellectual Tradition* (1960).

M. Brown, *Scientific Organisations in 17th Century France* (1934).

L. Brunschwig, *René Descartes* (1937).

W. F. Church, *Constitutional Thought in Sixteenth-Century France* (1941).

A. R. Hall, *The Scientific Revolution, 1500-1800* (1954).

G. Milhaud, *Descartes savant* (1921).

J. F. Scott, *The Scientific Work of René Descartes* (1952).

H. Sée, *Les idées politiques in France au XVIIe siècle* (1923).

B. Willey, *The Seventeenth Century Background* (1934); especially valuable for treatment of Descartes.

A. Wolf, *The History of Science, Technology and Philosophy in the Sixteenth and Seventeenth Centuries* (1935).

RELIGION

N. Abercrombie, *Origins of Jansenism* (1936).

A. Adam, *Sur le probleme religieux dans le grand siècle (1946 première moitié du XVII siècle)* (1959).

H. Brémond, *L'histoire litteraire du sentiment religieux en France depuis les guerres de religion* (12 vols., the first of which appeared in

1916). A classic in the field of popular exposition of Catholic spirituality.

L. Cognet, *Le Jansenisme* (1961). Short study in the *Que sais-je?* series.

E. Daniel-Rops, *l'Eglise des Temps Classiques* (1958).

A. Huxley, *Grey Eminence* (1941). Father Joseph is the subject of this essay in psychology and mysticism.

R. A. Knox, *Enthusiasm* (1950). Especially for chapters on Jansenism.

E. Leonard, *Le Protestant Français* (1955).

E. Mortimer, *Blaise Pascal* (1959).

J. Orcibal, *Les origines du jansenisme,* vol. ii, *Jean Duvergier de Hauranne, Abbé de Saint Cyran, et son temps, 1581-1638* (1947).

J. Pannier, *L'Eglise reformée de Paris sous Henri IV* (1911).

A. Perraud, *Le Cardinal de Richelieu, évêque, théologien et protecteur des lettres* (1882).

E. Préclin et E. Jarry, *Les luttes politiques et doctrinales aux XVIIe et XVIIIe siècles* (1955).

L. Prunel, *La Renaissance Catholique en France au XVIIe siècle* (1921).

Saint-Beuve, *Port Royal,* 7 vols. (1930 edition).

W. J. Stankiewicz, *Politics and Religion in Seventeenth Century France* (1960).

H. F. Stewart, *The Secret of Pascal* (1935); *The Holiness of Pascal* (1940).

G. R. R. Treasure, *Seventeenth Century France* (1966).

THE ARTS

A. Blunt, *Art and Architecture in France, 1500-1700* (1953).

G. Brereton, *A Short History of French Literature* (1954).

R. Crozet, *La Vie Artistique en France au 17me Siècle (1598-1661)* (1954).

W. D. Howarth, *Life and Letters in France* (1965).

A. Lagarde and L. Michaud, *Le XVIIme siècle* (1962; in the series *Textes et Litterature,* with extracts and illustrations).

T. E. Lawrenson, *The French Stage in the 17th century* (1957).

M. M. McGowan, *L'Art du Ballet de Cour en France 1581-1643* (1963).

D. Maland, *Culture and Society in Seventeenth-Century France* (1970).

H. Peyre, *Qu'est-ce que le Classicisme?* (new edition, 1965).

G. de Reynold, *Synthèse du 17me siècle* (1962).

G. Snyders, *La Pédagogie en France aux XVIIe et XVIIIe siècles* (1965).

V. L. Tapié, *Baroque et Classicisme* (1957).

M. Turnell, *The Classical Moment* (1947).

R. H. Wilenski, *French Painting* (1931).


## ARTICLES

| Abbreviations: | | |
|---|---|---|
| | *Past and Present* | *P & P* |
| | *Revue historique* | *R.H.* |
| | *Bulletin de la Societe d'études de XVIIe siècle* | *Bulletin* |
| | *Revue d'histoire moderne et contemporaine* | *R.H.M.C.* |
| | *Revue d'histoire moderne* | *R.H.M.* |

I have found the following especially useful or interesting:

L. Batiffol, 'Richelieu et la question d'Alsace', *R.H.*, 1921.

P. Blet, 'Richelieu et les débuts de Mazarin,' *R.H.M.C.*, 1959.

D. J. Buisseret, 'A Stage in the Development of the French *Intendants*: the reign of Henry IV', *Historical Journal*, 1966.

A. Degert, 'Le mariage de Gaston d'Orléans et de Marguerite de Lorraine', *R.H.*, 1923.

M. Deloche, 'Testament Politique du Cardinal de Richelieu', *R.H.*, 1930.

P. Deyon, 'A propos des rapports entre la noblesse française et la monarchie absolue pendant la première moitié du XVIIe siècle', *R.H.*, 1964.

J. H. Elliott, 'The Decline of Spain', *P & P*, 1961.

G. Fagniez, 'L'opinion et la presse sous Louis XIII', *Revue des questions historiques*, 1890.

P. Goubert (trans. P. Rudé), 'The French Peasantry of the Seventeenth Century: an Example from the Beauvaisis', *P & P*, 1956.

E. J. Hamilton, 'The Decline of Spain', *Economic History Review*, 1938.

P. Jeannin, Review of Mousnier's *Les XVIe et XVIIe siècles*, *R.H.*, 1964.

L. Lalanne, 'Un récit inédit de la mort du Cardinal Richelieu', *R.H.*, 1964.

R. Major, 'Henry IV and Guyenne. A study concerning the origins of royal absolutism', *F.H.S.*, 1966.

A. G. Martimort, 'Comment les français du XVIIe siècle voyaient le pape', *Bulletin*, 1955.

J. Meuvret, 'Circulation monetaire et utilisation économique de la monnaie dans la France du XVIe siècle et du XVIIe siècle', *R.H.M.C.*, 1947.

J. Meuvret, 'Comment les français voyaient l'impôt', *Bulletin*, 1955.

C. Michaud, 'François Sublet de Noyers, Surintendant des Bâtiments de France', *R.H.*, 1969.

R. Mousnier, 'Comment les français voyaient la constitution au XVIIe siècle', *Bulletin*, 1955.

R. Mousnier, 'Etudes sur la population de la France au XVIIe èsicle', *Bulletin*, 1952.

R. Mousnier, 'Recherches sur les soulèvements populaires en France avant la Fronde', *R.H.M.C.*, 1958.

R. Mousnier, 'Sully et le Conseil d'Etat et des finances. La Lutte entre Bellière et Sully', *R.H.*, 1941.

R. Mousnier, 'Le conseil du roi de la mort de Henri IV au gouvernement personnel de Louis XIV', *Etudes*, 1947-8.

R. Mousnier, 'L'opposition politique bourgeoise à la fin du XVIe at au début du XVIIe siècle', *R.H.*, 1955.

R. Mousnier, F. Bluche and others, 'Serviteurs du Roi. Quelques aspects de la fonction publique dans la société française du XVIIe siècle, *Bulletin*, 1959.

J. P. O'Connell, 'A cause célèbre in the history of treaty making. The refusal to ratify the peace treaty of Regensburg in 1630', *British Yearbook of International Law*, 1967.

G. Pagès, 'Le Conseil du roi sous Louis XIII', *R.H.*, 1937.

G. Pagès, 'Autour du grand orage. Richelieu et Marillac, deux politiques, *R.H.*, 1937.

G. Pagès, 'La vénalité des offices dans l'ancienne France', *R.H.*, 1932.

G. Pagès, Essai sur l'évolution des institutions administratives en France du XVIIe siècle à la fin du XVIIe siècle., *R.H.M.*, 1932.

E. Porchnev, 'The Legend of the Seventeenth Century in French History', *P & P*, 1955.

E. Préclin, 'Edmond Richer (1559-1631), sa vie, ses œuvres, son gallicanisme', *R.H.M.,* 1930 (two articles).

A. Rebelliau, 'Un épisode de l'histoire religieuse au XVIIe siècle: la compagnie du Saint-Sacrement, *Revue de Deux Mondes,* 1903.

M. Prestwich, Review article on subject of popular revolt, *English Historical Review,* 1966.

V. L. Tapié, 'Comment les français du XVIIe siècle voyaient la patrie', *Bulletin,* 1955.

H. Trevor-Roper, 'The General Crisis of the Seventeenth Century', *P & P,* 1959 (see also other articles cited on pages 187 n. and 189 n.

H. Weber, 'Richelieu et le Rhine', *R.H.,* 1968.

# Index

Abd-el-Malek, Sheikh of Morocco 211

Absolutism, progress checked 38; development of 43, 49-50, 148-9; and idea of Christian prince 45, 240-1; theories 46, 240-1, 245; resistance to 47-8; and Parlement and the Estates 159ff, 259; and the army 177-9; and the navy 179; and the 'general crisis' debate 188-9; Richelieu and 240-1, 286-7

*Académie de Peinture et de Sculpture* 244-5

*Académie Française*, the 158, 249; foundation and aims of 249, 251, 252

Academy, Cadet School 10

Acadia 209

Acarie, Mme 14; and Fr Joseph 233

Admiral, Office of 200, 202

Agen 145

*Aides* 54, 63, 145

Aiguillon, Marie Madeleine de Vignerot du Pontcourlay, duchesse d', *see* Pontcourlay

Aix-en-Provence 140; riots in 140

Alais, peace of 105-6, 110, 143, 166

Albert, archduke 79

Albret, Isabella d' 98

Albret, Jeanne d' 32

Alsace 36; Bernard of Saxe Weimar and 268; Richelieu's designs upon 268ff

Altmark, Truce of 128-9

Ameixial, battle of 266

Amsterdam 96

Angélique, Mère (Jacqueline Arnauld) 224

Angers 30

Angoulême 142

Angoulême, Charles de Valois duc d' 84, 102

Angoumois, revolt in 138ff, 141-2

Anne of Austria, Queen of France 154; Infanta 19, 20; and Louis XIII 28, 85, 108, 274, 275-6; and Richelieu 231, 274; and relic of St Isidore 271; character and problems of 274; intrigues with Spain 274; birth of sons to 276; at Louis XIII's death-bed 285; Regent 286-7

Anneçy 122

Antoine de Bourbon 32

Antoinette d'Orleans 17

Antwerp 81

*Armateurs* 210

Army, the French (*see* also references to campaigns); indiscipline of 135, 175ff, 177; and billeting 138-9; reforms of 176ff, 179; under Servien 177; under Sublet de Noyers 177-9; recruitment for 178-9; Richelieu, view of 247

Arnauld, Antoine, the elder 224; the younger 224, 225

Arnoux, Père 30

Arras, capture of 272, 280, 283

*Arrière-Ban* 54, 139, 144, 169n, 178

Artois 36

Aubeterre, Marquis d' 143

Audebert, Fr. 215

Augsberg, settlement of 75

Augustine, Saint, theological influence of 221, 224, 226; his *Treatise on Virginity* 226

Augustinians, Convent of 22

Auvergne 117; remoteness of 138; grands jours d' 202

Avaux, Comte d' 236; bargains with Swedes 266

299

m T